ENVY AND GRATITUDE REVISITED

PSYCHOANALYTIC IDEAS AND APPLICATIONS SERIES

Wolfgang Loch—The Art of Interpretation: Deconstruction and New Beginning in the Psychoanalytic Process
edited and commentary by Peter Wegner

The Unconscious: Further Reflections
edited by José Carlos Calich & Helmut Hinz

Escape from Selfhood: Breaking Boundaries and Craving for Oneness
Ilany Kogan

The Conscious in Psychoanalysis
Antonio Alberto Semi

From Impression to Inquiry: A Tribute to the Work of Robert Wallerstein
edited by Wilma Bucci & Norbert Freedman; associate editor Ethan A. Graham

Talking about Supervision: 10 Questions, 10 Analysts = 100 Answers
edited by Laura Elliot Rubinstein

ENVY AND GRATITUDE REVISITED

Edited by

Priscilla Roth & Alessandra Lemma

Foreword by

R. Horacio Etchegoyen

Psychoanalytic Ideas and Applications Series

KARNAC

First published in 2008 by
The International Psychoanalytical Association

This edition published in 2008 by
Karnac Books
118 Finchley Road
London NW3 5HT

British Library Cataloguing in Publication Data

A C.I.P. for this book is available from the British Library

ISBN: 978-1-85575-735-6

Edited, designed, and produced by Communication Crafts

www.karnacbooks.com

CONTENTS

PSYCHOANALYTIC IDEAS AND APPLICATIONS SERIES

IPA Publications Committee

The Publications Committee of the International Psychoanalytical Association continues, with this volume, the series: "Psychoanalytic Ideas and Applications".

The aim is to focus on the scientific production of significant authors whose works are outstanding contributions to the development of the psychoanalytic field and to set out relevant ideas and themes, generated during the history of psychoanalysis, that deserve to be discussed by present psychoanalysts.

The relationship between psychoanalytic ideas and their applications has to be put forward from the perspective of theory, clinical practice, technique, and research so as to maintain their validity for contemporary psychoanalysis. The Publication Committee's objective is to share these ideas with the psychoanalytic community and with professionals in other related disciplines, in order to expand their knowledge and generate a productive interchange between the text and the reader.

Special thanks are due to the editors, Alessandra Lemma and Priscilla Roth, and to all the contributors, for their remarkable work.

Leticia Glocer Fiorini
Chair, IPA Publications Committee

ACKNOWLEDGEMENTS

This book would not have been possible without the enthusiastic engagement of all the contributors. We would like to thank them for agreeing to be involved. We would also like to thank the IPA Publications Committee for supporting this project. For us, it has been a pleasure and a privilege to edit this collection. The editors would also like to thank the Melanie Klein Trust for their support and permission to reprint Melanie Klein's photograph. The editors would also like to thank Klara King for her invaluable help with the production of this book.

Robert Caper wishes to thank Michael Paul and Priscilla Roth for their helpful comments and suggestions.

Heinz Weiß would like to express his thanks to Mike Gibbon and John Steiner for looking through and discussing different versions of the manuscript.

Finally, the Editors would like to thank Nick and Jeremy.

Priscilla Roth & Alessandra Lemma

EDITORS AND CONTRIBUTORS

Irma Brenman-Pick is a training analyst and child analyst of the British Psychoanalytical Society, and author of several papers, particularly, "Working in the Countertransference".

Ronald Britton is well known internationally as a psychoanalytic writer, teacher, and clinician. His books include *The Oedipus Complex Today, Belief and Imagination,* and *Sex, Death and the Superego.* In addition to his clinical papers, he has written on the relationship of psychoanalysis to literature, philosophy, and religion. He was a former Chair of the Department for Children and Parents at the Tavistock Clinic, President of the British Psychoanalytical Society, and Vice-President of the International Psychoanalytical Association.

Robert Caper is assistant clinical professor of psychiatry, UCLA School of Medicine; the author of *Immaterial Facts: Freud's Discovery of Psychic Reality and Klein's Development of His Work* and *A Mind of One's Own*; instructor in the Department of Psychoanalysis, California Graduate Institute; and is in private psychoanalytic practice in Beverly Hills, California.

H. Shmuel Erlich is past-President and former Chair of the Training Committee of the Israel Psychoanalytic Society. He is a training analyst and faculty member at the Israel Psychoanalytic Institute; Sigmund Freud Professor of Psychoanalysis (Emeritus) and former Director of the Sigmund Freud Center at The Hebrew University of Jerusalem. He served two terms as European Regional Representative on the IPA Board and is currently Chair of its Education Committee. He is in private psychoanalytic practice in Jerusalem and Tel Aviv.

R. Horacio Etchegoyen, MD, Universidad Nacional de La Plata, is a training and supervising psychoanalyst of the Buenos Aires Psychoanalytic Association. He previously served as chairman of Psychiatry and Medical Psychology at the Universidad Nacional de Cuyo and was a Doctor Honoris Causa (Universidad Nacional de San Luis), Past President of the Buenos Aires Psychoanalytic Association, and President of the IPA, 1993–1997. He is the author of numerous articles. His book *Fundamentos de la técnica psicoanalítica* [Fundamentals of Psychoanalytic Technique], has also been published in English, Portuguese, Italian, and French, with a German edition in preparation.

Michael Feldman is a training and supervising analyst of the British Psycho-Analytical Society. In addition to his clinical work and teaching in London, he regularly works with analysts in several European countries and in the United States. His papers have explored some of the theoretical and technical issues that arise in the interplay of transference and countertransference, the patient's use of projective mechanisms, and the pressures both on patient and analyst towards defensive action rather than thought. He has published a number of papers and, with Elizabeth Bott Spillius, co-edited *Psychic Equilibrium and Psychic Change: Selected Papers of Betty Joseph* (1989).

Peter Fonagy, is Freud Memorial Professor of Psychoanalysis and Director of the Sub-Department of Clinical Health Psychology at University College London; Chief Executive of the Anna Freud Centre, London; and Consultant to the Child and Family Program at the Menninger Department of Psychiatry and Behavioral Sciences at the Baylor College of Medicine. He is Chair of the Postgraduate Education Committee of the International Psychoanalytical Association and a Fellow of the British Academy. He is a clinical psychologist and a training and supervising analyst in the British Psychoanalytical Society in child and adult analysis. He has published over 300 chapters and articles and has authored or edited several books.

Florence Guignard was elected Full Member of the Paris Society in 1979 and Training Member in 1982. She has been a Member of the COCAP (Committee on Child and Adolescent Psychoanalysis) since its foundation and was elected directly by the IPA as a child analyst in 1997. She is running several clinical and theoretical seminars, both at the Institute of the Paris Society and in private practice. Together with Annie Anzieu, she created in 1983 the Association pour la Psychanalyse de l'Enfant (APE) and, in 1993, a European structure, the Société pour la Psychanalyse de l'Enfant et de l'Adolescent (SEPEA). She is the Head of the Editorial Board of *l'Année Psychanalytique Internationale*. She contributes to conferences, seminars, and supervision in several countries. She has published more than 200 papers and two books: *Au vif de l'infantile* (1996) and, *Épître à l'objet* (1997).

Alessandra Lemma is a psychoanalyst and a consultant clinical psychologist working in the Adolescent Department of the Tavistock and Portman NHS Foundation Trust, where she is also the Head of Psychology. She is a Senior Member of the British Association of Psychotherapists and a Member of the British Psychoanalytical Society. She has published several books on psychotherapy and psychoanalysis.

Edna O'Shaughnessy is a child and adult training analyst and a Fellow of the British Psychoanalytical Society. She is a supervisor for the Child and Family Department and also works for the Adult Department of the Tavistock Clinic, London. She has published many papers on the analysis of adults and children.

Caroline Polmear is a training analyst of the British Psychoanalytical Society. She worked in the past at the Brent Centre for Young People and retains an interest in psychoanalytic work with young people through supervision of therapists in university student counselling services. She co-wrote (with Milton, Polmear, and Fabricius) *A Short Introduction to Psychoanalysis* and has also published on the subject of the psychoanalytic treatment of Asperger's syndrome. She is currently centrally involved with the Psychoanalytic Training at the Institute of Psychoanalysis in London.

Priscilla Roth is a Training and Supervising Analyst at the British Psychoanalytic Institute, where she is currently head of training. She is the author of several psychoanalytic papers and the editor of *Bearing Unbearable States of Mind: The Work of Ruth Malcolm* and the co-editor, with Richard Rusbridger, of *Encounters with Melanie Klein: The Work of Elizabeth Spillius.*

Henry F. Smith, MD, is a training and supervising analyst at the Psychoanalytic Institute of New England, East (PINE), and a member of the Boston Psychoanalytic Society and Institute. A frequent contributor to the literature on the theory and practice of psychoanalysis, he is currently Editor-in-Chief of *The Psychoanalytic Quarterly* and Chair of the Program Committee of the American Psychoanalytic Association.

Ignês Sodré is a training analyst at the British Psychoanalytical Society. She has taught extensively in the United Kingdom and abroad. She has written several papers on psychoanalysis and on literature and has co-authored a book (with A. S. Byatt), *Imagining Characters.*

John Steiner is a training analyst of the British Psychoanalytical Society and works in private practice as a psychoanalyst. He is the author of several psychoanalytic papers and a book entitled *Psychic Retreats* (1996).

Heinz Weiß, Prof. MD, Psychoanalyst (DPV, DGPT, Guest member Brit. Psychoanal. Soc.), is Director of the Department of Psychosomatic Medicine, Robert-Bosch-Krankenhaus, Stuttgart, Germany. He worked as a visiting scientist in the Adult Department of the Tavistock Clinic, London (1992/1993), and is a Member of the Editorial Board of *Psychoanalytic Psychotherapy.* As author and (co)editor he has published several books: *Der Andere in der Übertragung* [The Other in the Transference] (1988), *Ödipuskomplex und Symbolbildung* [Oedipus Complex and Symbol-Formation], a Festschrift for Hanna Segal (1999), *Perspektiven Kleinianischer Psychoanalyse* [Perspectives of Kleinian Psychoanalysis], *Vols. 1–12* (1997–2004), and *Projektive Identifizierung. Ein Schlüsselkonzept der psychoanalytischen Therapie* [Projective Identification. A Key-Concept of Psychoanalytic Psychotherapy] (2007).

FOREWORD

R. Horacio Etchegoyen

During the Nineteenth International Congress of Psychoanalysis held in Geneva, Switzerland, at the end of July 1955, Melanie Klein presented a paper entitled "A Study of Envy and Gratitude". Two years later, following the development of certain themes and the addition of clinical material, this paper became a book: *Envy and Gratitude*.

This volume of barely one hundred pages was the culmination of almost 40 years' work, and at the same time constituted both a drastic shift and a new starting point within psychoanalysis. For it was here that Klein introduced her audacious and revolutionary concept of primary envy—one that would cause great commotion among psychoanalysts, who have since then not ceased to study and discuss it.

Although the notion of envy can be found throughout the work of Klein, and naturally in the writings of Freud and his followers, the envy that is presented in this small yet highly significant book is something completely new, and for this reason it arouses admiration, rejection, controversy—and even envy!

In my view the key is in the adjective "primary", which Melanie Klein defines in the book's brief introduction and opening chapter: envy is primary because it is directed towards the primary object, the breast; it is primary because it is part and parcel of the individual and is constitutional; and it is primary because it is endogenous and intrinsic and does not depend on frustration.

In this text, Klein argues that object relations and the ego are there at the outset (something that Freud never—or hardly ever—accepted), and also that we come equipped with instincts, drives, and tendencies, just as Freud always said.

Half a century after it was first published, no one can doubt the influence of this little book on psychoanalytic theory and technique, or on our understanding of complex human beings and their social lives. Indeed, the passage of time and the continued study to which it is subjected are proof positive that this is a perennial and fundamental work.

To my mind, it is no coincidence that as *Envy and Gratitude* passes its half-century, a number of books are appearing that study it from different angles: for example, the book by Mabel Piovano, which I had the pleasure of presenting to the Argentine Psychoanalytical Association a few months ago, and the present volume, for which I am equally delighted to be writing a prologue.

Envy and Gratitude Revisited is a collection of valuable essays that Priscilla Roth and Alessandra Lemma have wisely compiled in order to illustrate the rich ideas of key psychoanalysts from the northern hemisphere. With intelligence and passion and from a wide range of perspectives—or vertices, as Bion would say—this collection considers the two issues that most concerned Klein towards the end of her life: envy and gratitude. The fourteen chapters, all of considerable interest, address the nature of envy, its relationship to the death instinct and destructiveness, the ever complex relationship between envy and jealousy (Othello ever-present), the similarities and differences between envy and greed, the relationship between envy and the negative therapeutic relationship, the theoretical dilemma concerning envy and narcissism, the ongoing struggle between the child and the mother's care, the complex relationship between envy, on the one hand, and guilt and repetition on the other, and the vicious circle of guilt and envy, contrasting it with gratitude, reparation, and creativity and always in relation to dependence. I could go on listing the issues addressed by this stimulating collection, but fortunately, for both readers and myself, the book's excellent introduction summarizes the papers and interweaves them in a critical and precise way.

Whoever is familiar with the work of Melanie Klein and has read and re-read *Envy and Gratitude* will find in this valuable selection, put together by Priscilla and Alessandra, a marvellous opportunity to reflect upon and rethink these issues. I recommend it with heartfelt enthusiasm.

Buenos Aires, 20 January 2008

ENVY AND GRATITUDE REVISITED

Introduction

Priscilla Roth

Envy

This collection of essays is an exploration of Melanie Klein's *Envy and Gratitude* and a testament to its fruitfulness and complexity. Written just a few years before the end of Klein's life, the elaboration of her mature views on love and hatred marked a culmination of her previous work and a radical addition to it.

The work begins with an assertion of Klein's conviction that all psychological development evolves from the experience and the internalization of the first relationship to the mother:

> Throughout my work I have attributed fundamental importance to the infant's first object relation—the relation to the mother's breast and to the mother—and have drawn the conclusion that if this primal object, which is introjected, takes root in the ego with relative security, the basis for a satisfactory development is laid. Innate factors contribute to this bond. [Klein, 1957, p. 178]

Everything that follows in *Envy and Gratitude* reflects this conviction. It is impossible properly to understand Klein's discussion of the destructive power of envy separate from her belief that its perniciousness lies precisely in its fundamental interference with the establishment of the loved and loving good object within the ego—"the foundation for hope, trust, and belief in goodness". She believed that an expectation of this "inexhaustible" breast was inborn and that it soon begins to stand for life and for creativity. She also believed, following Freud, that the early months of life were characterized by the struggle between the life instinct, represented by love for breast and mother, and the death instinct, represented by envy of the breast's "intolerable goodness".

Envy and Gratitude was immediately surrounded by controversy, focused on what was seen to be Klein's insistence on the constitutionality of envy and its relation to the death instinct. In fact, Klein is clear that "the capacity for both love and for destructive impulses is, *to some extent,* constitutional, though varying individually in strength and *interacting from the beginning with external conditions*" (p. 180, emphasis added). However, the juxtaposition of the power of the relationship to the breast with the deadly destructiveness of an innate hatred of the very goodness of the breast sent a shudder through the British psychoanalytic community, presenting to some readers a drama of stark contrasts, easily reduced to a battle between good and evil. In fact, the issues are far more complicated and multidimensional and, in spite of the controversy, continue to engender important developments in psychoanalytic understanding and to be of enormous clinical value—as will be clear from a reading of the chapters in this book.

All of the contributors to this volume find Klein's descriptions of the manifestations of envy clinically essential, but they have different ways of thinking about the notion of a death instinct. Peter Fonagy and Shmuel Erlich explicitly applaud Klein for embracing, developing, and emphasizing internal innate factors over external ones; unlike some others, they don't find the issue of constitutionality irrelevant. Michael Feldman and John Steiner also agree with the concept of the death instinct; Steiner describes it quite specifically as a destructive instinct that is *anti-life,* meaning hostile to the fundamental realities of life: the goodness of the feeding breast, the creativity and exclusiveness of the parental couple, the painful and immutable facts of dependence, separateness, limitation, and difference. In this work he sees the repetition compulsion as a particularly powerful manifestation of, and defence against, an envious hatred of dependence, difference, and creativity. Feldman would, I think, agree with this, though he sees envy itself not as an expression of the death instinct but as a provoker of its sadistic impulses. Ron Britton prefers the term "destructive instinct" to death instinct; he sees destructiveness as originally "directed outwards and in the course of development internalized" (Britton, 2003, p. 3). Exploring destructive narcissism, envy, and guilt, he considers that envy exists as a compound of various elements in the personality, including, especially, the disillusion of narcissistic and self-idealizing phantasies and the recognition of difference and differentiation: such a compound, he suggests, can form at the threshold of the depressive position and can, when combined with "a powerful quota of innate hostility", create a "potentially pathological envious complex". Both Robert Caper and Henry Smith are uncomfortable with what they see as the moralistic duality of Klein's emphasis on opposing instincts. Caper finds untenable and incomprehensible an instinct "built into the mind that is aimed precisely and exclusively at killing the mind"; he sees envy as one part of a more general defence against the overwhelming anxiety caused by "endangered narcissism"—a defence felt to be necessary for self-preservation but which is, incidentally though tragically, catastrophic to the mental life of the self. Smith contrasts Klein's emphasis on pure states of mind—pure goodness, pure envy—with her more clinically derived and, he feels, clinically meaningful insights into more complex and multi-determined states of mind. Caroline Polmear, working in the Independent tradition, also rejects the notion of a death instinct, understanding destructiveness and aggression to arrive somewhat later in development.

The question of when envy first emerges is not insignificant. Klein's view that it is "operative from birth" has theoretical consequences: primary envy is so singularly pernicious, its effects so far-reaching, because it prevents bi-polar splitting, the infant's first and essential defence. The argument goes like this: In order for the infant to deal with both powerful internal conflicts and the frustrations and demands of external reality, its ego must gradually strengthen and develop. Random sensations, perceptions, and impulses must, little by little, become structured and comprehensible—this requires an ego of some strength and cohesion. The first task for the infant, then, is the organization and structuring of its ego and the organization of its experience, so that it can begin more or less accurately to perceive and manage internal and external events. Capable of perceiving and responding to objects from the beginning of life, the infant is also capable from the beginning of experiencing events and objects felt to be attached to them, as good (e.g. a warm, full tummy) or bad (hunger pains, colic). The infant begins internalizing, incorporating, identifying with good experiences from the first: they "take root in his ego", and gradually his ego coheres around these repeatable, and eventually expectable, experiences of his good object. In other words, he gradually begins to have an unconscious sense of himself, largely based on and dependent upon his sense of his good object in good experiences. Binary splitting allows the infant to protect his sense of his good object, on which his growing sense of himself is based, from his own feelings of hatred and rage—his innate hatred as well as the rage growing out of inevitable frustrations—thereby safeguarding his mind to allow it to develop and strengthen. If envious feelings during these earliest weeks prevent the good breast from being experienced as good (ideal), its introjection is impeded. Since it is the identification with an internalized good (ideal) object that leads to a strengthening of the ego, enabling it to begin to cope with increasing increments of reality, an interference by primary envy with this identification has profound effects on all future development.

There is, however, a problem with this argument. The infant, in Klein's view, splits the world not only into Good and Bad, but, simultaneously, into Me and Not-Me, and these splits overlap: Me is felt to be everything good, including the good object; everything bad (bad self/bad object) is felt to be Not-Me. This being so, during the period when an infant's *experience* is one of unity with his ideal object—whether this is primary or secondary (defensive)—the ideal object is experienced as Me. The question, then, is how can the breast be "intolerably good" if it is experienced as Me? How can envy interfere at this stage? I think one can conceptualize this if one thinks of mini-moments of a recognition of otherness—tiny moments of awareness of a gap from the beginning. But if we were to think of envy as powerful enough to prevent any internalization and identification with the good (ideal) object at this early stage, we would need to imagine not only a particularly strong quantum of envy, but an underdevelopment of the infant's primary defensive organization: his ability to protect himself from the invasiveness of the world, in the most fundamental, life-serving way: his ability to feel that he and his good object are one.

Several of the contributors take up and emphasize Klein's brief discussion of the significance of external experience in the development of an envious personality: Lemma, Polmear, Brenman-Pick, and O'Shaughnessy all discuss the importance of the object's ability to contain and work through disturbed and disturbing states of mind; some—particularly, Alessandra Lemma and Caroline Polmear, each in a different way—giving this factor more weight than Klein explicitly did herself, pointing out that "deprivation" includes deprivation of this vital containment. Brenman-Pick and O'Shaughnessy, particularly, emphasize the complex interplay between the innate qualities of the infant and the experiences provided by their environment. Florence Guignard writes about the effects of developments within contemporary Western society on the young child's ability adequately to process developmental tasks and on the way particular qualities in mothers impact on their infants. Of particular interest is her description of the defensive manoeuvres that an infant needs to employ when he is envied by his mother: such an infant will have to both identify with an envious external object and endure the prohibitions of an envious internalized primary object. Fonagy writes of the "colonization" of envy; the way that, in its projective power, it establishes peculiar, highly ambivalent and lasting links between the envious person and the one he envies. This of course is particularly catastrophic when the couple envious/envied are a mother and her small child. Lemma's paper describes this process in detail.

All the contributors write about actual qualities of the analyst whose real capacities or difficulties will affect the patient's—as the real mother has affected the infant's—capacity to deal with his envy. As O'Shaughnessy writes, "The nature of the patient's internal objects, his love and his hate, affect his perceptions of the analyst . . ."; but, she notes, they are also affected by the actual qualities of the analyst. For these writers, as for several others (Steiner, Sodré, Erlich, Feldman, Smith) the patient's experience, in analysis as well as, though perhaps differently, in infancy, is a complex mixture of perceptions, projections, introjections, re-projections and new perceptions, though some (Polmear) put more weight on external and some (Fonagy) put more weight on internal factors.

All of the contributors describe and emphasize the way that envy as a force within the personality is always complicated by other emotional experiences—particularly, in these chapters, jealousy and guilt.

Unity, narcissism, separateness

Experiences of envy and experience of gratitude depend on an awareness of separateness—an awareness of the otherness of the other. It is hard to formulate a concept of envy which could take place within a relationship of absolute fusion between self and object; so long as what is Good is Me, what is experienced as good need not be envied since it belongs to me. Envy can only arise at the moment—however brief and however fleeting—when the individual becomes aware that what is Good is not Me. Similarly, gratitude can only be experienced in relation to another person—a not-Me. Klein believed that momentary awareness of the separateness of the object begins from birth. She believed that infants have an inborn awareness of a separate, bountiful object—a pre-conception in Bion's (1962a, p. 89) terms—which is met at the first feeding experience by the reality of the breast. The goodness of the breast, as Shmuel Erlich points out in these pages, is not in the first instance to do with its actual qualities, it is to do with the infant's projection into it of an ideal munificence. It is the arrival of what has been expected. The first, original Messiah. However much the capacity for gratitude or the propensity for envy may be constitutional—may be manifestations of the life and death instincts—and Klein certainly believes they are—*experientially* these emotions cannot exist in their true form until there has been some, at least momentary, awareness of separateness whether this arrives, as Klein obviously thought, at or just after birth, or whether such momentary awareness arrives some weeks later. Issues of separateness, then, are fundamental to the exploration of the concepts of envy and gratitude.

Both Caroline Polmear and Shmuel Erlich write about an experience of union between self and other, each in a different way. Polmear describes a picture of infantile development in which the early weeks of the baby's ordinary experience are characterized by a complete emotional and physical dependence on the mother, such that there is a merging of the psyches of the two and a perfectly normal lack of differentiation between the wishes of the mother and those of the infant. In this view, the ordinary mother is able to perceive, understand and empathize with her baby's needs as if they were her own. Under these (optimal) conditions, the baby's experience of himself and mother as one is not interfered with or invaded by his mother's variant expectations. Serious psychological disturbance, in this view, is a result of the insufficient provision in early infancy of such necessary "holding" and a premature incursion into the developing sense of self of the child. The merging between mother and baby in the early weeks, and the permitted experience of merging between analyst and patient at some points in some analyses, are not understood as defensive organizations, but as developmentally necessary stages. In *Envy and Gratitude*, Klein (1957) emphasized that envious and hateful impulses are frequently split off from the patient's awareness, and that re-introducing them to the patient requires great sensitivity and care and "only becomes possible after long and painstaking work". Polmear's work with her patient is a demonstration of this kind of effort.

Shmuel Erlich also disagrees with some of Klein's views on separateness and unity; in his essay this focuses on a disagreement with Klein's juxtaposition of envy and gratitude. While he agrees that envy is a drive derivative, he sees gratitude—and the love which fuels it—as a coming from a different order of experience. He suggests that these positive feelings derive from an "experience of unity", togetherness, which he suggests may be linked to the "pre-natal unity" described by Klein. Erlich does not see the experiences he describes as defensive, or an illusion—he differentiates them from defence-driven identifications which he also explicitly recognizes—but, rather, feels that such positive feelings of gratitude and love have their own kind of truth, and are a manifestation of integration at a different level of the personality. He links this with Freud's comment that "the attitudes [relations] of love and hate . . . are reserved for the relations of the *total ego* to objects" (1915c, pp. 133–137).

Two contributors, Caper and Fonagy, discuss envy as it emerges in groups; both remark that institutions—including psychoanalytic institutes and organizations—frequently reject independence of thought and creative insights because such creativity and autonomy stir up envy and also, I think, anxiety. Such anxiety results both from guilt about the envy, and from a terror of the loss of the group's cohesion. And Guignard suggests that the antipathy to otherness that is so central in envy may be reinforced at a societal level by the increasing dominance of virtual communication/virtual reality, thereby creating the illusion that there are no differences between the sexes and the generations such that the experience of envy is denied and therefore never processed.

Thus, issues of separateness—about narcissistic organizations and how they operate, or a capacity to allow a differentiation between self and object—run through almost all the chapters, and this is an accurate reflection of an increasing interest in these issues among Kleinian and non-Kleinian writers (Spillius, 2007b). At the same time, there is a growing sense of the complexity and interweaving of concepts, so that an examination of envy leads to the part it plays in narcissistic disorders and repetition compulsion, in fears of object loss and guilt, and in defensive organizations that include idealization, self-aggrandizement, contempt, and omnipotence.

Defences

Any study of envy is at the same time a study of the defences constructed against envy, and these defences are constructed not only because envy is an inherently painful emotion, nor because it is felt to be so reprehensible and guilt-inducing. The experience of envy is defended against because it is an acknowledgement of the otherness of the other, with all the terrifying consequences that arise from such an acknowledgement: foremost, dependence on an object who is not under one's control.

There is something particularly onerous about envy. Envious feelings—mental pain at the recognition that another person possesses something valuable, and the wish that this not be so—are experienced as bad and blameworthy, but can also create intolerable feelings of inferiority, humiliation, and hatred. Because the experience of envy is so painful, it is powerfully defended against in many ways, and it is the defences we erect to prevent ourselves from feeling envious that are most pernicious. These defences always involve a destructive spoiling of the object. This spoiling can be predominantly in the mind of the subject, or it can be played out so that the object herself is actually attacked and her most enviable qualities spoilt. And there are different types of spoiling: spoiling can be denigrating and diminishing, or it can be over-valuing, idealizing. In either case, what is being spoiled is the recognition of the object's true, real qualities and real value. Furthermore, these attacks may be overt and even conscious—though not consciously recognized as envious (Sodré on Iago) or they may be subtly undermining and more unconscious (the patients of Steiner, Feldman, Brenman-Pick, and

Smith). While our picture of how this may work between a mother and her baby—in both directions (see the chapters by Lemma and Guignard)—is largely theoretical, in analysis we can watch how it works more closely and accurately and begin to have ways to address the process.

The phantasy of being eternally combined with the object is a self-protective defence against what can feel like overwhelming anxiety. When such a narcissistic phantasy is enduring, interfering with relations with real, important objects and overriding the perception of reality, it becomes characterological—what Rosenfeld called a *narcissistic organization* (Rosenfeld, 1971) and Steiner has termed a *pathological organization* (Steiner, 1993). Rosenfeld (1987) and Britton (2003) have written about the difference between those narcissistic disorders that are largely defensive (libidinal), and those that are largely destructive. Examining narcissism in illuminating detail, Caper is primarily writing about the former: the way in which certain people are so powerfully threatened by having to recognize their dependence on an object whose importance is unquestionable but who is not in their control that they must maintain an illusion of possessing or being their object.

Many of the analysts writing in this book (Sodré, Britton, Steiner, Weiß, Feldman, Brenman-Pick, Smith) describe such organizations as they become manifest in analysis or in characters from literature. It is, of course, characteristic of such systems that they can be intractable in analysis, as analytic attempts to influence the destructive narcissistic process often lead to what is simply a mutated form of the same basic narcissistic structure. Heinz Weiß's chapter is an excellent illustration of a particular such arrangement within an analysis. His patient creates a "romantic perversion of timelessness", constructing in her analysis an unchanging world of admiration and adoration in which there are no limits, in order that there be no perceivable gaps between herself and her analyst, thereby obviating envy. When an analytic interpretation intrudes into this idealized situation, the patient entraps the analyst in a sado-masochistic entanglement: the two states are equally dictated and equally imprisoning—neither allows the presence of two separate individuals interacting with each other. They are equivalent ways of obliterating the facts of life: differentiation, separateness, dependence, and, of course, the limits of time. Henry Smith's chapter, too, beautifully demonstrates the entanglements between patient and analyst that often take place in an analysis where the patient's over-riding need is to prevent any experience of separateness between them; describing in detail the movements in the session, Smith shows us how the patient cuts off meaningful contact—with her own feelings or with her analyst—and can thereby maintain a state of mind in which nothing changes.

Steiner writes about exactly such intransigent and repetitive situations in his chapter. He quotes Freud as saying, "The decisive thing remains that the resistance prevents any change from taking place—that everything stays as it was". It is this everything-stays-as-it-was quality that characterizes so many of the defences against envy: the object is controlled, imprisoned, possessed; ennobled, punished, or secretly despised. But it is not to be allowed to move from the position into which it has been placed by the subject and therefore is not allowed to be alive. And the world in which this goes on, in the patient's psyche and then in the analysis, is a world of endless enactment of a primal phantasy. The timelessness of these phantasies is part of what marks them as having their roots in the most primitive mental events, where, when hunger, rage, or terror overwhelms, it is felt to exist forever. Sodré's chapter is a powerful exploration of such a state of mind: she demonstrates how Iago's mental picture of Othello and Desdemona together—"Even now, now, very now . . ."—is a nightmare vision of togetherness: precisely the other side of the coin of an idealized, unchanging, unlimited union.

Steiner himself describes a case where the emotional atmosphere was very different from that in Weiß's or Smith's, but which often seemed to be equally unalterable: in the place of endless love or a morass of sado-masochism, his patient resolutely denied having any feelings at all about his analyst. Here the repetition compulsion seemed to have its roots in the patient's envious hatred of the emotional link between himself and his object, a fear and intolerance of dependency and receptivity that the patient saw as weak and feminine. Steiner describes the way the patient often used projective identification to bind his analyst in a narcissistic organization and suggests that if the analyst can bear to be receptive to such disturbing experiences, some progress may take place in the analysis.

Michael Feldman follows an analytic session in close detail, illustrating the specific moment-to-moment working of a negative therapeutic reaction made up of envy, manic defences against the experience of envy (with its accompanying feelings of smallness, humiliation, and dependency), and the persecutory guilt that follows.

This is beautifully encapsulated in the opening "act" of the session when the patient, having been late (for the third day running), then becomes manically cavalier and pseudo-analytic about the lateness and is then plunged into an identification with an analyst now felt to be weakened and unemployable.

Feldman discusses the relative weights of guilt and envy in producing negative therapeutic reactions; several contributors make the point that the close relationship between envy and guilt means that it is sometimes difficult to know whether what interferes with the patient's progress at any given moment are the consequences of guilt or of envy. Smith makes the point that negative therapeutic reactions are participated in by both analyst and patient, emphasizing that "there can be no working through . . . that does not pass through this place of mutual torment".

Many of the patients discussed seem to deal with their envy of their analyst by themselves being the one who can elevate the analyst by their appreciation: the patient Brenman-Pick describes believes that she herself "ennobles" her analyst by making her a "genius". Sodré, writing about small babies, suggests that the baby feels that his mother can give endlessly because he feeds her by sucking from her breast, thereby making her milk flow. A patient discussed by O'Shaughnessy praises his analyst in a way that is partly genuine and partly *creating* her as praiseworthy, bestowing a gift on her. These are subtle, mixed experiences: partly, of course, the baby's love *does* reassure his mother about his goodness and her own; partly the supervisee's patient *is* grateful to his analyst. On the other hand, the patients in these scenarios could also be seen to be in projective identification with an idealized object: any gratitude is projected, so the analyst must be grateful for being "ennobled" and elevated by the patient's appreciation, as the breast is felt to be filled by the baby's sucking. Steiner's discussion of the issues of giving and receiving come into this: receiving is often felt to be inferior and even humiliating, and giving—whether milk, analysis, or praise—is felt as superior and powerful (see also Spillius, 2007b). Each of these contributors emphasizes the component parts of such experiences and draws our attention to what is almost always the complex interaction of conflicting motives, often difficult for the analyst to disentangle. Smith addresses this issue most directly; and, of course, as Polmear proposes, different analysts will choose to address different aspects of the material, each according to his own theory and personality.

Triangularity

One of the issues that emerges frequently throughout this book is that of triangularity. Klein herself explicitly refers to envy as being a two-person experience, differentiating it from jealousy, yet in earlier papers she had described at some length the infant's phantasies of its parents combined in an intercourse of continuous oral, anal, and genital satisfaction:

> oral frustration arouses in the child an unconscious knowledge that its parents enjoy mutual sexual pleasures and a belief at first that these are of an oral sort. Under the pressure of its own frustration it reacts to this phantasy with envy of its parents . . . an unconscious knowledge of this kind about sexual intercourse between the parents . . . already emerges at this very early stage of development. . . . Oral envy . . . soon cease(s) to be directed against the mother alone and become(s) extended to the father . . . [and infants] imagine that his penis is incorporated by her during oral copulation and remains hidden inside her [Klein, 1932, pp. 130–132]

And in *Envy and Gratitude* she refers to envy arising during "the earliest stages of the Oedipus complex", which includes the "phantasies of the mother's breast and the mother containing the penis of the father" (1957, p. 197). A number of contributors write about the ways in which envy is actually always an experience in which there are three figures, but the point is emphasized and explored particularly by Ignês Sodré and Ron Britton.

The notion of the triangularity of the envious experience rests on the assumption that envy proper emerges only at a moment of differentiation—the gap in which separateness between self and object is momentarily perceived. It is this perception of separateness that creates the belief that the goodness of the object, now not belonging to the self, is being given to an Other, a third, even when this third is perceived to be other aspects of the self or the object. Sodré describes this moment as a movement from the belief, "The breast *is* goodness" (presumably including "and the breast is me"), to a picture that "the breast *has* goodness" (presumably including "and I don't have it, since the breast is *not* me").

This notion of triangularity—the presence of the third—contains the seeds of what will become the full-blown Oedipus complex, but in its earliest appearance it concerns primitive phantasies of oral and anal as well as genital satisfactions, and it begins with the couple breast/baby. Wilfred Bion famously wrote about attacks on the links between the mother–baby couple that are motivated by aggression and envy (1959, p. 105). In the present volume a number of contributors, influenced by the work of Bion and of Rosenfeld, describe situations in which a part of the patient enviously attacks the link between a trusting, infantile part of himself and his analyst: Sodré, Caper, Steiner, Weiß, and Feldman all describe how an envious part of the self can separate itself from the analyst/patient couple and, taking up an observing, critical role, attack the link between them. Sodré locates the roots of this process firmly in the early mother–baby feeding relationship, where, at moments of separation, the infant who is not feeding, observes/remembers himself at the breast and perceives the feeding infant–himself as an Other. "Love", she writes, like milk, is "something fluid, that flows from one person to the other, forming a live link between the two". It is this link, she says, that feels unbearable to the excluded, observing child, the infant not happily sucking, now an envious third.

Alessandra Lemma presents clinical material that vividly illustrates the situation where the "third" is felt to be the mother herself. For her patient, Mother *has* the goodness—milk and also, importantly, her love, her attention, her capacity to cure—which she keeps *from* her infant and *for* herself. For this patient the situation is immensely complicated by the real probability that her actual mother did deprive her of her maternal goodness.

But, of course, even a very envious infant doesn't *only* envy his mother; he also, we have always to remember, deeply loves her, since she is the embodiment of all the goodness that he knows. Indeed, his envy is a consequence of his experience of her as all the goodness in the world. And his sense of her as profoundly good means that his envy and hatred of her, and of her link with him, or with her own good internal objects, including his father's penis, creates powerful feelings of guilt in him. This is one of the vicious circles that Klein describes: the envious part of the self attacks the baby–mother or patient–analyst couple, and this leads to a sense of guilt, a painful feeling of being bad and of being neither loving nor lovable. And this, of course, leads to despair about the self and then to such defences as persecution (Polmear, Lemma, Britton) or erotization (Sodré, Weiß). Brenman-Pick, describing the way envy, jealousy, and guilt interact with each other, points out that because envy is felt to be so unforgivable, the Other, the third—other children, other patients, the wife or husband—is felt to be more lovable and loved, painfully increasing envious feelings. Britton's discussions of Trollope's Reverend Mr Crawley, of Milton's Satan (*Paradise Lost*), and of the relationship between the ego-ideal, the ideal ego, and the superego also—and powerfully—make this point: envy creates guilt, and guilt increases envy, and someone else is felt to have been anointed, to be living in a perfect envy- and guilt-free paradise with the object (and the superego), and "we feel our own merit to be lessened thereby". Weiß's patient, as a child, would, when she expected harsh punishment from her father, retreat to a hiding place where she would bite into her arms and longingly suck blood from herself. This reminds us of Britton's patient's dream in which a baby is eating itself. In both these patients one sees, in the background, a very desperate child biting herself, concretizing the internal experience of biting and feeling bitten by the breast, and then eroticizing it. In the psychological history of both these patients one imagines a child that endlessly feels herself to be less loved and therefore feels full of hideous "stuff" (like Feldman's patient) and thus "impaired" and *justifiably* less loved.

Later, the observing self also observes the primal scene: the parental couple felt to be in constant polymorphous sexual contact, endlessly engaged with each other sexually in every sphere. In analysis, as in infancy, the mother/analyst is felt to be able to give generously because she contains her own internal object supplying her with goodness. In this situation, the baby who is not being fed and who yearns for the breast feels that it, and all the experiences connected with it, are being given to this object (father, internal penis) who simultaneously feeds, excites, and perpetually satisfies mother. This is Klein's notion of the combined parental couple, forever locked together in passionate bliss from which the baby is excluded, and it is tellingly described by Guignard as "the scandal" of the mother's sexuality. Seen through the hurt, angry, envious, and jealous eyes of the excluded child, such a couple can appear to be ugly, hateful, tantalizing, and torturing: Sodré reminds us that Klein's little patient Erna saw any signs of tenderness between her parents as designed specifically to torment her, the observing child, and that Iago transforms the real love between Othello and Desdemona into grotesque bestiality. Brenman-Pick describes a patient who, after some progress in analysis, wants to create an excited panic when she has to observe a rival giving a theatrical performance; Brenman-Pick points out that the patient is jealous of the rival, but that her jealousy is enormously compounded by an envious attack on her own progress, which she will spoil by her panic. This same patient idealizes cruelty, which she then feels guilty about and then, envying the analyst's capacity to think about her cruel attacks, becomes placating and idealizing—thereby nullifying what might otherwise be real admiration for her analyst's capacity to help her. For this patient, cruelty seemed often to be expressed in relation to someone's child: someone's child was ill, or killed, and the patient found that she felt excited and triumphant in her violent, excited, envious attack on the mother–baby and analyst–patient couple. Thus the mother/analyst is punished by having to watch her child suffer or die; and the patient is excitedly participating in an intercourse felt to be cruel and violent. In her fine reading of Othello, Sodré convincingly illuminates the nature of the violence of Iago's attack on Othello's mind and on his love. She argues that, ultimately, envious attacks are always attacks on love—the love of the baby and mother for each other, love between the parents, and love between the loving couple.

What is gratitude?

Edna O'Shaughnessy is the only one of our contributors who chose to focus explicitly on gratitude, though gratitude is recognized as a concept with far-reaching implications by Fonagy, and its absence is of central concern in Lemma's chapter. O'Shaughnessy accepts Klein's view of "gratitude"—"essential in building up the relation to the good object and . . . the appreciation of goodness in others and in oneself" as the conceptual equivalent of envy, envy's potential "mitigator", and she examines the ways it can arrive within an analysis. Klein saw gratitude as the protector of loving feelings, opposing it to greed. Her argument is interesting: she saw greed as directed originally precisely towards the breast's specific contents: the milk that quells hunger. The appeasement of greed, Klein insisted, cannot bring gratification. It can bring satiation, a feeling of lack of hunger, an absence of appetite. But gratification, according to Klein, concerns experiences beyond the satisfaction of hunger: pleasure and delight from smell and from touch, from gazing and being gazed at, from being held comfortably and safely. It contains all the budding sensory and psychological experiences that will gradually become what we know as love. If greed can be understood to be about getting all the goodness for oneself—Klein links it with gorging and sucking out the contents of the breast—then gratification can be seen to be about an experience of closeness and intimacy—what Petot (1993, p. 199) calls "disinterested love". And repeated experiences of gratification can lead to gratitude.

Gratitude is the acknowledgement, recognition, and enjoyment of the fact that something good has been received—"a gift". Gratitude therefore requires an other: the gift is given me by an other. Gratitude proper arises at the moment of the gap—the moment it is recognized that the gift comes from another person, not from the self. At this moment, when hatred of the object—because it is other, because it is not-Me—appears, gratitude is a mitigator of such hatred and a protector of loving feelings. Gratitude, then, is not just for a full belly, but for the multitude of experiences involved in the process of feeding and loving, being fed and loved: smell, touch, held, gazed at.

Alessandra Lemma writes about patients whose capacity to feel grateful has been severely curtailed by their experiences. The patients she writes about are young women whose own mothers deeply resented their birth, and who were fed and cared for without pleasure and without generosity. These patients rarely had an experience of a bounteous, loving breast and were thus unable to internalize and identify with a generous object. Without such an internal object, able to protect them from internal impulses and external disappointments, these young women remain, instead, in a fixed identification with a cruel superego—the bitter, resentful internal object—and in this identification later resent and deprive their own infants. As an infant begins to be aware of the separateness of the object, hatred towards this separate, different object is powerful. Experiences of gratification at the breast allow the awareness of separation to take place by opposing love—gratitude—to the hatred. Elizabeth Spillius, in her paper on "Varieties of Envious Experience" (2007b), has described the relationship between the "giver" and "the receiver", and her views correspond closely with those of Lemma: when what a child receives has been given reluctantly, he will be deprived of sufficient proper gratification, and he will be deprived of the opportunity to feel grateful as well. This will fundamentally affect his capacity to internalize a generous, loving, and loved internal object. Such a child may well grow up unable to dis-identify from a cruel and remorseless superego. There is an obvious link between the dilemma of the patient Lemma is describing and that of Milton's Satan, as described by Britton: each feels turned out from Paradise, while watching someone else able to live in perfect union with his object. In the patient's case, it is her mother's (and later her analyst's) "calm" "carefree" life she envies—a phantasy that her mother/analyst lives in perpetual harmony with her own superego while she has been banished to the hell of her own disturbing feelings.

When love is given reluctantly, gratitude is impossible. And when love is believed to be false, it is also impossible, as Sodré, O'Shaughnessy, and Steiner point out. It is also true, as several writers describe, that envy can falsify the perception of love: such is the case with Klein's little Erna, Sodré's Iago, and Weiß's patient.

Both Caper and Erlich question Klein's conceptual equation of envy with gratitude. Erlich sees gratitude, as mentioned above, as an aspect of love; he feels that both love and gratitude represent feelings and mental integrations that are at a higher level than the drive-directed emotions such as envy, hunger, passion. Caper has a different point of view about this. Following Bion, he understands envy to be one example of a more general hatred of reality, a hatred that, by its very nature, attacks the links that connect one person meaningfully to another or one idea meaningfully to another. He feels that what envy leaves in its wake is a general and widespread constriction of experience, and this leads him to believe that the damage caused by envy is significantly wider than the undermining of gratitude emphasized by Klein. He suggests that the real object of the envious attack is independence of thought and creativity.

Fonagy takes a different view. He sees Klein's opposition of envy and gratitude to be a significant conceptual contribution in that, insofar as it posits constitutional differences to exist between infants in their ability to receive love and experience gratitude for it, it takes important issue with theories about development that are based on the assumption that destructiveness is a direct result of environmental failure.

For Klein, it is gratitude that marks the movement from narcissism to object love and *establishes* it—as opposed to opposing it, denying it, obliterating it. Goodness felt to be coming from the self, requiring no gratitude, is, as Britton describes in these pages, narcissistic union between the self and the superego. Gratitude is the recognition and appreciation of otherness and is thus the marker of the capacity to internalize an object known to be separate from oneself.

At the end of her chapter on gratitude, O'Shaughnessy writes about transience—about the perpetually moving and changing quality, the fluidity, of all our experiences. We are reminded, then, of Steiner's description of the opposite experience: the interminable, intractable quality of the whole variety of repetition compulsions, where "everything stays as it was". It is because of the painfulness of the first that one must have sympathy for those who resolutely retreat to the safety of the second.

The idea for this book came from Alessandra Lemma, and I am very grateful to her for including me in its realization.

Reading these thirteen chapters, abounding in thoughts, hypotheses, images, opinions, conclusions all engendered by one short work, one has a sense of how psychoanalysts must have struggled without *Envy and Gratitude.* It is a measure of Klein's lasting bequest that so much flows from it—like a bountiful well from which any number of vessels can be filled. This book is *ipso facto* dedicated to Klein's work and to the psychoanalysts who have been inspired to enjoy, explore, examine, and expand it.

1

"Even now, now, very now . . ." On envy and the hatred of love

Ignês Sodré

Even now, now, very now, an old black ram
Is tupping your white ewe. Arise, arise!

Othello (I.1.88–89)

Sight hateful, sight tormenting! Thus these two
Imparadised in one another's arms
The happier Eden, shall enjoy their fill
Of bliss on bliss, while I to hell am thrust.

Milton, *Paradise Lost, Book IV,* v. 505–508 (1975, p. 99)

Othello, Shakespeare's great tragedy of domestic violence, provides the most powerful example in literature of how destructive envy involves a triangular situation in which the envious self is the tormented outsider and consists in an attack the aim of which is to obliterate love itself. For Iago, the sight of love between two people is so unbearable, so utterly tormenting, that it must not be allowed to exist in his mind. To prevent it, he must constantly debase it by creating an obscene—to him exciting rather than tormenting—version of intercourse, which must also be projected into the lover's mind.

Othello is tormented by delusional sexual jealousy that is fuelled by Iago's constant pornographic projections; his love turns into hatred, and he commits murder. But Shakespeare's beautiful play ultimately shows us what Othello's profound despair is about: it is the idea of goodness itself, of love, being not only lost forever but felt as never having really existed, that causes his descent into madness.

In this chapter I address the question of triangularity in envy. I examine the centrality of the most primitive version of the primal scene, the involvement of jealousy in the unconscious envious attack, the role of what Klein calls early genitalization as a defence against primitive envy, and the question of what is the ultimate object of envy, which, I think, is love itself. To illustrate these points, I use as an example Shakespeare's extraordinary portrayal of the functioning of Iago's mind.

Envy and triangularity

Klein's Envy and Gratitude, postulating the importance of envy as a manifestation of the destructive instinct, caused a controversy that continues to this day. It is a work of great complexity, and many of its insights have become definitive for the understanding of the mind. Klein says that "Envy is a most potent factor in undermining feelings of love and gratitude at their root, since it affects the earliest relation of all, that to the mother" (Klein, 1957, p. 176). And: "I consider that envy is an oral-sadistic and anal-sadistic expression of destructive impulses, operative from the beginning of life, and that it has a constitutional basis" (p. 176). These ideas, derived from the concept of the death instinct, inevitably cause a resistance: it is painful to conceive of an inborn wish to destroy what is good because of—rather than in spite of—its goodness. Klein saw evidence of such destructiveness in her clinical work with adults and with children and emphasized this in her published work. She also emphasized—a fact that is perhaps not sufficiently taken into consideration in controversial debates—the amount of suffering that these destructive states of mind cause in its subject, and her belief that this acute suffering could be diminished through interpretation. Interpretation of envy was meant to alleviate mental suffering by leading to greater integration and a strengthening of the ego—though, of course, insight connected to having to acknowledge in oneself a wish to attack goodness cannot but be extremely painful. (Somehow the need to make the point about envy being an essential part of human nature led to an overuse of the words "innate" and "constitutional" attached to envy, in a way that I think became unhelpful—as if an extra condemnation were attached to it: after all, we don't talk of innate jealousy or innate Oedipus complex—we just assume that these are all part of human nature. The conflicting emotions we are all born with are, as most analysts would agree, love and hate; what is controversial is the question of destructiveness—as opposed to aggression.)

The theoretical question of whether envy always involves a primitive form of triangularity to some extent is a complex one. In the case of little Erna, first described in 1924, Melanie Klein (1932) places great importance on oral envy of the primal scene. Erna's experience of being tormented by the primal scene is central to her psychopathology: "her oral envy of the genital and oral gratifications which she supposed her parents to be enjoying during intercourse proved to be the deepest foundation of her hatred" (1932, p. 46) Erna believed that any expression of her mother's tenderness towards her father had one chief purpose, which was to arouse the child's envy and to wound its feelings" (p. 39); and when she played at being the mother herself, she made it clear that "tenderness was a pretence" (p. 46).

Petot (1993), in his scholarly exposition of Klein's theory, does an excellent job of disentangling the various changes and developments in the theory of envy since 1928, which culminates in *Envy and Gratitude*; although there is no space here to describe this, for the purpose of this chapter it is important to keep in mind that for Klein "envy is born of the gap between the greedy expectation accompanying the fantasy of an inexhaustible breast, and reality, which inevitably brings deprivation" (Petot, 1993, p. 212). The envious attack has at its aim to suppress "inside and through omnipotent phantasies *the intolerable goodness of the frustrating breast*" (p. 215; emphasis added).

> [E]nvy relates to a dyadic situation, whereas jealousy can appear only in a relationship involving the subject and two objects. Envy, then, appears earlier than this triangular situation, as the latter is the condition of the transformation of envy into jealousy. But the Kleinian notion of envy is inseparable from an early form of the triangular situation, one which concerns not relations between two objects, but conflict with the object that is centered on a *third thing*. [Petot, 1993, p. 217; emphasis added]

This third thing is an *imaginary part object*, a constant inside mother (father's penis). Linking this to combined parents doesn't change this significantly: this is about the two parents combined, enjoying themselves and their contents, depriving the child. But, to start with, "it is because the relationship with the breast is already triangular in a certain sense that the feeling of frustration can arise at all" (p. 219).

This triangulation is discussed by Riviere in her 1932 paper in which she analyses a pathologically jealous patient's "dominant phantasy":

> this consisted of an impulse or an act on the patient's part of seizing and obtaining from some other person something she greatly desired, thus robbing and despoiling him or her. In her phantasy such an act or impulse presupposed a "triangular situation"; if not necessarily in the sense that two other *persons* besides herself were required to fulfil its terms, at least two *objects* were essential in it. (Both objects might be persons or one might not be). [Riviere, 1932, p. 107]

> The "search" or the "loss" [of love] can be traced back to *oral envy* and to the deprivation of the breast or the father's penis (as an oral object). . . . This . . . [is the] basis for the acute and desperate sense of lack and loss, of dire need, of emptiness and desolation felt by the jealous one in the triangle. [p. 112]

How can one conceptualize the most primitive form of envy, how can one imagine the infant in that state of mind? Petot points out that the concept of innate envy appears in relation to the idea of the preconception of a good breast (something that exists as a given, to satisfy all needs and desires): "Melanie Klein affirms that the infant suspects the breast of keeping for itself its milk and its love, but she never troubles to account for the formation of this belief" (Petot, 1993, p. 217). He thinks that the idea is that, unlike with other versions of the breast, this belief happens without projection. This does not really seem possible—a breast that keeps it all to itself is necessarily bad and must be created by the projection of the infant's possessiveness. I suspect that the lack of clarity about the conceptualization of this process was part of the need to make envy "purer" of influence from experience and therefore more fit to be the main representative of destructiveness. I don't think this works, though.

The only way I can imagine this is to suppose that envy appears the moment a sense of separateness appears, and up to that moment breast and baby are the same; when there is a sense of baby looking from the outside, then it is possible to imagine a goodness as belonging to the breast and not to the baby. I think that may be the moment in which the breast ceases to *be* goodness and becomes something that *has* goodness, as a possession. (Only then can it conceivably "keep it all to itself"). At this moment, then, love stops being a total state of endless bliss and becomes a substance (a "third") that flows between one person and the other. At this moment, generosity can exist, and gratitude, and envy, and jealousy too.

Love (like milk) is always something fluid, flowing from one person to the other, forming a live link between two; it is this link that, seen by the envious third, is unbearable and must therefore be enviously debased. What Petot (1993) calls "the intolerable goodness of the breast" must fundamentally be not only its riches but its generosity: the willingness to part with these riches must connect to the belief that the breast will be continuously replenished. The mother/analyst/breast can give generously because they contain their own internal object, which is endlessly supplying them with goodness. The supply is also inexhaustible (in this version of things) because of the mutuality of love between mother and baby: it is the baby's sucking that creates more milk, it is gratitude that creates generosity, not just generosity that creates gratitude. The separated/separate baby, in an envious/jealous state of mind, cannot maintain in his internal world a continuity in time of the good feeding experience; a rupture with that—caused by faulty introjection or by unbearable frustration/deprivation—creates a state of mind in which the self as the loved-baby-at-the-breast is perceived as *another baby*; so the link between mother and baby needs to be attacked, as it provokes unbearable envy and jealousy. A vicious circle is established, because the more the excluded envious part of the self attacks the couple baby-at-the-breast and mother, the more unlovable it feels and the greater the despair about the survival of love.

What is preserved in an idealized form as perfect love is not necessarily just oral—although the life-giving union of nipple–mouth is its most powerful link. Klein, of course, believed that what is longed for as the ideal state is that of the baby in the womb—and that this loss can be accepted only through the introjection of the good breast: "the infant who was first inside the mother now has the mother inside himself" (1957, p. 178). This is symbolized by the experience at the breast, with the milk filling the baby up, creating contentment and gratitude; what we call "good breast" stands for the total experience, which includes the mother's arms, the warmth of her skin, her eyes and smile, her voice, and so on. (I don't think the breast here should be called part-object; I don't believe "part-object" is at all a good description: if the baby relates just to the breast, it is because breast and mother are the same. I think part-object should be reserved for something that is the product of splitting, not for the original object of love and desire; splitting of a part from the whole, and of course splitting of good—that which I invest with love, and experience as loving—and bad—that which I invest with hatred, and experience as hating.)

When love given to another—even when the "another" is oneself a moment ago, before separation or before the realization of separateness—is a "sight tormenting", envy must destroy it by making it not exist: the mind's eye will be prevented from seeing it, contemplating it as this greatest good to which the self has no access now—and will, therefore, never have. As we know, these states of mind are felt to be forever. It is the growing capacity to experience the continuity of good experience in the mind—when the satisfying experience is felt to be going on existing in the internal world (which is what gratitude means)—that will ensure that destructive envy will not be stirred up in such a way; it is the forever-ness of the loss, the unbearability of separateness as opposed to the temporality of separation, that creates the eternal now-ness of the primal scene. With development, separation will be felt to imply temporary loss; the loss becomes total in the case of the death of the object, or if the object is felt to be entirely possessed by another. What cannot be "cured" in further development is separateness—its existence as a fact of life can only be warded off by delusion. Although the experience of falling in love—with a lover, or with a new baby, or with one's mother, the bliss-on-bliss merging of the experience of all-encompassing love of "imparadised in each other's arms" (see Milton quote above)—is an illusion that has the intensity of truth, we know it is a passing stage. At best, idealization will be succeeded by lasting ordinary goodness. The establishment of an internal sense of continuity of time, which ensures a continuity of identity, is an essential development that both fosters and is confirmed by the advent of the depressive position: the experience of separation and of separateness is only bearable if the frustrated baby is able to know that the contented baby-at-the-breast was himself in the past and therefore can be himself in the future. Joan Riviere says that everything starts with a comparison:

> For as soon as the need for much is strong, comparisons have begun to enter in. Now a comparison between ourselves and others is no primary, simple situation in itself. It is, however, a more developed and complicated version of the primary situation I described earlier, when the baby feels the *difference* between pleasant good states of well-being in itself and painful dangerous feelings and states. All comparisons began with that comparison. [Riviere, "Public Lectures", 1937, p. 184]

The same experience can be felt as: the breast has been given to another (thus rage, envy, persecution); or it was mine and I lost it (sadness, guilt, pining); at best, I will have it again (= I am still loved).

Envy and the negative therapeutic reaction

From a conceptual point of view, the change from "the breast *is* goodness" to "the breast *has* goodness" (which it may keep all for itself) is already a form of triangularity—both in terms of goodness becoming the *third thing* and in terms of mother having herself as her love object. When trying to isolate envy, specifically, as an object of clinical study, we could think schematically of various triangular configurations, in which the self can experience being the excluded third watching some form of the primal scene. All these provoke psychic suffering, giving rise to various painful affects and causing various defensive manoeuvres. In the consulting room, we see these most clearly in negative therapeutic reactions, which happen often in minimal ways, though sometimes more dramatically creating a therapeutic impasse. In some patients, serial negative therapeutic reactions seem to become a way of life—which we must therefore understand as their only way to survive psychically.

Here are various possible triangles:

1. The binary "the breast *is* goodness" becomes the triangular "the breast *has* goodness" and "keeps it for itself"—for example, the

analyst who is, or is felt to be, narcissistically invested in the therapeutic success.

2. The mother feeds the baby because she is fed by her internal object (breast, penis); one negative version of this is the analyst too wedded to theory.
3. The baby eternally witnessing part object parental oral intercourse—the analyst seen as excited by his own ideas.
4. The baby observing himself at the breast can't tolerate separateness and envies baby and breast together; this manifests as a difficulty in allowing analyst to enjoy working with the patient and a sense of unfairness that "it is all so easy for the analyst".
5. The frustrated, separated baby observes and finds intolerable the sight of himself at the breast, loses the continuity in time of baby-at-the-breast was me a moment ago with the present state of baby-not-at-the-breast self, and sees baby-at-the-breast as *another baby*. This results in envy of another part of the self and attacks on linking of good breast with contented baby. In the consulting room, this can be seen when what seems like real contact is suddenly broken, and the interpretation is treated with contempt. An atmosphere of cold cynicism ensues, which is ultimately an attack on the dependent, loving part of the patient.

In terms of clinical work, the denigration of the—nursing or parental—couple through the envious/jealous attack on the fluid link between them creates a state of mind characterized by cynicism, arrogance, and triumph over and contempt for dependent, vulnerable aspects of the self; love disappears because it is seen always to be false, with the parental intercourse seen as perverse (deliberately projecting envy, and obscene because devoid of love). The manic defence has to be kept going to hide the despair that ensues, so this constellation is perpetuated.

In more perverse patients, with a serious lack of stability in the good internal object, the analyst sees an almost continuous negativism: the tiniest bit of insight begins to be felt as only a trap, presented solely to give the analyst hope that can be instantly dashed. The patient is then in projective identification with a cruel, tantalizing mother, offering baby a taste of milk, only to be able to pull it back into dependence and therefore into humiliation and bitter deprivation. In these patients a pseudo-jealousy situation can be repeatedly stirred up in the mind, providing the erotic excitement to fuel the envious attack.

This relates to one of the points I want to illustrate with Iago: hatred of the loving couple in the primal scene causes it to be denigrated through contempt and over-sexualization, making it obscene; this connects to Klein's idea, already present very early on (in little Erna) but more clearly conceptualized in *Envy and Gratitude*, of precocious genitalization being both a result of and a defence against primitive envy.

According to Klein:

> Excessive envy interferes with adequate oral gratification and so acts as a stimulus towards the intensification of genital desires and trends. This implies that the infant turns too early towards genital gratification, with the consequence that the oral relation becomes genitalized and the genital trends become too much coloured by oral grievances and anxieties . . . genital trends interfere with oral ones at a stage when normally the oral desires are uppermost. . . . Genitality based on a flight from orality is insecure because into it are carried over the suspicions and disappointments attaching to the impaired oral enjoyment. . . . For the lack of primary enjoyment introduces into the genital desires compulsive elements, and . . . may lead to sexual sensations entering into all activities, thought processes, and interests. [Klein, 1957, p. 195]

Iago's character powerfully illustrates—as we often also observe in perverse and delusional jealousy—how erotization provides the energy for a continuous intrusion into and attack of the primal scene. This means that what I consider to be the necessary connection of envy with jealousy is two-fold: first, that primitive envy is always connected to triangularity, and, second, that sexual jealousy is hijacked into the situation to help provide fuel for the envious attack—erotization heats it up and provides the perverse excitement that increases the power of the projections, literally propelling the envious self right into the primal scene (Bloom, 1999, calls Iago a "moral pyromaniac", "setting fire to reality"). By keeping the obscene primal scene going endlessly, with erotic excitement as its fuel, the real "sight tormenting" of love—that which is most envied—is constantly obscured.

The debasement of love as a defence against envy

Within minutes of the beginning of *Othello*, Iago makes a vicious attack on the primal scene, transforming a love marriage that is about to be consummated into a cause for hatred and contempt through his imagery of bestiality and obscenity. Ideal love is violently debased and becomes pornography in Iago's mind and in the minds of those he projects it into: in this scene, Brabantio, Desdemona's father. Later in the play, when he makes Cassio drunk and orchestrates a brawl, he again interrupts Othello and Desdemona's repeat-wedding night, when, having failed to consummate their marriage in the first night [Iago: "he hath not yet made wanton the night with her" (II.ii.15], they retire to bed and are literally taken out of it by the interruption. (Some critics think that the marriage may in fact never have been consummated—for instance, because logically Othello would then have had to know that Desdemona was a virgin.) And the climax of the play, the third primal scene, is the transformation of passionate love into murder, with Othello, corrupted by Iago's perverse projections, killing Desdemona in the marriage bed. It seems clear that Iago is set to destroy the loving primal scene by causing the death of one of the partners; but because here the object of his hatred is love itself, simply organizing the murder of one or both partners would not be enough: he must destroy love in the mind of the lover by transforming it into hatred. The excitement that gathers momentum and results in murder is that of poisoning and corrupting—perverse sexual excitement.

Through an exploration of Iago's character I want to illustrate some of the core features of envy that I have been describing: Iago's experience shows powerfully how love in the original configuration of the primal scene is the central provoker of envy, and that malignant envy is not consciously experienced as envy but as contempt and repulsion. Significantly, we can see how at the height of the envious attack the primal scene is experienced as being permanently in the present—"even now, now, very now . . ."—and therefore must be constantly attacked and debased to prevent the conscious self from experiencing the "sight tormenting" of a love union that excludes the self.

One of the fascinating aspects of Iago's complex character is that, ultimately, he doesn't know why he does what he does, although he is aware that he is full of hatred and thoughts of revenge; he is proud of his nastiness and of his capacity to trick others into believing he is "honest" (Empson, 1951). Destructive envy is, by definition, unconscious: he can't know that he can't stand the sight of love, since he does not know it exists, and only sees it as "(Brabantio's) daughter covered by a Barbary horse", "in the gross clasps of a lascivious Moor" "making the beast with two backs". He is obsessed by his pornographic fantasies, which are constantly reactivated to prevent himself from catching a glimpse of a sight that otherwise he would find unbearably tormenting.

Critical opinion has always been divided on the matter of Iago's motives: since Coleridge (1813) wrote of Iago's "motive-hunting of motiveless malignity", there is, roughly speaking, one camp that believes in Iago's stated motives, and one that believes, instead, that Iago fabricates motives to convince himself with: "Iago [is] the dramatist of his own psyche no less than that of Othello" (Nuttall, 2007, p. 282). Iago's stated motives are jealousy and revenge because Othello chooses Cassio as his lieutenant and Iago has to accept the lesser post of ensign; and jealousy of Othello "twixt his sheets" with his (Iago's) wife Emilia:

> I hate the Moor,
> And it is thought abroad that 'twixt my sheets
> He's done my office. I know not if't be true
> But I for mere suspicion of the kind
> Will do as surety.
>
> [*Othello,* I.iii.375]

He even suggests a thought of Cassio in his "nightcap". This sexual jealousy is particularly unconvincing—nothing in Iago's relation with Emilia indicates it—and the fight for preferment ought to have ended after he succeeded in making Cassio lose Othello's love and Iago himself became lieutenant. (There is no sense of satisfaction in getting Cassio's job: clearly what he wants is not the position of Othello's lieutenant but that of omnipotent master of Othello's thoughts; Cassio's demotion becomes just a useful fact to be manipulated to further his monstrous plot.) It is clear that Iago chooses to stir up his own jealousy as fuel for erotization, to heat up the situation in his own mind, thus adding strength to the pornographic projections. Coleridge's "motiveless malignity" sounds very much like innate envy, and the critics seem embroiled in veritable controversial discussions on this subject (see, e.g., Bradley, 1904, or Leavis, 1952). I think this is a clear example of what one sees in patients when the real jealousy that is intrinsic in the triangularity of unconscious envy is hijacked and transformed into exciting pseudo-jealousy, increasing the strength of the phantasy of being right in the middle of the primal scene. It is, of course, Iago who is projecting himself into his puppets' "nightcaps" and perversely enjoying being "twixt their sheets".

Although Iago, because of his cold cynicism, is particularly revealing about his perverse motives (he has eight soliloquies), he plots Othello's downfall from the position of a sadistic, omnipotent puppeteer and is caught up in it, moving "from contingency to contingency" (Wain, 1971, p. 13), never entirely knowing where it is all leading to, He is caught up in his plot's own momentum, stirs up his own emotions, and, as happens in perverse excitement, is taken over by an orgy of destructiveness.

> How? How? Let's see.
> After some time to abuse Othello's ear
> that he [Cassio] is too familiar with his wife.
> . . .
> The Moor is of a free and open nature,
> That thinks men honest that but seem to be so,
> And will be as tenderly led by th' nose
> As asses are. I have't! It is engendered: Hell and Night
> Must bring this monstrous birth to the world's light.
>
> [*Othello,* I.iii]

And now it is clear that the "monstrous birth" will drive out of existence a creative, loving one, through the abuse of Othello's mind.

Othello and Desdemona convey in their language and in their contact both passionate *coup de foudre* and spiritual love:

> She loved me for the dangers I had passed,
> And I loved her that she did pity them.
>
> [*Othello,* I.iii.165)]

> My heart's subdued
> Even to the very quality of my lord:
> I saw Othello's visage in his mind,
> And to his honours and his valiant parts
> Did I my soul and fortunes consecrate.
>
> [*Othello,* I.iii.250]

> I therefore beg it not
> To please the palate of my appetite,
> Not to comply with heat—the young affects
> In me defunct—and proper satisfaction;
> But to be free and bounteous to her mind.
>
> [*Othello,* I.iii.265]

Iago is as crude as it is possible to be. We see "the Iago-spirit gnawing at the root of all the *Othello* values, the *Othello* beauties; he eats into the core and heart of this romantic world, worms his way into its solidity, rotting it, poisoning it" (Wilson Knight, 1930 p. 96).

As the plot begins to work, Othello starts doubting Desdemona and asks himself why did ever married:

> O curse of marriage,
> That we can call these delicate creatures ours,
> And not their appetites! I had rather be a toad
> And live upon the vapour of a dungeon,
> Than keep a corner in the thing I love
> For others' uses.
>
> [*Othello,* III.iii]

As uncertainty becomes unbearable, he starts demanding proof of her unfaithfulness:

> Villain, be sure to prove my love a whore!
> Be sure of it; give me ocular proof
>
> [*Othello,* III.iii.360]

His mind begins to fill up with obscene thoughts:

> Were they as prime as goats, as hot as monkeys,
> As salt as wolves in pride
>
> [*Othello,* III.iii.405]

The deterioration of Othello's mind as it becomes contaminated by Iago's envious projections is clear in the fragmentation of his language: "Pish! Nose, ears, lips! Is't possible? Confess? Handkerchief? O devil!"; "Fire and brimstone!" "Goats and monkeys!" (IV.i.255). Moments of melancholic sorrow, as in "but yet the pity of it, Iago; O Iago, the pity of it, Iago!" are followed by savage "I will chop her into messes".

Iago has triumphed in his desire to transform love into hatred, through utter corruption of Othello's mind: he rids himself of envious suffering at the sight of love through continuous, brutal "tupping" of Othello's mind with obscenities. The corruption is only temporary: Othello commits suicide after the murder, because he has become sane again.

The "double-time" of reality and phantasy:

The three "primal scenes", the only nights Othello and Desdemona spend together as a married couple, seem to belong together as they take our minds into what we, the audience, experience as three consecutive days (although in fact the sea-voyage from Venice to Cyprus separates the first night from the second). The impact of Iago's seduction and corruption of Othello and his consequent madness takes place between the second night and the third: in the first there is union but no consummation due to the interruption orchestrated by Iago. In the second, equally disrupted, there is union and (probable) consummation, and in the third there is the murder on the bed made with the marriage sheets (which Desdemona, as if predicting her death, asks Emilia to make into her shroud). Symbolically it is always the same wedding-night bed.

In this way, the primal scene transformation of love into murder happens in a rapid continuum that feels almost like real time in the immediacy of the play. As the inevitable tragedy unfolds, past, present, and future are but yesterday, today, and tomorrow. But a longer-time plot is present simultaneously, even though to the audience this does not seem illogical and it is hardly noticed. In fact, one does not necessarily notice this strange anomaly even when reading the play carefully.

For instance: Desdemona, whom Othello has just married as a virgin, becomes "that cunning whore of Venice" who has been having this adulterous affair with Cassio—although there is no time when it could possibly have taken place. Emilia claims her husband Iago has asked her "a hundred times" (III, iii) to steal the handkerchief that has just become of interest to Iago a moment before. When referring to "Cassio's" dream—which he has fabricated, as "proof"—Iago says: "I lay with Cassio lately" (III.iii); in the "other time" Brabantio has become ill and died, and political changes have taken place in Venice, which include Othello being commanded to return to Venice (IV.i). And near the end, Othello says:

'Tis pityful, but yet Iago knows
That she with Cassio hath the act of shame
A thousand times committed.

[*Othello*, V.ii]

Although of course Othello is exaggerating because of his rage, a sense of a long past is clearly implied.

The causes for this double-time have been very much part of critical debate over the centuries (Allen, 1968). What is its meaning? Is it Shakespeare's mistake or a product of his genius? To my mind, it conveys the double-time of reality and phantasy: Iago, driven by malignant envy, is in thrall to a need to destroy love by his constant, ultimately successful, attack on the primal scene, which invades his mind: love is unbearable and must be destroyed. To the jealous–envious outsider, the primal scene is permanently in the present and ubiquitous, and so has to be attacked continuously; so in the "place" that it occupies in the internal world, it is forever "even now, now, very now". To us analysts the coexistence, on the one hand, of a long time span in which ordinary events follow each other and developments take place and, simultaneously, on the other, a powerful endless present-time where a terrible disturbance repeats and repeats without ever changing seems only natural. There is no time in the unconscious, no time in primary process, as Freud discovered. But we can also see the link with the question of time in Klein's conceptualization of envy: Erna, like Iago, cannot bear the sight of love, presumably because there is no internal continuity in her sense of being, on and off as it were, the baby at the breast. Instead, the mind is stuck in the torture of exclusion. Erna, getting better, says "mother is not really like that, is she?" Iago, "in reality", has a loving wife.

Shakespeare portrays in Iago a mind that cannot bear the sight of love and must therefore destroy it, so that it will not only cease to exist, but cease to *ever* have existed. If envy proves that all love is a sham, then the past where it once existed also ceases to be. This kind of omnipotent phantasy destroys time. The provocation to this literally unbearable sight is ideal romantic love. It is the very fact that Othello and Desdemona are, from the point of view of the outsiders, "mis-matched", both racially and in age (so much more mismatched than Romeo and Juliet, troubled by family-feuds, but otherwise equal) that makes the claim for perfect love more powerful and therefore more unbearable. The fact that the "trifle" that is central to the plot, the handkerchief, is anchored in, and symbolic of, the creative primal scene version of the parents must contribute to the envy: Othello's mother gave it to him, and it is destined to be given to the woman whom he will love—it had been a present from his father, also reminiscent of the breast, white and embroidered with strawberries; in another version, it had been given to the mother by a woman—a gipsy "magician" mother, who wove it. (Red stains on white linen is also, of course, proof of the bride's virginity on the wedding night—see Cavell, 2003.)

The success of the loving couple, "imparadised in each other's arms" (I quote Milton's Satan's consciously envious speech about the unbearability of the sight of "those two, Imparadised in each other's arms, bliss on bliss" as the best description of what Iago would see if for a moment he were to stop his concerted effort to debase love), implies therefore an identification with a successful parental couple whose intercourse produced a loving child: Othello the blissful lover is also the beloved child of his mother. So everything about him is experienced as provoking envy by Iago. By contrast, Cassio is able to know about it and accept it—which perhaps is what makes Iago say the most un-Iago-esque thing about him: "he hath a daily beauty to his life which makes me ugly".

In terms of development, the excluded child who can bear the feeling of jealousy "pines", longs for the recovery of paradise in mother's arms. When envy has the upper hand, the "sight tormenting" is unbearable, and thus ceases to be borne. It is diminished by contempt, falsified, robbed of its good qualities; it is consciously experienced as a sham. Long before she wrote *Envy and Gratitude*, Melanie Klein showed this very clearly in little Erna's case: in her despair, Erna does not believe in the reality of feelings of love: tenderness is a fake. One assumes that unconsciously guilt and despair ensue, which must be kept constantly at bay by manic triumph, perpetuating the situation where no good coupling is ever allowed to exist.

2

Envy, narcissism, and the destructive instinct

Robert Caper

It has been 50 years since Klein published *Envy and Gratitude.* While it has not had the impact of such fundamental works such as "Notes on Some Schizoid Mechanisms" (Klein, 1946), which laid out the paranoid–schizoid position and described projective identification, or "A Contribution to the Psychogenesis of Manic-Depressive States" (Klein, 1935) and "Mourning and Its Relation to Manic-Depressive States" (Klein, 1940), which laid out the concept of the depressive position, it does crystallize her thinking on two subjects that have become prominent in the Kleinian tradition ever since its publication: envy and the destructive instinct.

Klein begins her work by setting out unambiguously just what she proposes to discuss:

> I consider that envy is an oral-sadistic and anal-sadistic expression of destructive impulses operative from the beginning of life, and that it has a constitutional basis [Klein, 1957, p. 176].

While she does not attempt a comprehensive account of what it is that envy is supposed destroy, she does emphasize that it is "a most potent factor in undermining feelings of love and gratitude at their root, since it affects the earliest relation of all, that to the mother" (Klein, 1957, p. 176).

For Klein, the significance of this early relationship cannot be overestimated:

> Throughout my work I have attributed fundamental importance to the infant's first object relation—the relationship to the mother's breast and to the mother—and have drawn the conclusion that if this primal object, which is introjected, takes root in the ego with relative security, the basis for a satisfactory development is laid. Under the dominance of oral impulses, the breast is instinctively felt to be the source of nourishment and therefore, in a deeper sense, of life itself. [Klein, 1957, p. 178]

In Klein's view, then, envy attacks the ability to value and appreciate life at its source. Since it also operates from the beginning of life and has a constitutional basis, it seems to be a fairly straightforward clinical expression of the destructive instinct.

The destructive instinct is a concept that Klein accepts without hesitation in this work. After referring to her analyst Karl Abraham's "A Short History of the Libido, Viewed in the Light of Mental Disorders" (Abraham, 1927), she points out that, although he did not himself use the concept of the destructive instinct, his analysis of the first manic-depressive patients was "based on insight which was taking him in that direction", implying that he would have arrived at it had he not died prematurely. She then says,

> as I am about the publish *Envy and Gratitude*, three decades after Abraham's death, it is a source of great satisfaction to me that my work has contributed to the growing recognition of the full significance of Abraham's discoveries. . .

thus not only providing an illustration of what she means by gratitude, but also laying a claim that she is fleshing out the idea of a destructive instinct latent in the work of the analyst whom she loved and admired. Her work on envy is, therefore, among other things, her most detailed exposition of her ideas about the destructive instinct.

But as she penetrates deeper into the infant's relationship to the breast, Klein begins to apprehend problems that, at least on the surface, have little to do with envy. Writing of the infant's earliest relations to the breast, she observes that the

> . . . mental and physical closeness to the gratifying breast in some measure restores, if things go well, the lost prenatal unity with

> the mother and the feeling of security that goes with it. . . [Klein, 1957, pp. 178–179]

However,

> while the pre-natal state no doubt implies a feeling of unity and security, how far this state is undisturbed must depend on the psychological and physical condition of the mother, and possibly even on certain unexplored factors in the unborn infant. We might, therefore, consider the universal longing for the pre-natal state also partly as an expression of the urge for idealization, and we find that one of its sources is the strong persecutory anxiety stirred up by birth [i.e. by the intrusion of the post-natal, extra-uterine world]. . . .
>
> I would not assume that the breast is to [the infant] merely a physical object. The whole of his instinctual desire and his unconscious phantasies imbue the breast with qualities that go far beyond the nourishment it affords.
>
> We find in the analysis of our patients that the breast in its good aspect is the prototype of maternal goodness, inexhaustible patience and generosity, as well as of creativeness. [Klein, 1957, pp. 179–180]

From this it is clear that the breast that is the prototype of goodness, patience, and generosity, the relationship to which restores the pre-natal security of the womb, is an idealized object, and the longing for it is, as she puts it, "an expression of the urge for idealization".

The model—and, for all we know, the genesis—of such an idealization would be the pre-natal experience of the placenta, which is normally nothing if not good, patient, and generous from the point of view of the fetus. But from any other point of view, it is impossible to regard it in this light without great irony: the actual placenta is a fetal organ—a part of the fetus—the function of which is to parasitize the mother's physiologic resources, serving the interests of the fetus at the expense of the mother. This means that its goodness, patience, and generosity are extracted, like the goods that flow from a colony to its colonizer, at the mother's expense, without her consent, and on rare occasions even at the cost of her life. [David Haig of Harvard University and Ananth Karumanchi of Harvard Medical School have offered evidence that preeclampsia, a potentially fatal disease of late pregnancy treatable only by delivery of the baby, may be due to proteins normally secreted into the mother's blood by the fetus in order to divert more of her blood supply to itself (Zimmer, 2006).] This is not really maternal goodness, patience, or generosity: it is fetal invasion, occupation, and exploitation. It only appears to embody these maternal virtues if one is able to ignore the fact that the fetus extracts these goods from its mother willy-nilly.

We are of course discussing psychology here, not biology, but the analogy does seem to hold: the idealized (mental) breast of early infancy—the prototype of goodness, patience and generosity—seems to be part of a narcissistic system, meaning one in which the self is felt to be able to invade and control the object (via projective identification in psychic reality), obviating frustration, just as the placenta invades and controls the uterus. In this system, the needed object is felt to be part of the self, while the real, external, non-self object that provides mental sustenance for the infant—e.g., the real mother's capacity to contain and detoxify its mental states—is pushed into the background.

I can clarify what I mean when I refer to the infant's lost pre-natal unity with the mother as a narcissistic system if we consider William Blake's perspective on another lost paradise. Reading Milton's *Paradise Lost* in what he called "th' infernal sense", Blake concluded that Lucifer was not an envious creature who rebelled against God because He was so good, but an independent soul who could not abide living in a dictatorship, no matter how benevolent. If we regard the lost paradise of infant/maternal union in the same way, we arrive at what I mean by a narcissistic system. In this system, the infant plays the role of God, and the mother is allowed to remain part of his paradise only as long as she is a good angel.

A breast that restores the lost prenatal unity with the mother, that is, with a mother who is viewed, so to speak, as the fetus might view the invaded uterus, is a captive object—an object that is treated as though it were part of the self, and at the complete disposal of the self—and is therefore persecuting (since it is felt to invade and control the self in return). Klein recognized that an idealized object is not the same as a good one: ". . . a good object which is well established, and therefore assimilated, not only loves the subject *but is loved by it.* This, I believe, is characteristic of the relation to the good object, but does not apply, or only in a minor degree, to an idealized one" [emphasis added] (Klein, 1957, p. 218).

When Klein says that the good object is loved by the subject, she is not referring to what is known as cupboard love, which is not love of the object, but only a desire for what can be obtained from it. This type of love forms a part—however subtle—of the relationship to the idealized object, but it is not true object love.

I am not suggesting that this idealization is a bad thing. It isn't, and in fact splitting and idealization are a part of normal early development that is necessary to defend against frustration that is too painful to tolerate. But idealization has its drawbacks, and a sense of persecution by the split-off bad object is one of them. Another is confusion between good and bad objects, since idealization, by eliminating the experience of frustration at the hands of the object, makes bad ones seem more or less like good ones. This impedes the development of judgement and the ability to think for oneself. These drawbacks need to be overcome in the process of maturation by later integration of the object, for which early splitting and idealization (paradoxically) pave the way. Only if this later integration fails is development endangered. Klein wrote in this connection that the "capacity for love gives impetus . . . to *successful* primal splitting" (Klein, 1957, p. 191, emphasis added). The success of this early splitting depends on its not being too wide. But excessive persecutory anxiety leads to too-wide splitting-and-idealization, resulting in the formation of an extremely bad object and an extremely idealized one. Both are persecuting in their own way, and so a vicious cycle is established. Splitting that is not too wide—which, as Klein recognized, is a function of sufficient capacity for object love and the ability to tolerate frustration—can more easily lead to later integration.

To the degree that the primal good object is idealized—that is, to the degree that its goodness, patience, and generosity are available without frustration—it is a narcissistic good object, that is, it is a narcissist's good object: something that may be treated with impunity as a part of the self. This kind of idealized relationship is not a sufficient basis for development in Klein's scheme, not only because an idealized object is persecuting (as she recognized), but also because it is hardly possible to see how an object such as this, which is experienced as part of the self, could be an object of the gratitude that Klein felt was so essential to normal development. One does not feel grateful to one's hand for doing what it is supposed to do.

Until one loses function in that hand. This adds the element that is missing from the narcissistic system and that is needed for the establishment of the good (not idealized) internal object, one that may serve as the basis for true post-natal security and psychological development. This object is not simply a paragon of goodness, patience, and generosity. It is good, patient, and generous, but it is also prone to disappear from time to time. Such an object must not only be appreciated (i.e. met with gratitude) if it is to form the core of the ego, it must also be tolerated:

> . . . a child with a strong capacity for love and gratitude has a deep-rooted relation with a good object and can, without being fundamentally damaged, withstand temporary states of envy, hatred, and grievance, which arise even in children who are loved and well mothered. Thus, when these negative states are transient, the good object is regained time and time again. This is an essential factor in establishing it and in laying the foundations of stability and a strong ego. [Klein, 1957, p, 187]

From Klein to Bion

For Klein, the conflict between envy and gratitude was a crucial battleground of development, and development proceeded in an approximately normal fashion if gratitude was able to revive the good internal object repeatedly, after it had been lost as a result of envious attacks. For Bion, the crucial battle was fought over what he called the decision to evade or modify frustration—that is, to evade or modify reality, whose hallmark is its habit of frustrating at least some of one's wishes.

In this regard, he was focusing on the movement from a system of narcissistic object relations (i.e. with idealized—non-frustrating—objects) to a system of real relationships (i.e. with real—frustrating—objects): the cultural equivalent of this transition being that from belief in a personal God to a scientific view of the universe. What is crucial for development from this point of view is the capacity to bear reality, which means tolerating frustration. This was not a fulfilment of Klein's work in the sense in which she meant to consummate Abraham's but, rather, a generalization that transcended envy, founded less on her work than on Freud's "Formulations on Two Principles of Mental Functioning" (Freud, 1911b), which contains the observation that the distinguishing feature of the reality principle (as opposed to the pleasure principle) is the tolerance of frustration.

Klein believed that envy was dangerous because it prevented the good object from being fully enjoyed, which, in turn, prevented the subject from experiencing gratitude for what the object brings and therefore from being able to use what it brings and to incorporate it into the ego as a source of life by introjection. From Bion's point of view, envy is deadly because it is one species of a more general phenomenon—attacks on linking. The latter undermine the ability to form a relationship not just with the good breast, but also with the bad breast and with all of the good and bad breasts' psychological successors (i.e. all objects). Envy is dangerous because it destroys links and therefore destroys the capacity for thought and creativity and, along with them, the ego's capacity to repair itself, which depends on them (Bléandonu, 1994, p. 133).

For Bion, envy poses a danger to development because it embodies a hatred of reality, which cuts one off from the experience of the object. The damage to ego development stems not just from envy's undermining of gratitude, but from the constriction of experience brought about by envy's effect of severing the ego's links to, and hence its appreciation of, certain important realities. While being cut off from reality—external and internal—obviously destroys creativity in a general way, what is particularly damaging is envy's attacks on the creative links that objects form with one another, of which the combined parental object, with its melding of strength and beauty, is the prototype. The combined parents' creativity is a particular victim of envy because it is itself so particularly enviable. The consequent oedipal blindness to the parents' connection deprives the ego of the capacity to observe other meaningful connections between objects or ideas. The overall effect of this is to constrict the powers of thought and observation (contact with reality) that the ego needs to repair itself and to grow.

Klein was aware, or course, that envy opposed creativity when she wrote that "envy of creativeness is a fundamental element in the disturbance of the creative process" (Klein, 1957, p. 202), and that it seeks not only to greedily scoop out, suck dry, and devour the breast, but "also to put badness, primarily bad excrements and bad parts of the self, into the mother, and first of all into her breast, in order to spoil and destroy her. In the deepest sense this means destroying her creativeness" (Klein, 1957, p. 181). But she viewed gratitude, not creativity, as the main countervailing psychological force against envy. For Bion, it is primarily creativity (in the sense elaborated in the following paragraph) that mitigates and neutralizes the effects of envy.

Bion held that the prototypical object of envy's destructive attacks was not the breast *per se* but, rather, the parental couple, whose combination of paternal strength and maternal beauty (as Donald Meltzer put it) allows it to contain the split-off, discarded, or violently projected aspects of the infant's personality while maintaining a balanced outlook. The capacity to entertain strange and disturbing ideas and feelings without losing one's mental balance is very near the essence of what Bion meant by creativity. (This view of creativity was nothing if not experience-near for Bion: it is precisely what an analyst does when he is functioning well. It is also an apt description of artistic and scientific creativity.) Containment of the infant's unbearable anxieties, so vital to its survival, triggers off feelings that the containing object providing such relief is one of great strength and almost unbearable beauty. This, in turn, precipitates powerful feelings of love, along with the most violent envious attacks on the containing couple. The latter render it difficult for the infant to introject the parental couple as an intact container and therefore to grow, meaning in this case to develop its own capacity to think. The infant's envious attack on precisely what it needs for its own development gives a good insight into the nature of envy and is a good argument for linking it to a deadly force within the psyche.

Envy and the defences against it

It is important to pause here and consider that, although we are used to regarding envy *per se* as an enemy of development, a closer examination shows that this is not so. It is not envy that causes damage but, rather, the devaluation of loved objects and the destruction of linking that occurs as a kind of pre-emptive strike designed to obliterate the occasion for envy to arise. Attacks on linking are not expressions of envy but defences against it, and are due to fear and hatred of it. In *Envy and Gratitude* Klein presents a catalogue of these defences (pp. 216–219), which include idealization of the object, confusion between good and bad objects, flight from mother to others, devaluation of the object, devaluation of the self, greedy internalization of the object (narcissistic identification), stirring up envy in others, stifling of love and intensification of hate, acting out (to prevent integration), "and many others".

All of these defences are variations on the theme of killing off love for objects that are worthy of love. They are themselves, however, not direct expressions of envy, but only indirect ones whose purpose it is to suppress the experience of envy. Acknowledged envy, envy that is not split off and not defended against, is not destructive *per se*: in fact, acknowledgement of it is a sign of mental health. If we can say of someone who is beautiful, intelligent, kind, rich, charming, witty, generous, modest and compassionate, "I can't stand people like that"—we are envious, but we don't have a problem with envy: our hatred is not so strong and frightening that we have to assuage it by trashing the object.

Such humorous or rueful acknowledgements of envy mean that we are not taking ourselves too seriously. This is why it is a sign of mental health: it indicates that our narcissism has its limits and that we can face them.

Envy and narcissism

Experiences with external objects always produce a certain amount of anxiety associated the novelty and unpredictability of the experience. This is especially true with loved objects, because only loved objects are allowed to penetrate deeply enough into one to elicit substantial anxiety. (In this context, a loved object is an object that one admires, would like to be like, and wants to—but does not—possess.) If this anxiety may be compared to an immune response, something that protects us from being injured by what we allow inside ourselves, then envy would be an allergic reaction to contact with loved external objects—a self-destructively exaggerated defence against something that is not only benign, but necessary and unconsciously recognized to be so.

If we ask ourselves what is it that might react in this way—what is it that is threatened when we allow ourselves to have an experience with an object that we love and feel is beautiful, it is difficult to escape the conclusion that it is our narcissism. If awareness of an object that one admires, would like to be like, and wants to possess (but does not) is unbearable, then one will quite often defensively (delusionally) feel that one *does* possess it, or (even more delusionally) feel that one *is* the loved object. This is a common aspect of projective identification (see Klein, 1955). These delusional states eliminate one's awareness of one's love for the loved object, with consequences that are quite harmful to one's development but leave one's narcissism relatively intact.

But if this defensive identification breaks down, then the only remaining way of safeguarding narcissism is to attack and devalue the object. As Susannah Isaacs-Elmhirst has observed, envy is a "weird compliment". Inherent in its violent hostility towards the envied object is a recognition of the object's beauty. Defences against envy offend against the beauty of the object, the source of one's envy towards it, by devaluing and defacing it. This breaks one's ties with the loved and beautiful object, and is therefore a step towards death-in-life.

What I have so far written here about narcissism may make it appear as a kind of perverse or indulgent self-love, existing in opposition to object love. I do not believe this to be necessarily the case. The emergence from narcissism is one of the major tasks of psychological development, and it is difficult because, among other things, the awareness that one's life depends on others over whom one has ultimately little or no control is a source of terrible anxiety. Emerging from narcissism means confronting this reality and the terror that accompanies contact with it. I believe that this is what Rilke had in mind when he wrote, in the *Duino Elegies,* that, "Beauty is the beginning of terror that we can only just still bear." Narcissistic defences against anxiety such as concrete identification with the needed object, or, failing that, attack and devaluation of it, are essential to prevent the psyche from being faced with anxiety that would overwhelm it. But if excessive, they also prevent the personality from having the experiences that would enable it to emerge from narcissism. Envy, or rather the defences against it, act on the psyche like auto-immune disease act on the body. A certain amount of inflammation is good and necessary when survival is threatened, as for example by an infection, but inflammation directed against one's own healthy tissues is taking a good thing too far. [Segal (1983), in considering the relationship between envy and narcissism, arrived at conclusions different from mine, which space precludes me from discussing.]

Envy and the destructive instinct

The destructiveness of the destructive instinct consists of its tendency to drive one to attack links to real external and internal objects and thereby to cut oneself off from external and internal reality. A mind cut off from both realities is a dead mind.

Attacks on linking take two broad forms. The first, hysterical attacks on linking, takes the form of narcissistic identification with objects. Narcissistic identification is the type that produces the delusion that the subject somehow *is* the object. What might have been a link to an object is replaced by a fusion with it, a perverse relationship that destroys links. This type of identification may be seen between those members of groups who mindlessly adhere to the group ethos, having lost their capacity for critical, independent thought. The destructive nature of this phenomenon may be seen in the group's hostility to anyone who departs from the group's ethos—that is, anyone who is linked to the group in the sense of having a relationship to it while still maintaining the capacity for critical independent thought. I have described elsewhere (Caper, 1997) how this type of identification may also be seen in the analytic dyad, where examining the analytic relationship, as opposed to merely being in it, elicits hostility. Narcissistic identification leads one to feel that one has the attributes of the loved object, is in fact just like it, and therefore one has no need for it and no love for it. The real (non-self) object is thus devalued precisely because it is non-self.

The second form, psychotic attacks on linking, involves splitting or fragmentation, which results in the subject being cut off from reality and is instrumental in bringing about psychotic states.

Both psychotic and hysterical attacks on linking provide an escape from the anxiety, insecurity, and conflict associated with having links to objects that are both needed and felt to be non-self (beyond one's control). But since links to these objects (whether internal or external) are what in fact constitute one's *real* mental life as a person, such a fundamental attack on them is self-destructive.

But there is obviously a difference between a psychological force constitutionally targeted to destroying one's mental life and a psychological force that destroys one's mental life incidentally in the pursuit of some other goal, even if it does so regularly. Klein views envy (attacks on links to the good object) as a constitutionally destructive force. If we look at envy as she does and ask ourselves what psychological good it is, we would be hard pressed to come up with an answer.

But, of course, as a constitutional force, it is not supposed to make psychological sense—it is metapsychological (literally, "beyond psychology"). We can, however, ask if a constitutional destructive force is a necessary hypothesis. In Klein's way of looking at it, it seems to be quite close to sin (she quotes Chaucer that "envy is the worst sin there is, for all other sins are sins against one virtue, whereas envy is a sin against all virtue and all goodness" (Klein, 1957, p. 189). Its depredations are incomprehensible and unmotivated, and it seems to be a manifestation of pure spite and meanness, destructive purely for the sake of being destructive.

The idea of a destructive instinct has proven extremely controversial, despite the confidence with which Klein treated it, and one of the roots of this controversy is, in my opinion, the dissatisfaction of many psychoanalysts with the idea of evil for evil's sake as a fundamental force in mental life. For them, it smacks too much of theology.

Many writers, perhaps in an attempt to make the destructive instinct comprehensible within a context of human motivation, have treated it as though it were somehow the same as aggression. But aggression is not inherently destructive in itself: after all, one can aggressively defend one's life, or the lives of those one loves, in which case the aggression is in the service of life, not of death. Conflating the destructive instinct with aggression does justice to neither.

If we were to look for a literary exemplar of envy, we could do no better than Klein did in *Envy and Gratitude* when she chose Iago. Shakespeare was able to convey the ambivalence and ambiguity of his characters' mental lives more vividly and succinctly than any other writer in English. Iago is perhaps unique in Shakespeare's work because he lacks ambivalence and ambiguity and seems therefore more like a representation of pure, malicious envy as a simple psychological force—a part object—than like a real human being. We are so horrified by his destruction of Othello and Desdemona partly because it is difficult to understand *why* he is so destructive. This is what makes him such a strange figure in Shakespeare's work.

Walter Cohen has written of Iago that, although Shakespeare indicates that Iago believed that Othello had passed him over for promotion and suspected him of having slept with his (Iago's) wife,

> Iago also enjoys the sport of ruining Othello's life. In this respect, he descends from the Vice figure of the earlier morality plays—a semi-secularized version of the devil . . . in one view, Iago is plausibly driven by resentment: "I know my price, I am worth no worse a place"—and by an obsessive jealousy that "doth . . . gnaw my inwards". He is thus part of the psychological drama, afflicting Othello with what he himself feels . . . alternatively, however, Iago has no fixed essence at all: "I am not what I am." Operating inside and outside the narrative movement of the play, Iago, like Vice before him, sometimes seems more a dramatic function than a psychologically realized character. [Cohen, 1997, p. 2093]

Cohen notes that Coleridge "accurately described the villain's behavior . . . when he saw in Iago the 'motive-hunting of a motiveless malignity' (p. 2093).

If we compare Iago to another Shakespearian villain, Richard III, his singularity becomes even clearer. Unlike Iago, Richard does not at any time seem to be pure, unmotivated malignity: his depredations, if not justified, are at least comprehensible, and he even charms us more or less against our will, evoking in us a certain grudging admiration for his machinations against a fate that cheated him. While he is undoubtedly a nasty character and full of envy of those less "curtail'd of fair proportion" than he, we can identify with him even as we deplore him. Richard is envy with a human face:

> But I,—that am not shap'd for sportive tricks,
> Nor made to court an amorous looking-glass;
> I, that am rudely stamp'd, and want love's majesty
> To strut before a wanton ambling nymph;
> I, that am curtail'd of this fair proportion,
> Cheated of feature by dissembling nature,
> Deform'd, unfinish'd, sent before my time
> Into this breathing world scarce half made up,
> And that so lamely and unfashionable
> That dogs bark at me as I halt by them;—
> Why, I, in this weak piping time of peace,
> Have no delight to pass away the time,
> Unless to spy my shadow in the sun,
> And descant on mine own deformity:
> And therefore,—since I cannot prove a lover,
> To entertain these fair well-spoken days,—

> I am determined to prove a villain,
> And hate the idle pleasures of these days.
>
> [*Richard III*, I.i]

Our reaction to depictions of sin in the morality plays is supposed to be fear, loathing, and horror, and our reaction to Iago is along those lines. But what are we to feel when Shakespeare has Richard quite plausibly seducing the grieving Lady Anne (and the audience) at her father-in-law's funeral, despite her (and our) full knowledge that Richard had not only murdered him, but Lady Anne's husband as well, only a few months before? Whatever we are meant to feel, it's something far more nuanced and ambivalent, and more fully human, than simple horror at sin or evil.

In his grasp of human ambivalence, ambiguity, and complexity of motives, Shakespeare anticipated the spirit of psychoanalysis (as did Terence when he wrote, "I am a man, and nothing human may be alien to me"). The destructive instinct seems unpsychoanalytic in the same way as Iago seems unshakespearean. This has nothing to do with the humanistic ethic that Terence expressed but, rather, with the fact that it is not our job as psychoanalysts to be theologians, moralists, ethicists, or humanists. It is our job to be observers—to make observations with the goal of gathering enough information to render what we are observing comprehensible in a human sense. We can try to make observations as keen and subtle as Shakespeare's (while at the same time curbing our narcissism by recognizing how rare such genius is), and when we find ourselves arriving at something that is humanly incomprehensible, we can try to recognize it as a sign that we need to observe more before venturing a guess at what we're observing.

An instinct built into the mind that is aimed precisely and exclusively at killing the mind is not comprehensible in a human sense, any more than is pure evil. [I think Freud recognized this when he treated the destructive instinct so diffidently in *Beyond the Pleasure Principle* (1920g) as a biological phenomenon instead of a psychological one.] To conclude that there is such a thing as a destructive instinct or unmotivated envy (as opposed to the epistemologically more modest position that there is something that appears to be so) is, to my way of thinking, an abandonment of the empirical rigors and uncertainties of psychoanalysis for the comfortable certainties of dogma. We would do better, when faced with such a situation, to adopt Freud's verdict of *non liquet* (it is not clear).

If we view envy not as something that brings death and evil into the world, but as a manifestation of endangered narcissism—of an endangered autistic system threatened with breakdown by being forced to live in relation to a needed, but ultimately uncontrollable, object, and counterattacking whatever is breaking it down—it becomes comprehensible in human terms, and a destructive instinct becomes an unnecessary hypothesis. Development requires us to be dragged out of a state of mind dominated by narcissism and the pleasure principle into one in which we can acknowledge the reality of dependence on objects: other people, creatures not of our making and beyond our control in some vitally important way. Envious devaluation is a reaction against this dependence on good objects, operating by making them appear anything but good, and, while it does undermine the capacity to need and depend on them, and in this sense qualifies as an anti-developmental—and, therefore, anti-life—force, it is still firmly within the realm of psychology.

But if we subscribe to the idea of envy as a direct clinical manifestation of a destructive instinct, we move out of the realm of psychology, where the idea of envy is useful because it gives us something to explore, into a realm where it is useless because it gives us only something to fear and deplore. Furthermore, if we picture gratitude as the opposite or antidote to this version of envy, it becomes an uncontextualized goodness in opposition to the uncontextualized badness of envy, and we are then in danger of falling back up into Milton's paradise, where there is plenty of room for goodness and badness but very little for creativity, a force that is so unpredictable, uncontrollable and subversive of our plans, pre-conceptions, and certainties that it bears a strong resemblance to life itself.

3

Envy and Gratitude: some current reflections

H. Shmuel Erlich

The invitation to take part in the present volume presented me with the opportunity to reread one of Melanie Klein's undoubtedly most seminal contributions. It stirred up feelings and memories, as well as questions and reflections. I will try to present these as best I can, but I must confess that it is a difficult task. What makes it difficult is not the dearth of issues but, quite to the contrary, their multitude and encompassing nature. The metaphor that comes to mind is musical: it is like listening to a symphony, where one may be taken with the emotional and spiritual totality yet at the same time become aware, especially after repeated listening, to specific themes, developments, interactions, and harmonious relationships that contribute to the overall grandeur of the construction.

Rereading *Envy and Gratitude* was for me a lively experience of meeting once again with Klein's unique way of thinking, and interacting with it in a flowing and continuous way: each and every page and paragraph is an occasion for strong reactions, most of them happy reunions with long-familiar friends and relatives, some producing raised eyebrows or puzzlement, and a few bringing up sharp disagreement. It would be impossible as well as inappropriate to try to go through all of them here, since this would require—what I would really mostly wish for—a page-by-page reading accompanied by exegesis, questions, and discussion. Obviously, I would be much happier to do this in the form of a seminar discussion with colleagues than within the confining frame of a written work. Having accepted the task and challenge, however, I will try to focus on a few issues that are, to my present way of thinking, major issues, yet with the constant feeling that in no way can this substitute for or capture the richness of this clinical–theoretical masterpiece. I begin with some personal feelings and memories and proceed to more general theoretical and clinical issues, stressing especially their contemporary relevance.

I

My personal statement is in the nature of a full disclosure: Melanie Klein was largely absent from my early psychoanalytic exposure in the United States. At the time, the attitude to Klein's concepts and treatment approach, though not really well known or understood and lacking direct exposure to its practice and application, might best have been described as to a bad object. The little that was known or said about it was tantamount to calling it wild analysis. It was accused of lacking any regard for the development and functioning of the ego, the mental apparatus, the existence of defences that needed to be carefully dismantled and worked through before depth interpretations could be offered, and so on. It seemed both frightening and exciting.

Perhaps because of this combination of the forbidden and exciting fruit, I became more interested in Klein and read some of her major papers. Their impact on me was considerable and is demonstrated in the following story. As senior candidates, close to the end of our training in the Israel Institute of Psychoanalysis, we were given the opportunity to conduct an elective reading seminar. My suggestion to my fellow candidates that we read Klein's "The Origins of Transference" (1952) was met with surprise and interest. Up to that point in time, Klein's contributions were simply not present in our Institute's curriculum, and my classmates were quite ignorant of her work. The aftermath was rather dramatic: all of us became very much identified with object relations thinking and practice, and several went on to develop a deep and abiding interest in the Kleinian approach. Nowadays, of course, the Institute's curriculum includes a number of courses on Kleinian thought.

I believe this personal story demonstrates what has happened in most, if not all, psychoanalytic institutes and thinking: over the past several decades, Klein's thinking has not only been exonerated and reintegrated into the mainstream of psychoanalytic thinking and is no longer a bad object, but has actually become, together with Freud, a major constituent of what is frequently misnamed "classical" psychoanalysis—a point I return to later.

II

Let me turn to some of the theoretical questions that came up for me in the course of this rereading and are reflective of my own present focus and concerns. A central issue is the way Klein conceptualizes the relationship between subject and object. Her views contain certain propositions, fundamental to her thought, which are clearly defined, well articulated, and firmly maintained. At the same time, however, these propositions seem to include some less clearly thought-through theoretical aspects. One such major issue is her conception of the inherent separateness of subject and object. Klein starts out from the fundamental and central (Freudian) place of the dual drives in psychic dynamics and economy. In pursuing this line of thought, it is fundamental that the relationship of the subject to its object always emanates from the gap that yawns between them: the force that moves the subject towards the object, whether focused on internally or externally, issues from this gap. The object of desire is not yet fully within the purview of the subject, which is what gives rise to the desire, the passion, or what Freud termed "attraction". Once the object is attained, the desire can be consummated and subsides. The implication, which is a fundamental characteristic if not a precondition for Klein's thinking, is the inherent separateness of subject and object. This is, of course, clear in the case of envy, which she describes as the desire to possess the object and especially its goodness and supplies. This separateness is again illustrated, though not mentioned, in the following sentence, which is frequently repeated, with some variations: "the infant feels that [the breast] possesses everything *he desires* and that it has an unlimited flow of milk and love which *the breast keeps for its own gratification*" (p. 183, emphasis added). Everything here hinges on this dimension of the differentiation, the gap, or the absence of the object of desire.

I wholly agree with Klein's way of understanding this dimension. It is fully consistent with the conceptualization of the drives in general and by Freud in particular. If we conceive of the relationship between subject—ego or self—and object along these lines, it is a necessary corollary assumption. It is this issue that formed a leading theme in the "Controversial Discussions" and has served as the basis for major attacks and criticism of Klein's theory, since it implies a degree of separateness at a developmental stage that many were unable to conceive of, let alone grant. Without getting sidetracked into this ancient debate, it can be safely said that this idea of an early separateness is more acceptable today and seems to find support in infant research (Stern, 1985). Yet the basic issue it represents still colours significant aspects of contemporary psychoanalytic thought.

It is fascinating that at the very end of his life Freud engaged briefly with this issue. In a posthumously published note that might be directly related to Klein's theorizing, he said:

> July 12 [1938]. "Having" and "being" in children. Children like expressing an object-relation by an identification: "I am the object." "Having" is the later of the two; after loss of the object it relapses into "being". Example: the breast. "The breast is part of me, I am the breast." Only later: "I have it"—that is, "I am not it." [Freud, 1941f (1938)]

Freud speaks to the issue of possessing the object, which is so much at the core of Klein's discourse on envy. "Having" or wishing "to have" the object or its attributes must come from a psychic position that is not identified with it, that perceives the object as a "not-me" that "I" so badly wish to incorporate in the various ways Klein describes. This kind of object relation, says Freud, is a later development. It is preceded by what he describes as *"being* the object". The latter is an undifferentiated position that does not allow for craving, because "I *am* the object". If one *is* the object, one cannot envy it in the way Klein describes. Freud clearly differs from Klein on the issue of the developmental timing of this separateness, which alone is what can give rise to the envy she describes. I must add that to my mind this issue is not resolved by relegating the entire relationship to the realm of the unconscious and unconscious phantasy, where it does not involve "cognitive" or "knowing" awareness of separateness. Of course we are not dealing with cognitive issues; but we are postulating the possibility, perhaps the necessity, of separation of subject from object at a deep psychic level.

Yet Klein also makes several statements that seem to contradict her fast-held proposition of separateness and to allude or hint at a simultaneous lack of separateness. She begins with the reflection that "even a happy feeding situation cannot altogether replace the pre-natal unity with the mother" (1957, p. 179). Pre-natal unity—I assume it refers to psychic unity—must therefore exist at birth, yet it is unclear what happens to it so soon afterward, when "the infant feels that. . . . [the breast] possesses everything he desires . . . which [it] keeps for its own gratification" (1957, p. 183), implying a clear separation of infant and breast. The fate of the pre-natal unity is even more troubling, since in other respects, even with regard to the capacity to love, Klein postulates the operation and manifestation of innate factors: "But the internal factors underlying it" [i.e. the relation to the mother] "—above all the capacity for love—appear to be innate" (1957, p. 188). Envy is "also constitutional" (1957, p. 229). If envy, greed, hate, and persecutory anxiety all have an innate basis (1957, p. 229), then why not the unity with the object, which presumably pre-existed *in utero*?

The issue becomes yet more complicated when Klein introduces the other side of the coin: positive feelings of love and gratitude. While the development and destructive impact of envy, greediness, and hate, as well as the persecutory anxiety and guilt aroused in their wake, are clearly outlined and established as derivatives of oral- and anal-sadistic drives, as well as the death instinct, the positive side of the equation is not as well established. Undoubtedly love and gratitude have something to do with the good object and the relation to it, as the following quote illustrates:

> In contrast with the infant who, owing to his envy, has been unable to build up securely a good internal object, *a child with a strong capacity for love and gratitude has a deep-rooted relation with a good object* and can, without being fundamentally damaged, withstand temporary states of envy, hatred, and grievance, which arise even in children who are loved and well mothered. Thus, when these negative states are transient, the good object is regained time and time again. [Klein, 1957, p. 187, my italics]

In this passage, the existence of love and gratitude are already taken for granted, and their ameliorative and detoxifying effect can be counted on. But how did they come about? A bit earlier we are told: "For it is *enjoyment* and the *gratitude* to which it gives rise that mitigate destructive impulses" (Klein, 1957, p. 187, italics in original). And again: "A full gratification at the breast means that the infant feels he has received from his love object a unique gift which he wants to keep. This is the basis of gratitude" (Klein, 1957, p. 188). Gratitude is thus thought to stem from the enjoyment of the feed and the satisfaction in its wake. But how could this be the basis for gratitude, if the same enjoyment also gives rise to the envious attacks on the object? The answer, of course, is that the two experiences and feelings are simultaneous events, separated from each other by the primitive operation of splitting and projective identification. But this is still not fully convincing, nor does it account for the derivation of gratitude from the experience of enjoyment. Let me elaborate.

I think Klein herself is not fully convinced of the efficacy of the formulation, as illustrated in the caveat she issues a few lines down: "Doubts in the possession of the good object and the corresponding uncertainty about one's own good feelings also contribute to greedy and indiscriminate identifications" (Klein, 1957, p. 187). The existence of good feelings is, by itself, no guarantee for their persisting and withstanding the attacks on them, reflected in doubts and uncertainty about one's goodness and the good internal object. Furthermore, Klein links together love and gratitude as varieties of positive relatedness to the object. Freud, in his elaborate effort to account for love in terms of instinctual vicissitudes, eventually conceded defeat and admitted that

> We should prefer to regard loving as the expression of the *whole* sexual current of feelings; but this idea does not clear up our difficulties, and we cannot see what meaning to attach to an opposite content of this current . . . we become aware that the attitudes [relations] of love and hate cannot be made use of for the relations of *instincts* to their objects, but are reserved for the relations of the *total ego* to objects. [Freud, 1915c, pp. 133–137, italics in original]

The difficulty with Klein's formulation of gratitude as a variety of love is that it is indeed different from envy. Envy emanates directly from the desire set in motion by the oral- and anal-sadistic drives. Love and gratitude, however, do not emanate *directly* from the experience of enjoyment and satisfaction. What can be said to derive from this is *pleasure*, which represents an experience, a psychic state, or its mnemic residue; it does not represent the object of the drive, since the latter is already quiescent. Love and gratitude thus represent higher-order feelings and mental integrations at the level of what Freud described as the "total ego" or personality. These integrations enfold within them hateful and destructive impulses as well as love and gratitude in a post-ambivalent consolidation or, in Klein's terms, as an achievement of the depressive position.

This distinction between varieties of love, and hence gratitude, is illustrated and reflected in the understanding of the positive transference and how it is handled. We usually interpret positive transference when it is either idealizing (as Klein demonstrates), or conflictual, or when it masks erotic or destructive–envious attacks on the analyst. We would very rarely interpret feelings of love and gratitude where these are deemed to be genuine (i.e. non-idealizing) and to reflect the analysand's appreciation and gratitude for the analysis and the analyst's efforts. The non-interpretative stance in this case reveals that such feelings are of a different order. We regard them as an achievement of the analysis, and as not requiring interpretation. It is sometimes said that the love and gratitude Klein speaks of are of a primitive nature, and thus are mere precursors of the more mature feelings (Segal, 1979). But this does not fully clear up the difficulty: at the very least, it introduces an imbalance between gratitude and envy, where no such distinction is claimed between earlier and later manifestations.

There are several places where Klein hints at a somewhat different, perhaps added, dimension: it is not enough to speak of the desire or its satisfaction; there is also the question of *how this is experienced* that influences the outcome. The first such hint comes when she says that "greedy internalization disturbs the relation to the object" (Klein, 1957, p. 188). The implication is that when the internalization is experienced as greedy, when greedy desire permeates the *experience* of satisfaction, the result is coloured by it and might be deleterious. Again: "It is the very greed with which this internalization [of the breast] is carried out that contains the germ of failure" (Klein, 1957, p. 218). The following quote introduces quite clearly the idea of the significant role and place of *experience*:

> An overlapping between these various sources . . . of libido and of aggressiveness is normal. But when the overlapping amounts to *an incapacity to experience* sufficiently the predominance of either of these trends . . . then both later sexual life and sublimations are adversely affected [Klein, 1957, p. 195, emphasis added]

Allowing for such an additional *experiential* dimension that focuses not on the *contents* but on *how* the content is processed—that is, *in what experiential dimension* it takes place—can resolve some of the theoretical difficulties to which I have referred. I have proposed (Erlich, 2003) that psychic events and contents occur within *two* experiential dimensions: one based on the separateness of subject and object (*Doing*), the other on the unity of subject and object (*Being*). I also postulate the simultaneous and continuous presence and operation of these two dimensions from the very beginning of extra-uterine life. Klein's assumptions of the primary separateness of subject and object that give rise to envy, hate, and destructive attacks on the loved object are entirely within this frame of reference, in which everything to do with drives—which, as suggested, imply separateness of subject from object—takes place. It is precisely the gap that makes for the longing, as well as the rage and envy, that the infant experiences, as Klein has described.

On the other hand, at least a good part of what Klein describes as love and gratitude involves the *Being* dimension: that is, the *experience of unity* of subject and object. This experience accompanies everything that happens, often as a background quality. As Klein suggests, and I agree with her, it becomes a focus and an issue when it is damaged or disturbed, and "incapacity to experience" sets in. In such cases the capacity for experiencing unity is severely hampered, if not totally absent. But this is accompanied by other attributes and components of this dimension, which include feeling alive and existing (being) as well as *being a part of a totality or unity*. I find a hint at this in Klein's statement: "In the course of development, the relation to the mother's breast becomes the foundation for devotion to people, values, and causes" (p. 187). What Klein describes here is the experience of *belonging*—to a group, an idea, or an ideology, to a cause or a set of values—based upon one's immersion in and merging with them. It is this experience that makes for the good breast being part of one's self, in what Klein calls "assimilation". The crucial difference is that in my thinking this particular assimilation is not driven by drive, but by the experience of unity and the *Being* dimension.

The experience of *Being* or unity is sometimes understood in Kleinian thinking in the sense of identification (Klein, 1955), which is a defence-driven unity set up against losing the object or giving it up. Similarly, in projective identification there is also a component of feeling a unity with certain aspects of the object into which parts of the self have been evacuated and projected, but out of a defensive and often regressive need. In the *Being* dimension, in contradistinction, a non-drive experience takes place that is of a different nature and is a necessary backdrop for feeling alive and connected. I think this is exactly what Klein had in mind when she referred to the experience or state of "unity".

There are naturally consequences to this view. Perhaps the most important one is that we must make a distinction between what is drive- and separateness-based and its ramifications and what is not. I cannot find such a distinction in Klein's thought. There are also differences in what causes disturbance in either track or dimension. For example, I regard the effects of drive and conflict (the *Doing* dimension) to be precisely as Klein described them. In that sense, they are, as she suggests, largely internal and independent of "actual" environmental influences, which can only serve to ameliorate and ease their impact and render it less destructive. What transpires in the *Being* dimension, on the other hand, precisely because it is based on the experience of unity (and not on drive), is much more susceptible to the object's capacity for being in such unity with the subject. It is a dimension more sensitive to the fluctuations and willingness of the object to take part in what may be experienced (by the object) as giving up its own separate existence and merging with that of the infant or other. Clearly this might be a threatening experience for some, especially if they already suffer from difficulties in this dimension, thus contributing to an intergenerational transmission. We have seen such pronounced difficulties in the relation of Holocaust survivors with their children, or the second generation (Erlich & Felsen, 1990).

III

I have dwelt in some length on the issue of separateness and unity because I think it represents a fundamental psychoanalytic shibboleth, but also because it seems to reflect a lack of clarity in Klein's theorizing that has influenced others. I will now focus on those aspects of *Envy and Gratitude* that I find refreshingly current, pertinent, and enduring.

The first and most important of these is the place accorded to the internal world and psychic reality. Here Klein's position is unequivocal, firm, and consistent. As far as the impact of the drives on the psyche and its development is concerned, there is a clear priority of the internal and psychic over the external and actual. The "good object", longed for as a container for the subject's love, represents not an objective evaluation of its nature but the product of the life and loving aspects of the subject. This emphasis and her unwavering insistence on it serve as a much-needed beacon in the contemporary psychoanalytic world, in which this hierarchy has been rejected and supplanted in many quarters by the predominance of external factors, or by the substitution of actual object relations for phantasies as what populates the internal world.

The shift in emphasis has been in no small measure related to Klein's work, which paved the way for a clearer focus on object relations. For Klein, however, as for Freud, this meant object relations motivated and set into motions by the internal workings of drives and phantasies, not of interpersonal relationships and interactions. Though she does not eschew the role of the actual mother and environment, she makes it clear that it is the phantasy and inner dynamics, based as they are on innate factors, that are decisive:

> My accumulated observations . . . have convinced me that the impact of these external experiences is in proportion to the constitutional strength of the innate destructive impulses and the ensuing paranoid anxieties. Many infants have not had very unfavorable experiences and yet suffer from serious difficulties in feeding and sleeping, and we can see in them every sign of great anxiety for which external circumstances do not account sufficiently.
>
> It is also well known that some infants are exposed to great deprivation and unfavorable circumstances, and yet do not develop excessive anxieties. [Klein, 1957, pp. 229–230]

This position underlies much of what is currently controversial within psychoanalysis. While debates often centre on educational standards and varieties of clinical practice, it is transparent that the underlying fermentation stems from deeper disagreements on the role and substance of the inner world as against external influences and circumstances. This is the present-day version of the initial resistance to Freud's theories of infantile sexuality and the dynamic unconscious. There is simply no way in which such ideas can be accepted without resistance and/or attempts to bring them in line with ordinarily expectable, rational, and observable reality.

There is a further important consequence to the position espoused by Klein. While it is immensely difficult to accept the primary effects of the inner world and its projections, such as the inevitability of envy and destructiveness, there is also an inherent degree of optimism in it. While the internal struggle is inevitable and ever-present, it does imply autonomy, a degree of choice, and an ultimately personal responsibility. It is an ethical as well as a scientific position that marks those psychoanalytic approaches that are commonly referred to as "classical", implying that they are relatively passé in comparison to the so called "contemporary" approaches. On the one hand, the latter's tendency to reallocate responsibility in the actual external environment frees the patient from guilt and holds out greater promise for cure and revitalization, contingent upon experiencing the analyst as a "new" and better attuned object; on the other, in accepting this prospect, the patient must assume a victimized posture. Klein was aware of this in a surprisingly contemporary and modern way. In the first instance, she stresses that it is the patient who is unable to accept the good feed offered by the analyst–mother out of his greed and guilt: "In this situation the early guilt about rejecting milk and love offered by the mother is revived, because the analyst's help is not accepted" (p. 222). In other words, the offering or availability of milk and love, while mandatory, does not ensure acceptance by the infant, who is then a victim not of external deprivation but of his own envy and greed. Klein seems to speak directly to some contemporary analysts when she says:

> It makes great demands [both] on the analyst and on the patient to analyse splitting processes and the underlying hate and envy in both the positive and negative transference. One consequence of this difficulty is the tendency of some analysts to reinforce the positive and avoid the negative transference, and to attempt to strengthen feelings of love by taking over the role of the good object which the patient had not been able to establish securely in the past. This procedure differs essentially from the technique which, by helping the patient to achieve a better integration of his self, aims at a mitigation of hatred by love. . . . We find that . . . the patient's strong desire to receive evidence of love and appreciation from the analyst . . . is never completely given up. . . . In identification with his patient, the early need for reassurance may strongly influence his [the analyst's] counter-transference and therefore his technique. This identification may also easily

> tempt the analyst to take the mother's place and give in to the urge immediately to alleviate his child's (the patient's) anxieties. [Klein, 1957, pp. 225–226).

A further aspect of this de-idealizing stance is the de-idealization of analysis itself. Klein, in true Freudian fashion, sees the motivation for and the readiness to persist in analysis as deriving ultimately from the "desire for truth", which is deeper and more enduring than the desire to be helped. Furthermore, analysis does not lead to rebirth or to the cessation of conflict and suffering. It leads, in the best of outcomes, to better integration. Yet "complete and permanent integration is . . . never possible."

IV

Finally, I want to make a few points with regard to the clinical and therapeutic process as it comes through in this work. Some of its aspects were already touched on in the foregoing discussion, but some points need to be stressed. Contrary to the earlier prevailing picture of direct, abrupt, and insensitive interpretation, this is clearly not the case here. In the first place, Klein maintains that anxiety is the focal point of her technique. I believe that when anxiety is the focal point, we are more often than not on safe grounds, as well as in the right direction. Furthermore, she asserts that "In analysis we should make our way *slowly and gradually* towards the painful insights into the divisions in the patient's self" (p. 225, emphasis added). It seems that this cautionary note is meant to directly counteract projections of ruthless analysing.

Klein's technique as reflected in this work is anything but insensitive. It may be forceful, and it certainly comes from a place of "knowing" something about the unconscious. This is understandable, but also needs some precautionary remarks. On the one hand, the analyst in Klein's approach is quite vulnerable in that his unconscious, countertransference, and envy might seriously hamper the analytic process in many ways that parallel some of the patient's. On the other hand, the analyst must be able to transcend these and to focus clearly on the myriad ways in which the patient's envy aims to destroy the analyst and the analysis. The analyst must be ready and able to receive the patient's projections and to work with them analytically. It is difficult to conceive of the capacity to maintain the analytic posture and work under these stormy and dramatic conditions without holding on to something. This something is the analyst's conviction about the presence and nature of unconscious processes such as envy, greed, and destructiveness, including destructive idealization. Klein asserts this in a footnote: "Experience has shown me that when the analyst becomes fully convinced of the importance of a new aspect of emotional life, he becomes able to interpret it earlier in the analysis" (p. 214). The analyst's conviction in his knowledge is experiential, deriving largely from his own analysis, but also to a large measure theoretical. But while he might flounder and be lost without such convinced knowing, there is also the ever-present danger that such knowledge might turn dogmatic and exclusive.

In my own work, envy—in its destructive sense, which is typically dyadic—is often present. In severe cases it plays a much more dominant role than do jealousy or tripartite oedipal envy. What I have found most difficult is the resistance to this line of interpretation and insight. I find that it takes a very long time, often years of analysis, before this destructive and pernicious emotional force can be addressed—not only by me, but by the patient—without flight and denial. When this actually happens and envy is laid bare in its pernicious, totally irrational character, stemming from the inside and bearing little or no relationship to the outside, then a fundamental change has taken place in the patient and in the analysis, which is experienced as a moment of unity between analyst and analysand. I am convinced that this could not happen without Melanie Klein's seminal work, for which I am deeply grateful.

4

An independent response to *Envy and Gratitude*

Caroline Polmear

In her preface to this seminal work, Melanie Klein acknowledges her debt to Abraham and her satisfaction at being able to take his work forward with the publication of her own: *Envy and Gratitude*.

In rereading it myself, twenty or more years after first studying it, I realize how easy it is to forget my debt to her and others whose work has become part and parcel of my collection of theories, part-theories, and concepts upon which I rely in the consulting room. Sandler (1983) helpfully explored our relationship to our theory. He pointed out that we very seldom actually give up an old theory or concept, even when it has been superseded by new thinking. He also noted that our theories do not form a cohesive whole theory, an internally consistent paradigm, but, rather, await being "called up" from our preconscious when they are relevant to material that we are trying to understand in the consulting room. Indeed, in quoting Sandler in this way I am demonstrating his point. The notion of the preconscious is seldom used by Kleinian and Independent analysts, but we all know exactly what it means and feel at ease with it as a descriptive term. Regarding Klein's work under discussion here, I realize how often I am aware of the destructive power of envy and the damage to the development of a relationship to a whole other person in which there is a capacity for concern and an ability to both give and receive love. It is curious, though, that my acceptance of her particular view of development in the early weeks and months of life, so different in emphasis from that of Independent theorists, sits within me in relative comfort.

So why is it that my debt to her for her insights can so easily go unacknowledged? I suspect that the failure to consciously recognize our use of many illuminating theories, concepts, and observations has something to do with the posturing of the narcissism of minor differences involved in defining which group we belong to by virtue of describing which group and theory is not "us". In the process we deny the very nature of our use of psychoanalytic theory.

Klein's *Envy and Gratitude* is so rich that I could pick any one of many themes to explore. I intend, however, to restrict myself in this chapter to an examination of Klein's description of earliest development as described in this work. I will then describe Winnicott's observations and conceptual understanding of the same developmental period. In particular, I would like to explore the central importance he places on the infant's complete dependence on the mother or carer, his concept of "holding", and the area of separation into "me" and "not me". I will then explore some of the clinical and technical implications of the differences between these two views.

The first six months: Klein's developmental view

Klein (1957) tells us that she considers envy to be an "oral-sadistic and anal-sadistic expression of destructive impulses" and that it has a constitutional basis. She raises the question: how does the immature and weak ego make its first object relationship safe when it is conducted under the sway of the powerful destructive force of envy, linked as it is to the death instinct?

Her answer lies in the elaboration of the projective and introjective processes at work and the defences against annihilation employed by the infant. In this and in all her work she attributes fundamental importance to the infant's first object relationship: to the mother's breast and then to the mother. If this relationship is introjected with relative security, then the basis for satisfactory development is laid down. Early internalizations dominated by envy contribute to difficulty in building up a good internal object and the development of the capacity for love and gratitude.

In the first instance envy, or primary envy, is of the feeding breast. She defines envy as "the angry feeling that another person possesses and enjoys something desirable—the envious impulse being to take it away or to spoil it". (Klein, 1957, p. 181). The envious infant desires the breast as food and desires also to be freed from destructive impulses and persecutory anxiety. The envious attack on the breast increases the infant's terror of annihilation by an attacked and persecutory breast. The ego's first defence and first developmental achievement is to split the breast into good and bad. In this way, the ego disperses the destructive impulses and internal persecutory anxieties. This is the primary defence during the first few months of life. Life instinct and love gives impetus to this successful splitting and preserving and then later to successful integration. Excessive envy in the immature ego creates persecutory guilt, which cannot either be tolerated or worked through, and splitting becomes more fixed.

When a good object is fairly securely established and not overwhelmed by destructive impulses, it survives the phantasied attacks on it, the guilt is tolerable, and the move towards integration (depressive position) progresses. With the onset of the Oedipus complex, which Klein locates at between 3 and 6 months, the parent, at first a combined object, becomes gradually differentiated into a couple. When envy is not excessive, jealousy becomes a means of working through, which, in its turn becomes in itself a defence against envy.

Where development during these months is more troubled by excessive envy, omnipotence, denial, and splitting intensify. Split off bad parts are evacuated by projective identification into the other while the good breast is idealized, and then internalized by the infant. The interference felt with oral gratification can lead to a defensive flight into genitality.

The first six months: Winnicott's developmental view

The Winnicottian infant begins life in a state of lack of integration of the ego and in a state of total dependence physically and emotionally on its mother or main carer (I use the term "mother" for simplicity).

So the starting point in Winnicott's understanding of the infant is his utter dependency. The infant and the mother together form a unit during the first weeks. The infant's physical and emotional growth is dependent on a "facilitating environment" (Winnicott, 1963b), often referred to as "good-enough mothering" (Winnicott, 1960b).

With favourable conditions the infant moves from a state of absolute dependence, through relative dependence, towards independence. At the same time, three developmental steps are achieved: integration, personalization, and the beginnings of object relating.

The mother's function in the time of absolute dependence is encompassed in the term "holding" (Winnicott, 1960a). It is through holding that "the inherited potential" develops into a "continuity of being" a beginning of self (1960a). With failure of holding, "being" cannot develop. The alternative to being is reacting, which interrupts being and annihilates the developing self. Holding implies not only sensitive and attuned physical handling, but also total environmental provision prior to and overlapping with the beginnings of separation into a "me" and a "not me". Part of this provision involves giving "ego-support" to the infant's weak ego, having the child in mind as a whole person, before the child has its own sense of self (Winnicott, 1948) It is this aspect of holding that allows for the beginning of the "line of integration", or the "going on being". It allows, too, for lapses, for example during rest, to the un-integrated state. Through this vital "ego-support"—or put another way, using the mother's strong ego while the baby's ego is weak, defence-less, and un-integrated—the infant can, from time to time, allow isolation (as opposed to merger) and an experience of his own authentic impulses with the idea of another, an object who is the subject of his experience and whose existence makes it real. These are the first experiences of the self, and when they result in a communication of experience, a spontaneous gesture, which is responded to by mother, they become the first experiences of object relations and a beginning of the concept of "me" and "not me". So in the first holding phase, all being well, periods of "being" can be experienced without the need to react to external impingements and without annihilation.

From the external point of view, holding means meeting the infant's physical needs and thus, at this early stage, his psychological needs. Holding is reliable and depends for this on the mother's empathy or capacity to identify with her baby by projective identification—a process that begins during pregnancy and lasts for the first few weeks of life. It requires a "live adaptation to the baby's needs" (Winnicott, 1960a), a moment-to-moment responsiveness that can be clouded in experienced mothers, who may have done it so many times before that they no longer tune in to their baby's unique and personal communication. (The dangers of an analytic equivalent are all too painfully real). Holding protects the infant from physiological insult and takes account of the infant's skin sensitivity, visual sensitivity, sensitivity to falling or falling apart, and lack of knowledge of anything other than his self. Last and by no means least, holding includes the physical holding and handling of the infant, which is a way of loving and the mother's only way of expressing her love at this stage.

> The basis for instinctual satisfaction and for object relationships is the handling and general management and the care of the infant, which is only too easily taken for granted when all goes well. [Winnicott, 1960a, p. 49]

The phase of personalization follows the holding phase. Somewhat like Freud's (1923b) statement that the ego is "first and foremost a bodily ego", Winnicott locates an important aspect of integration in what he calls personalization. This includes the concept of the indwelling of the psyche in the soma. With empathic holding, the infant gradually gains an awareness of a "limiting membrane between inner and outer, between me and not-me" (Winnicott, 1960a).

At the same time as separating inner from outer, the internal integrative process means that with empathic handling a psychosomatic partnership can be established.

> Handling describes the environmental provision that corresponds loosely with the establishment of a psychosomatic partnership. Without good-enough active and adaptive handling the task from within may well prove heavy; indeed it may actually prove impossible for the development of the psychosomatic interrelationship to become properly established. [Winnicott, 1962, p. 62]

Winnicott further states that in adaptive handling the mother "is able to manage the baby and the baby's body as if the two form a unit" (Davis & Wallbridge, 1981; Winnicott, 1969).

The developmental third phase features primitive object relating and the experience of omnipotence. Again holding in this phase is vital, although now the mother is required to respond to her infant's need for more independence of action as he is moving more frequently from "being" to "activity". When the infant initiates action from his own impulses and mother responds, the infant assumes that the satisfaction has come from himself. Winnicott sees this as an essential stage in the development of the self. The id event, the hunger, greed, and need for the breast is made, by the mother's attuned response, into a valuable and meaningful experience. Winnicott links this with Freud's notion of the infant hallucinating the breast and finding it right there for him. Once the infant has initiated the good experience, he will have an idea of what he needs now, and have the satisfaction of it being presented. The importance of this period of omnipotence lies in its creating a sense of being real and of being able to affect the environment.

Winnicott states that it is only at the point of some ego organization and of some recognition of the existence of another that Klein's work on primitive mechanisms of projection and introjection become important. This recognition comes about gradually and with the gradual disillusioning by mother who will know, for example, when her baby can wait for a while before being fed. It is sometimes referred to by Winnicott as the state of "living with" rather than being merged with the mother. Interestingly, unlike other theorists interested in the early months, Winnicott speaks of father's role. Father, unbeknownst to the infant, deals with the environment for the mother while she does the holding. So father "holds" mother in a sense, so that she can focus on the baby. Part of the infant's recognition of his separateness also depends on the growing awareness of father, mother, and the infant living together.

With the first "I am" moments and the recognition that everything else is not me comes an expectation of persecution. The assertiveness of "I am" feels like an aggressive attack on the mother and is experienced by the infant as a "raw moment", a feeling of infinite exposure. Only if the infant is safely held can the moment be risked. Without this security and trust in the mother's reliable holding, the infant will comply, regress to a merged state, or disintegrate in anxiety. Important, then, for Winnicott's infant is the achievement of separateness and the aggression that this carries with it. It follows that breakdown of support at these moments leads to a breakdown of integration.

Winnicott describes the beginnings of a capacity for concern when the infant is about 6 months old. He enumerates the conditions for its emergence: the integration of the ego and a sense of a self, a whole person with an inside and an outside; object relating in which there are elements of love and destructiveness perhaps well characterized in "I love you; I eat you", and a mother now seen as a whole separate person who is in the process of becoming permanent in the infant's mind.

Like Klein, Winnicott describes a split that needs to be brought together if the capacity for concern is to develop. But Winnicott's split is in the infant's view of his "two" mothers: the "object mother" and the "environment mother". The mother as object or owner of the part object, the breast, is the mother the infant experiences as satisfying his id drives. The object mother is used ruthlessly and aggressively by the infant. "The fantasy that goes with full-bloodied id-drives contains attack and destruction" (Winnicott, 1963a). The environment mother is the recipient of all his love, affection, and "sensuous co-existence".

With the development of object relating, the infant experiences anxiety because if he consumes and destroys the mother, he will lose her and/or may be attacked by her. But he also observes that he contributes to the environment mother—we could say he brings her joy. With this knowledge the quality of his anxiety changes and becomes guilt. With his knowledge of the reparation he makes through contributing to the environment mother, guilt can be withstood. In favourable cases, where the mother demonstrates through her reliable presence and response that she can withstand the ruthlessness of the baby, the infant becomes bolder in experiencing his id drives, thus freeing up the baby's instinctual life. The two mothers can gradually become one mother. Guilt lies dormant and only appears as sadness or a depressed mood when there is no opportunity for reparation.

So the Kleinian baby and the Winnicottian baby have both come, via different routes, to a similar position and by about the same time in their lives.

Klein's and Winnicott's approaches: similarities and differences

First it cannot have escaped the reader's attention that it took far fewer words to describe Klein's developmental schema as outlined in *Envy and Gratitude* than Winnicott's. Klein is describing one aspect that affects early development. She never says at any point that it is the only one. Winnicott is describing a more complex, fuller picture of a mother–baby unit and in his work pays attention to all the aspects that he observes, bringing them into the picture in numerous different papers.

Perhaps it is the very different tone, use of language, and emphasis that makes them seem so different. In fact, although Klein's picture is of an internally driven process governed by the need to defend against destructive and spoiling envy linked with the death instinct, she acknowledges at several points in her work the importance of environmental factors on healthy development: "External circumstances play a vital part in the initial relation to the breast". She goes on to refer to difficult births with complications such as a lack of oxygen in the baby.

> Furthermore, whether or not the child is adequately fed and mothered, whether the mother fully enjoys the care of the child or is anxious and has psychological difficulties over feeding—all these factors influence the infant's capacity to accept the milk with enjoyment and to internalize the good breast. [Klein, 1957, p. 179]

Then again, she says: "deprivation increases greed and persecutory anxiety" (p. 183) and "It is clear that deprivation, unsatisfactory feeding, and unfavourable circumstances intensify envy because they disturb full gratification, and a vicious circle is created" (p. 187, fn) So it is not true that this is a baby without a mother. Rather, Klein is investigating and teaching her audience about those processes at work in the internal world at a crucial time for laying down the foundations of health or ill health. She comes across as one with an urgent message for analysts to really understand and believe in the internal world and urgency to connect early failures in developmental achievement at this stage with severe mental ill health. I am sure that we all see in our borderline, schizoid, narcissistically damaged, and schizophrenic patients the clarity of the interplay between the processes she describes and the damage to personality development and to the development of love that ensues with failure at this stage. It is as if she is describing the failure to integrate and the domination by envy that is the very outcome of early developmental failure and is what we see clinically in those ill patients.

While Klein was addressing an audience of psychoanalysts, aiming to take forward the understanding of the development of the internal world and the dynamic processes at work in its formation, Winnicott addresses a wide-ranging audience in different papers. He emphasized the importance of the environment when talking to psychoanalysts with a wish to influence psychoanalysis away from what he saw as a single-minded study of inner conflicts. He was against the tendency to "explain all that can be known about babies in terms of the baby alone" (Winnicott, 1970). At other times he wrote for mothers, health visitors, teachers, social workers, and probation officers.

His picture encompasses the internal world of the infant while keeping his complete dependence on his mother firmly in the picture. He acknowledges the value of Klein's work while locating it at a later developmental stage than Klein does. For Winnicott, the earliest weeks before ego integration and awareness of a me and a not me precede the early defensive activity and object relating that Klein is describing.

Winnicott's elaboration of the merged state of dependence is central in Independent thinking. Balint (1959) describes a similar idea slightly differently in his phase of "primary love" in which the baby and mother remain in an almost pre-natal state of "interpenetrating mix-up". In the phase of primary love, both infant and mother desire the same thing, so that the infant need not be aware of his demands or the effect he has on mother. That knowledge comes after the first few weeks as in Winnicott's schema. This sensitivity to the early period that Independent analysts tend to stress is worth thinking about clinically. A lot has been written about regression and the management of regression, so I don't want to go down that path. Rather, I am thinking about the manifestations of early failure of holding in a more day-to-day way.

In a supervision a sensitive and experienced therapist brought a session that she thought had "gone badly". We set about trying to understand what "going badly" meant.

Her borderline patient had come back after a week away due to work commitments and reported rather unemotionally some things that he had been thinking about. The content suggested some fresh and meaningful thinking while the therapist experienced something irritating and un-engaging. She tried to work out what to take up and registered that she felt confused and provoked. The patient had brought new information, but it came with a mismatched feeling. He couldn't take the therapist's silence while she was thinking and demanded that she should speak now. Despite both patient's and therapist's best efforts, the session quickly degenerated into a "scratchy" to and fro, with the patient upset and angry that he had tried to bring something new and important and had experienced his therapist as not responding. The patient referred to wanting to leave the therapist out, just as he always felt left out by the therapist, and so on. This content drew the therapist into three-person thinking in a way that became intellectual and didn't relieve the patient.

The therapist recovered the situation by saying that she thought she had made a mistake and that something had "misfired" between them. Gradually, as they tried to unscramble the painful mess, the patient communicated how his therapist made him feel as if everything wrong was all his problem and his fault and felt that the therapist couldn't accept what he was bringing.

Hearing the way the therapist described the atmosphere and the confusion and pain in the room, coupled with the patient's extreme anxiety masked by a demanding provocation, I felt that the patient was bringing the trauma of impingement into the session. Mostly he brought it by making his therapist feel confused, provoked, and misunderstood. He had been away and missed his sessions but had done some work on himself in his time alone. In his fear of not being met with a satisfying response on his return, he tried to make a spontaneous gesture towards his therapist/mother but at the same time, acting in the transference, brought also the expectation of traumatic failure of holding and lack of an attuned response. What came to be played out was the failure of active and responsive holding and the defensive flight into precocious intellectual defence while they both scratched away at each other, trying to be the one who could "understand". The reference the patient made to feeling it was made out to be all his fault—so familiar when working with borderline conditions—points, I think, to the failure to allow merger during the first phase of development. There is a too speedy a rupture between infant and mother, which leaves behind it insecure boundaries and feelings of vulnerability to the other's projections into oneself.

I think the situation was rescued when the therapist could become a new object by saying that she thought she had made a mistake and engaging with the patient in trying to understand what had "misfired".

The term "new object" needs attention here, as it is an important cornerstone of my clinical approach to patients with early developmental failure. In the example above the therapist stepped out of the traumatizing transference role she had been assigned by her patient when she took him back to the point in the session when things had gone wrong. Strachey (1934) describes the nature of what is therapeutic in psychoanalysis as follows: the analyst's neutral reception of the patient's transferred id impulses leads to a new introject into the superego such that the patient's harsh superego now has a new imago within. Strachey sees it as at first an auxiliary superego that ultimately leads to a modification of the superego. The patient's id impulses towards the analyst can now become conscious through interpretation. He begins to see how his hostile id impulses are directed towards archaic fantasy objects and not real objects, and internal change comes about. So for Strachey the introjection of a new object is crucial to mutative change through interpretation.

Baker (1993) elaborates the concept of the therapeutic effect of the analyst as a new object. The analyst's survival as an analyst, maintaining the setting and analytic stance, gives the patient a new introject, a new object. In no way does this deny the importance of interpretation, and in no way does it encourage "corrective emotional experience" in analysis (Alexander, 1950), gratification of the patient's wishes, hand-holding, or any other form of seductive acting in by the analyst.

For our purposes, the new object might be one who can hear and feel the patient's complaints and criticisms about her real failure in holding (in the here-and-now transference) and can want to acknowledge it and think about it un-defensively and without critical attack on the patient.

To return to our two developing infants: the difference in emphasis on destructive forces is clear in the two accounts. Winnicott has no time for the death instinct. His thinking is that death has no meaning until the arrival of hate of a whole person. Only then can the person be hated and killed. Equally, the notion of castration comes into play at this stage, with the possibility that the person can be maimed while being kept alive. But his views on aggression scattered around in his various writings are by no means "soft". In "Hate in the Countertransference" (1947), Winnicott he puts forward the idea that it is only when the patient meets the analyst's hate that he can begin to feel love. With life comes aggression. The baby kicks in the womb as it first feels power in its body and takes pleasure in muscular activity. "At origin aggressiveness is almost synonymous with activity" (Winnicott, 1950, p. 204). At this stage the aggression is a matter of part-function and, as such, is not meant. But as oral aggression, such as biting of the nipple, begins to develop and some sense of separateness emerges, then aggression causes anxiety and guilt. This links with the emergence of the stage of concern. I described above how the emergence of the first "I am" moments so vital to development of the self are experienced as aggressive and give rise to anxiety. Anger at frustration also begins to appear. This is a meant form of aggression and will lead to anxiety if there is not sufficient security.

> He (the infant) has to reckon with his angry attacks, as a result of which he feels he becomes filled with what is bad or malign or persecuting. These evil things or forces, being inside him, as he feels, form a threat from within to his own person, and to the good which forms the basis of his trust in life. [Winnicott, 1950, p. 207]

Here Winnicott is describing a process in similar terms to Klein's but again dating it to a later stage than she did. It can only come about once the infant can differentiate what is inside him and what is external.

Some clinical and technical implications

Having laid out two different descriptions—Klein's and Winnicott's—of earliest development, it is a valid question to ask how they can helpfully coexist in me when I am with a patient. I think that Klein's clarity about the damaging effects of envy on the healthy development of the personality, of the limiting effects of the lack of integration when the depressive position cannot be achieved or maintained. and the powerful interplay of the projective and introjective processes form my basic understanding of the internal structure and dynamic that many of our more damaged patients bring. However. I tend to assume that as a result of an interaction between their inborn tendencies and early environmental experience. these patients bring to analysis traumatic early developmental failure that has resulted in the dynamic that Klein describes so well. The failure of holding will have been for a multitude of reasons, which can range from "a bad fit" between mother and child, to death or loss of the parent, to anxieties, depression, or losses in the mother projected into the child, to unmanageable ambivalence in the mother, to external pressures such as anxiety over debt or war, to societal pressures such as pressure on mother to get back to work so as not to give herself to her maternal preoccupation, and so on. There are as many possible reasons as there are mothers and babies. The patient brings an early trauma experienced as a lack of attunement at a time when he was not yet separate from mother and before he had a clear notion of me and not me. He knows it feels wrong and can complain vociferously but may have limited experience of good-enough holding to draw on or to know what he needs. The analyst is faced with the problem of unintentionally re-traumatizing the patient with everything she says, which in particular moments can feel to the patient as if it is coming from a *separate* person when he feels *merged* and needs a person who can stand to be undifferentiated from him. An accurate interpretation about envy and spoiling will only be helpful if it is received at a moment when the patient is aware of and able to tolerate mother/analyst's separate existence and has enough experience of being reliably held. If offered at a regressed moment often experienced as a raw or heated moment, it is experienced either as another impingement or as another distancing pushing away and traumatic separation by the analyst/mother on the raw and skinless baby—another nail in the coffin of the patient's hope for a different experience and a development of a true or core self through being received and responded to empathically.

Another clinical issue arising from Winnicott's view of the development of the self is the issue of authenticity in the mother/baby dyad. This depends on reliable-enough holding that enables the infant to experience his own bodily feelings and express them in a spontaneous gesture, which is responded to by an empathic mother. It requires a finding by the baby of his own experience, the expression of it in the spontaneous gesture, and a unique and appropriate response to it. By the same token, I think, patients who bring early traumatic failures in holding require the analyst to be able to use their analytic theory in an authentic and personal way, which is worked out between each analytic dyad. Just as the mother must not rely only on her experience of being a mother but must stay tuned to this different baby, so must the analyst. So if the patient complains "when you say that to me, it just makes me feel as if you are unable to take it!", then the analyst must really take this on board, however "right" the interpretation—otherwise the possibility of a real and spontaneous development of the self will be replaced with something compliant and false. This is another version of re-traumatizing the patient.

Mr X

I imagine myself in my consulting room with a patient—let us call him Mr X. Let us say he has been in analysis for some time, so we know quite a lot about each other's ways of thinking, being, and relating. I would describe him as borderline. He has shown me over and over again how impinged-upon and raw he can feel in certain terrifying states of mind and how he struggles with integration. His tendency to idealize in an effort to have a good object that can survive the hated, intrusive bad one leaves him very vulnerable to crushing denigration; usually it is I who am vulnerable to it in its projected form, in the first instance. At a more basic and developmentally earlier level, he struggles with a difficulty of going-on-being himself, a fundamental tendency towards disintegration, which increases his sense of lack of a protective skin or boundary to cushion him from what he experiences as my intrusiveness and my pushing all my failures and insecurities into him while denying them myself. The work can go through long periods when he finds it impossible to sort out what is I and what is he. His projections can feel violent and violating to me, and his terror of me can soar in these moments. In this terrified state he has to go on attacking me further, because were he to come back into a more integrated state, he would have to experience the guilt of what he has been doing to me. His envy of me and others troubles him enormously, and when the spoiling nature of it is pointed out, it can easily make him feel condemned by attack from his own psychotic superego.

In my mind I have an understanding of Mr X's difficulties, in tune with Klein's vivid and clear description. Sitting alongside this understanding, I have an Independent voice, a conversation in which I discuss how best to hold or handle him in the state he is in.

Mr X begins the session sighing and sounding rather miserable and letting me know that his symptoms have returned. I experience disappointment, and as he warms to his theme, I realize I feel criticized and attacked because I have not helped him. He talks with a little more animation about some wonderful insights he has gained from reading a chapter in a book. It is a really brilliant chapter, and he enumerates the things that have helped him. I am aware of various things. One is that I also have a chapter in this book, the second is that the topic has been the area of our recent work together, the third is that yesterday's session seemed to me to have been an illuminating one, after which I might have expected him to have felt relief, and the fourth is that, much as I don't like to admit it, I am feeling annoyed and provoked.

What goes through my mind as I try to organize my thoughts and feelings into an interpretation?

Should I interpret the envious attack at this stage? How will it be experienced by Mr X? I can hear in his measured delivery an effort to control his anxiety, which must be considerable in view of his unconscious attack. What I know of him is that he is very sensitive in this mood: our conversation could easily spiral down into a predictable stand-off where I feel I cannot hold him or get near to him, and he feels that I distance myself from him, leaving all the problems in him and not shared between us. I also wonder how he is today, in particular. I don't want to get stuck in thinking of him as if he hasn't developed since last month, when a similar thing happened. I want to keep my holding responsive, alive, and active. I wonder, too, about his reparative efforts. In the patient–analyst dyad based on a model of Winnicott's infant–mother dyad, is he making efforts to bring something enriching, and if so, can I recognize it? Does he perhaps fear that he can contribute nothing to me and is in a hopeless situation that he cannot make better in any way? As I think about this, I focus on the fact that he *is* bringing new and interesting material, he *is* telling me about the insights he has had and the work he has done between sessions, he *is* letting me know that he is ambivalent about yesterday's work in that he gained insight but was then left to cope with the new relationship to me it brought about. At the same time, his projective communication is an unconscious attempt to take us down a familiar path to re-enact his early traumatic impingements.

I would like to find a way of talking to Mr X about his envy, which gives him the experience of being held and not annihilated. Put differently, he will unconsciously be trying to repeat a terrible pattern of attachment, encouraging me to play out my part in it, while I will want to both recognize this with him and at the same time give him a different experience.

I would like to find a way of taking up his anxiety, that I will not appreciate that he is telling me about the helpful work of yesterday's session because I will be too quick to respond to his attack on me. Perhaps I could let him know that he might be afraid that if I realize how helped he felt, I will become too powerful and too separate to concern myself with him, and that keeping me in the dark is a way of holding on to my interest and of holding on to the me he needs to help him.

I would need to be careful in the way I spoke to Mr X that he didn't feel I was being seductively "nice". So I would need to make it clear that I knew by experiencing it that I had been attacked and that I could still want to go on thinking about him despite it.

Conclusion

In this chapter I have focused on one aspect of Klein's *Envy and Gratitude*: the development of object relations in earliest infancy. I have compared that with Winnicott's descriptions of the first weeks and months of life and have explored some of the technical implications of the Winnicottian view of development. I have also asked myself the question: how can these two views coexist within me in the consulting room, and I found, in an examination of my clinical thinking, that Klein's description of the dynamic structure of the internal object world of patient's with early developmental damage is invaluable to my understanding, while Winnicott's descriptions and emphases inform my technique in the consulting room.

5

On gratitude

Edna O'Shaughnessy

Envy and Gratitude, published in 1957, is one of Melanie Klein's last writings before she died in 1960. She begins the Preface to this marvellous short work by saying: "I have for many years been interested in the earliest sources of two attitudes that have always been familiar—envy and gratitude" (p. 176). The work is a distillation of reflections from her working life-time, and her reflections, in their turn, concern a whole life-time. She continues: "I arrived at the conclusion that envy is a most potent factor in undermining feelings of love and gratitude at their root, since it affects the earliest relation of all, that to the mother. The fundamental importance of this relation for the individual's whole emotional life has been substantiated" (p. 176). In her work she examines the role of envy more fully than gratitude, though this does not mean she thinks envy is more important than gratitude. Like Atlas carrying on his shoulders a whole world, envy and gratitude both bear a terrible weight: envy "interferes with the building up of a secure relation to the good external and internal object" (p. 239), and gratitude "is essential in building up the relation to the good object and underlies also the appreciation of goodness in others and in oneself" (p. 187).

In this chapter, about Klein's ideas on gratitude, I explore, in the circumstances of a psychoanalysis, some forms of the emergence of gratitude and also some of its problems. First, I would like just to note that there is no rule that envy must manifest itself before gratitude. Sometimes, in relation to the analyst, gratitude emerges before envy.

Leon

After his very first session, an 11-year-old boy left the playroom and went away. I was still in the room, putting away his box of toys, when I became aware he had returned and was standing at the door. I turned round to him, and he said with great seriousness "Thanks. Thanks. Thank you", and went away. What was he thanking me for?

When his parents had come to see me about an analysis for their child, they were distressed and at cross-purposes with each other. Father was in a panic that Leon (as I shall call him), nervous of all new prospects, would not be able to move to his new school in a few months, and for him it was urgent that Leon have an analysis. Mother was humbly dubious about this, insisting that Leon was just an ordinary boy, not academic, no trouble at all—but she was over-ridden by her husband.

As they had made no mention of depression, I was not expecting the very depressed child who arrived for a first session: a crushed, lumpy boy who sat himself down in front of me on a small bench, apparently not anxious about being with an unknown person for a strange purpose called "psychoanalysis". Indeed, he wore a conspicuous, incongruous air of "This is ordinary". When I spoke about how he needed to make everything ordinary to keep his fears away, Leon nodded assent. Then his face clouded and reddened, and he was weeping. After a while I asked him if it was that he did not know why he was crying, or was he crying for some reason he knew. He replied "The first one"—meaning he didn't know why he was crying—and I said he was letting me know there is a deep sadness in him and that he doesn't know what it is about.

He looked very depressed, and at the same time, his crying which continued, took on another quality: it was meant to make me feel sorry for him. So I spoke about how he also wanted me to

> see that, sent to me by his parents, he is suffering—he wants us all to feel sorry for him, and wrong for offering him analysis. He nodded again in assent. All the while his feet were moving out towards me and then retreating back under the bench; and at times he looked round the room, at the sink and the taps, and the box of drawing materials and toys with interest. I went on to say he had opposite wishes: he wanted to go away and he also wanted this new chance—though the wanting must be secret, from me and—I suspect—from his parents and brother at home. He nodded again. At the end of the hour his face puckered and his hands got shaky. Fear had flooded into him: for an instant he looked like a small baby. I said I thought that he, a big boy, felt he had a small child in him who was very afraid of me and unsure what this was all about. To this he nodded vigorously. He left, and then, as I described above, he came back, and said "Thanks. Thanks. Thank you" and went away.

I imagine we all have known patients who say a grateful "Thank you", not during the session, but after it. As split-off envy affects an analysis by its underlying negation, so split-off gratitude supports an analysis by an affirmation that is, for some reason, kept outside the session. Leon's gratitude showed itself at once; it was only later, when what turned out to be his watcher of events came into the sessions, that we discovered that this watcher could have other emotions, like contempt and envious gratification. In this connection, Hanna Segal (1979, p. 148) draws attention to a disagreement between Freud and Klein. As a consequence of his hypothesis of primary narcissism, Freud believed hatred of the object to be older than the love of it; Klein sees love and hate as present from the beginning.

What was Leon thanking me for? I think it was for addressing his psychic reality, for attention and interpretation, and for withholding from, as we say, "acting in" (Joseph, 1989) with him. He was grateful too that in this new circumstance of a psychoanalytic session, when he let me see his depression, fear, pleas to be softly pitied, I could—without denial or getting over-anxious or over-solicitous (i.e. without repeating his enmeshed object relations)—know his feelings and speak plainly about them. That is to say, I think he was grateful to me for doing my job. It also had for him the significance of his father giving to him something that he, father, who was himself in analysis, valued, and I think Leon was grateful for that too.

Melanie Klein writes of gratitude in infancy: "A full gratification at the breast means that the infant feels he has received from his loved object a unique gift which he wants to keep. This is the basis of gratitude" (1957, p. 118). She refers to Abraham, mentioning that "Abraham did not speak of gratitude but he described generosity as an oral feature" (1957, p. 176). Abraham describes generosity in a paper on manic character formation. He writes: "Generosity is frequently found as an oral character-trait. In this the orally gratified person is identifying himself with the bounteous mother" (Abraham, 1924, p. 403).

I think there is a continuum of psychic giving to which bounteousness belongs, a continuum that ranges from meanness and withholding at one end, to generous giving at the other. The bounteous mother with whom the generous person identifies is the bestowing loved object to whom gratitude can be felt. Of course "bounteousness" will have particular features in each instance. I shall give a sketch of a manic patient (known in supervision) whose objects had contrary, conditional elements in their bounteousness, as did also Mr M's generosity, which, even so, I think contained gratitude.[1]

Mr M

Mr M's work is to furnish interiors for affluent people and join them in social excitements with a blurring of boundaries and roles—a situation continuous with his early history. There was no father in the home, and he seems to have needed to excite his mother's "interior", and then, in mutual excitement, he and his mother had a sort of false high-living, which, he knew, had an underside where he was unaccepted, forgotten, and neglected. Currently, Mr M has a domestically neglectful partner; it is he who tends to the children, shops, cooks his "haute cuisine" for the family.

He had been on the verge of financial bankruptcy when he began analysis, and his analyst reduced her fee to what he could manage—a fact that he was aware of. In the first months Mr M might arrive too early, ring the bell too much, bring presents. He bounded into sessions, talked fast, went from one subject to another, made jokes, moved about on the couch—on his side, propped up on an elbow, onto his stomach to stare at his analyst, or sitting up in various places on the couch. Only for moments—and such moments had significance—could he lie on the couch in the ordinary way. His analyst had to struggle to maintain an analytic framework—both externally (e.g. find ways to deal with his times of arrival, or a gift), and also internally within herself. Mr M is used to designing "interiors", and with his speedy, profuse talk was adept at using warmth, cleverness, and jokiness to target and intrude into his analyst's mind. In Abraham's terminology, Mr M is a patient with a constitutionally high oral erotism. His speed and excitement made him difficult to contact, and his analyst had to struggle not to get excited or collapse with laughter—be almost forced into the patient's mania. At times Mr M, too, felt pulled to the place of analysis or into the analyst herself, his excitement almost uncontrollable, with a confused, anxious belief that excitement and mutual transgression was what the analyst really wanted, along with the knowledge—at times dangerously near to being lost—that there was a different reality of sessions with an analyst struggling with a needy patient excitedly defending himself from fears of an icy, vertiginous drop.

During this first year Mr M gradually became less excited and exciting in his way of communicating. He began to keep the boundaries of session times and bell ringing, and gifts stopped. In his work life he was notably more able to stand his ground with clients, and his money affairs were put into better order by a financial manager. As the first year drew to its end, he expressed his gratitude on two occasions. His analyst had called attention to his withholding payment of her bill; it turned out that he had the cheque in his pocket, but had not handed it over. Mr M then said "The thing is, I feel pathetically grateful to you. I'm embarrassed at how grateful I am, because I know I couldn't function without coming here. And I'm very grateful for the discount that you give me, and if someone did to me what I do to you, I'd be very pissed off . . . but I don't understand it, because I am so grateful, and I really hope you don't take it personally, because you know, more than anyone, it's a problem I have with everyone. [Consciously he meant his tendency not to settle bills]. I'm pathetically grateful for all of this." And again, on the last session before the Christmas holiday, after speaking about his anxieties about travelling and his dissatisfactions with his partner, he said how different it felt

> to have his finances in order before going away: how his current account was actually in credit, and all his suppliers had been paid; and he mentioned possible profitable business projects for the next year. With a jokey cover, he said to his analyst: "We're not doing Christmas presents this year, are we? I don't think I could cope with the talking about it for sessions on end anyway." And then seriously: "But I want you to know that you have something that only my children have, which is my deepest gratitude. 95% of this is down to you and my sessions. I am very clear about that. And maybe in the New Year we can talk about increasing my fees, because I am aware of the huge discount you give me, and I think I will be able to afford a little more." His analyst told me she was moved and thought Mr M was not—as so often—designing her interior, but expressing his gratitude.

Is Mr M's gratitude authentic? Or are the analyst, and the supervisor, too, deceived? When Mr M says "I want you to know that you have something that only my children have, which is my deepest gratitude. 95% of this is down to you and my sessions", is this sincere, in every particular, including that his gratitude is "*down* to you"—that is, he knows he is still high? Such questions are among the uncomfortable issues that recur in working with Mr M. As with all patients who are "bi-polar", Mr M's communications often have a dual aspect. Could Mr M, even as he expresses his gratitude, also be supplying it as the type of Christmas present he thinks the analyst wants, so interfering with and spoiling his gift of gratitude? Or is he, as the analyst took it, genuinely expressing his gratitude?

Taking it as she took it, I think Mr M's gratitude was foremost for her emotional struggle with, and containment of, the wild forces of his erotized excitement. I think he keeps his eye on her, watches and tests her, wants to see whether her acceptance of him is conditional on his doing what she wants or whether she can accept him as he is, whether she is sceptical and prejudiced against him or is able to discriminate and know when to trust him and when not to. In this analytic sense, has she the "bounteousness" for all?

Not unexpectedly, when the following year's work started, Mr M had a manic episode only just containable in the treatment. Several strands became clearer: the stimulation of the sequestered analytic situation; his mad hatred of its frustrations (e.g. that the analyst withholds from touching him or being touched); the nature of his destructive sexualized excitement, which, while it defends him from persecution by the analyst on whom he depends, also has a psychotic lure for him. Along with all of this, what he calls his "pathetic gratitude" continues.

The analyst

I shall now shift the focus from the patient to the analyst. Not all patients concentrate on the analyst's internal world to the degree that Mr M does. I think, though, that most patients scrutinize us and target our minds (Brenman-Pick, 1985) to find out how we attend and listen, whether we join in or withhold from acting "in", what we neglect and select for interpretation, and in what manner we bestow our interpretations. Under the patient's scrutiny will come our capacity and our incapacity to do analytic work, our narcissism, coldness, undue warmth, rectitude, whether we speak with or without conviction, from on high to a patient down below, and so on. The nature of the patient's internal objects, his love and hate, affect these perceptions of the analyst, and the scrutiny itself is anxious, concerning as it does the very nature of the analyst with the fear that the analyst may not tolerate the patient perceiving psychic things about him—especially the analyst's "no-go" areas.

"No-go" comes from a patient's dream reported during a supervision. An analyst whom I thought serious and hard-working, yet with a coldness about him, reported a patient's dream of a *frozen, snow-bound landscape in which there was a single small house. Near the house was a signpost saying "No-go"*. The analyst interpreted the dream not as his patient's perception of him, but as a representation of the patient's coldness and isolation. His patient made no objection to the interpretation, so accommodating the analyst. Easy, of course, to see such a "no-go" area of coldness, or narcissism, or whatever, in others; not easy, though, to see the no-go areas in oneself (Money-Kyrle, 1956).

If the analyst is cold, say, or narcissistic, a patient feels warmth to be withheld from him—in the case of narcissism, because the analyst bestows too much of his attention on himself. If these remain no-go areas, they interfere with gratitude. If it is possible for them to be talked about by patient and analyst, it can to an extent repair the situation; it can't, of course, take away the analyst's coldness or narcissism, but the patient may be grateful to have an analyst with the capacity to allow him the expression of such thoughts and feelings .

What, then, are our patients grateful to us for? There are some uncomfortable issues for the analyst here. Is it for the bounteousness of our invitation to bring all to us? Is it for the unique gifts we bestow upon them with our interpretations? If we start to think we are the bounteous bestowers of unique gifts, then we are, of course—as Freud warned—forgetting the phenomenon of transference. It is a dangerous area that can recruit our narcissism, seductiveness, tendencies to couple in spurious idealizations, our capacity for self-deception, or our mania—as is a danger with Mr M. And, as Gabbard (2000) notes, there also are the stresses for the analyst of the ungrateful patient. I think our patients perceive, and we communicate, such things about ourselves, which make it difficult for a patient to feel grateful—we are not bounteous enough; consider, in this regard, Mr M's expression of gratitude as a response to the contrarieties of his object. Moreover, our own fear of these things may cause us to shy away from gratitude when it is expressed.

Yet it is true, in a way that needs making clear, that a psychoanalysis offers a patient something unique. It is true simply in the sense that a psychoanalysis is the unique thing it is. "Everything is what it is and not another thing", said Bishop Butler. The circumstances for a patient to feel gratitude to a psychoanalyst, though not unconnected with the circumstances of gratitude in family, social, and working life, are different: they relate to conscious and unconscious meanings in a patient's external and inner life—that is, to psychic reality, and, as well, to the analyst as foremost a psychological object, and to the enterprise that psychoanalysis is, which has its own categories, which Bion called the "elements" of psychoanalysis. All this is a wide subject, and I leave it, as I also leave untouched the related question of the analyst's gratitude to the patient. I turn now to another patient, Dr Y, to inquire into a different area: the keeping, losing, and the internal regaining of gratitude, and all that comes with this.

Dr Y

Dr Y is a psychiatrist. Near the end of a long analysis, she told me the following dream: *In my dream I was looking for the text of Shakespeare's Hamlet. I knew there were some small volumes of the play, but I couldn't find one, and I was getting frantic. Then I saw someone, it seemed to be myself, calmly eating carrots with parsley, indifferent to my search and anxiety. The sight of such calm not helping, just going on eating, made me more and more anxious. My dream went on and on, and I got confused and agitated. I couldn't find the text, the little Shakespeare book I was looking for, and the dream was almost a nightmare.*

Without a pause Dr Y gave associations to her dream: obsessional neurosis. I was reading about obsessional neurosis yesterday in a bad paper, feeling I still didn't know or understand it. Hamlet was an obsessional neurotic. About the carrots and the parsley. It was the colours, bright and contradictory, red and green like traffic lights: Stop! Go ! It reminds me of trying to work on my paper yesterday (She is writing a paper for a conference). I stopped soon after I began. I felt tired, sleepy, went to get a coffee. Yes, that's it. That's the part of me that interferes, and I'll get no help from it.

Distressed and agitated, Dr Y continued:

I'm sorry, I know I shouldn't be like this at this stage. I know Hamlet must avenge his father's wrongful death but cannot. Like Hamlet with his obsessional neurosis, I, too, cannot. But is this right? I'd feel better if I could get on with my paper. I'm really sorry for being like this again so near the end of the analysis.

Dr Y was in distress, recognizing her regression to an old state of mind, which she at the same time queries. "Hamlet must avenge his father's wrongful death but cannot. Like Hamlet with his obsessional neurosis, I, too, cannot. But is this right?" she asks in agitated attempts, which she doubts, to find answers not in her own thoughts and feelings, but in Shakespeare's Hamlet. I noted the presence of the figure calmly eating red carrots and green parsley. I noted her guilt and apologies, her self-criticisms, and how in the same way she could not work on her conference paper, and still in the state of her dream, Dr Y was struggling on her own in the session, frantic and without resolution. She seemed to have no expectation of getting help from me, or that together we might try something. Foremost, she conveyed loneliness, inner and outer.

> After a while I spoke to Dr Y about how she felt alone and without help in her struggle with her dream and her agitation. I said she had lost the analyst she'd come to know over the long period of the analysis—myself, who is ending with her, but who is still here.
>
> A change of atmosphere followed. Dr Y began to cry and for a while could not speak. Then she said: "What you said made all the difference. You knew who I was."
>
> I think Dr Y had felt alone with only an obstructive self identified with an inhuman stop–go analyst who is indifferent to her search and anxiety. She had lost a good internal analyst with whom she has a long history. When I communicate to her that I remember who she is, I know she is my patient struggling with the ending of analysis, her inner state changes, and her mind works again. She cries with relief, I think, as she regains contact with her lost good object, and when she can speak, she generously expresses her gratitude: "What you said made all the difference. You knew who I was." Dr Y seemed to have life inside her again and she spoke to me in a hopeful way, even with enjoyment, about various things. However, her happier state did not last: I shall return to this in a moment .

Though loss and regaining were foremost, there are other crucial things. One is the figure eating red carrots and green parsley. Melanie Klein notes that envy—"the worst sin"—(Chaucer), and gratitude—"the father of the virtues" (Cicero), affect one another differently. Envy *interferes* with gratitude, while gratitude *mitigates* envy. Mitigation is more mysterious than interference. Is the figure of the carrot and parsley eater—present but *not dominant as it once was and now recognized for what it is*—an example of mitigation? Dr Y in her dream *"saw someone, it seemed to be myself, calmly eating carrots with parsley, indifferent to my search and anxiety. The sight of such calm not helping, just going on eating, made me more and more anxious."* And how in her associations she said "that's the part of me that interferes, and I'll get no help from it." Something notably different about Dr Y as her analysis moves towards its end is that she is not in the state of melancholic depression in which she began. Earlier, she was often like the figure in her dream: dissociated and depressed in a melancholic way, full of latent bitterness and envy, in identification with an uncaring "stop–go" object, who the analyst often was for her, a figure connected with undue losses and bitter neglects in her past, and with the ordinary losses that come with life as well.

The carrot and the parsley eater is still in Dr Y's inner world—but her relationship to it is different. It can influence her (e.g. her attempts to work on her conference paper are interfered with and turn into a "stop–go" as she goes for a coffee), but she is not predominantly identified with it, and she knows its nature. This is a central change that has taken place in the course of her analysis. Could we say that the weakening of the power of this figure is an instance of mitigation? Might Dr Y's gratitude to an analyst "who knew who she was" have mitigated—that is, *reduced the force and the ascendancy* of—envy and hatred in her personality?

The internal good object is impermanent thrice over: it is vulnerable to damage from internal attack and vulnerable to external circumstances and also to the passage of time. Klein says "the infant feels he has received from his loved object a unique gift which he wants to *keep*." (1957, p. 188, emphasis added). I think Dr Y is struggling to keep her good internal object. She apologizes for being anxious, agitated, and unable to work so near the end of her analysis. "I'm sorry. I know I shouldn't be like this at this stage", she says. She repeats "I'm really sorry for being like this again so near the end of the analysis." Consciously, she is guilty for losing her good object; unconsciously, she blames her analyst for this event and for her consequent state of anxiety and agitation. Just as externally, there is, in Klein's words "the infant's longing for an inexhaustible and ever-present breast" (1957, p. 179), so there is a longing for an *everlasting* internal object. Of course, the analyst can neither fulfil desires for an everlasting, inexhaustible object, nor provide the patient with an everlasting internal good object, and nor is it possible for the patient never to lose his good object or to effect an everlasting reparation. All are unrealizables.

Indeed, as we drew towards the end of the session, Dr Y lost her grateful state of mind that—to repeat Klein's words—"is essential in building up the relation to the good object and underlies also the appreciation of goodness in others and in oneself" (1957, p. 187). Her enjoyment of the session ceased, and she seemed more the way she had been at the start of the session: anxious and alone. Dr Y had been unable to keep her internal good object and was suffering an inner loss brought about by the impending loss of the external object (Klein, 1935) at this juncture when endings of sessions tended to foreshadow the final ending. I was not sure, though, of the direction of her anxiety. Had she turned away in search of some script, some small volumes of *Hamlet*? Or was she contending with something different: the loss and the pain of mourning the analyst at the end of the session? Was she trying to retreat from these via a regression to her old melancholic state, and yet found she could not—as in her dream she cannot find the text she is looking for, the little Shakespeare volumes of *Hamlet* with its murder of a father, maternal betrayal, and demands for impossible repair? Joan Riviere has described this domain: how "the immanent depressive position brings a sense of failure, of inability to remedy matters . . . so great, the belief in better things is so weak: despair is so near" (Riviere, 1936, p. 146). "all one's loved ones *within* are dead and destroyed" (1936, p. 144). Riviere stresses that in this scene in the inner world "it is *the love for his internal objects* which lies behind and produces the unbearable guilt and pain" (1936, p. 151).

I think that Dr Y, unable to regress to her former melancholic state and also unable quite to face the ending of the session, was lost somewhere between the condition that Riviere describes where the patient can neither repair nor escape from his damaged, dying, or dead objects, and the different depressive-position problems of the separateness of the self and object, the impermanence of the relation to the object, loneliness, and the pain of mourning the loss of the object. Of course, there is a whole interwoven area here of Dr Y's Oedipus complex, the demands she feels her objects to make of her—you will remember how she apologizes: "I'm sorry. I know I shouldn't be like this at this stage"—her conflicts over reparation, questions of what we have achieved and what hopes have been disappointed, issues of the analyst's failures. But more immediately, there is the end of the session, the painful reality that *time* has entered (Birksted-Breen, 2002), that the analyst really is a "stop–go" analyst.

Throughout *Envy and Gratitude,* Melanie Klein emphasizes that emotional life is characterized by losing and regaining the good object. Indeed, impermanence is a central aspect of what she means by her concept of position. Freud called it "transience" in his wonderful short paper, "On Transience" (Freud, 1916a): "Not long ago I went on a summer walk through a smiling countryside in the company of a taciturn friend and a young but already famous poet" (p. 305). Freud describes how the poet admired the beauty of the scene but felt no joy in it: "All that he would otherwise have loved and admired seemed to him to be shorn of its worth by the transience which was its doom" (p. 305). Dr Y is exposed to the transience of the analysis: the analytic session will end and the analysis will finally stop, with meanings that connect with the long human experience of transience and loss: birth out of the womb in the mother, weaning from the intimacies of feeding from a mother's breast, discoveries mother is not solely for you—she has other even greater sexual intimacies with father, and perhaps father and mother are parents also of others, and anyway they have more distant tasks, connections and pleasures in the home and out in society. In Dr Y's case, to this natural series of transience must be added early family separations, removals, and losses through death.

In his *Poem of the Deep Song*, Federico Garcia Lorca (1987) has this refrain:

> Ay, love
> that went away and never returned.

It is a refrain for the series of human loves that go away and never return. In a few months I will be Dr Y's former analyst, another entry in the series of her life's losses. Freud tells us in his paper how he debated with his companions, arguing that transience does not involve a loss of worth. "On the contrary", he said "an increase! Transience value is scarcity value in time" (Freud, 1916a, p. 305). He perceived, however, that he made no impression on them. Freud writes:

> My failure led me to infer that some powerful emotional factor was at work that was disturbing their judgement, and I believed later that I had discovered what it was. What spoilt their enjoyment . . . must have been a revolt in their minds against mourning . . . the mind instinctively recoils from anything that is painful. [Freud, 1916a, p. 306]

Well, could Freud convince us ? Can we keep our memories of enjoyment and gratitude, given the transience of nature and the pain of mourning its loss?

Note

Mr M is being analysed by Ms Natasha Harvey, who has given permission for him to be discussed.

6

Keeping envy in mind: the vicissitudes of envy in adolescent motherhood

Alessandra Lemma

What ties us to our objects? Is it love and gratitude—a sense that we have been given something freely, and that we value it and can tolerate that we need the other person to provide this for us? Or is it envy and grievance—a sense that we are locked in dispute with the one who, we feel, has deprived us of something good that *should* have been ours? Another way of looking at this is to ask whether the tie to our objects is one that supports our development and separateness or one that keeps us enslaved to the object by whom we feel deprived.

Klein's thoughts about love, gratitude, and envy have always deeply moved me as they speak so directly to the struggles we all face when we try to make sense of how love and hate shape our relationship to the good things in our life. Her ideas have been especially helpful to me in my work with adolescent mothers and the children born to young mothers (I am referring here to work with adult patients who were born to adolescent mothers), which is the focus of this chapter.

Envy and deprivation

In her seminal work Klein focused on a question we now all take so much for granted that it is difficult to imagine it not being somewhere in our minds when we are with a patient: How did the baby experience the breast? Was it felt to be full or empty? Was it joyfully offered and received? Or was it felt to be selfish, "mean" and "grudging", as Klein put it, becoming the source of envy and grievance?

In *Envy and Gratitude* Klein introduces her notion of an innate, "primary envy" defined by the attack being on a "good" object *because* of its goodness. The idea of innate destructiveness has courted controversy. Klein has, indeed, been criticized for either dismissing altogether or minimizing the impact of the actual mother on the development of the baby. This work, along with others, acknowledges that the "real" mother, not just the phantasy mother, plays an important part in helping the baby to manage his envy. Klein refers to how the mother's state of mind at the time of feeding, for example, may well impact on the baby's experience of the breast. Moreover, she discusses the relationship between deprivation and envy:

> If we consider that deprivation increases greed and persecutory anxiety, and that there is in the infant's mind a phantasy of an inexhaustible breast which is his greatest desire, *it becomes understandable how envy arises even if the baby is inadequately fed.* The infant's feelings seem to be that when the breast deprives him, it becomes bad because it keeps the milk, love and care associated with the good breast all to itself. [Klein, 1957, p. 183, emphasis added]

Although she refers to the unavailable breast as a source of deprivation and so as a trigger for envy, it is fair to say that Klein does not develop her ideas about this more reactive envy, lending primacy instead to envy deriving from an innate degree of the death instinct. Yet deprivation as an internal and actual experience figures in her thinking about envy and in her case material. Indeed, whatever assumptions we make about the origins of envy, the patient's experience as it appears in the transference is invariably one of feeling deprived in some way.

Although it is theoretically interesting to speculate about origins (and they can never be more than speculations), it is the patient's *experience* of envy and what she does with that experience that matters most in the consulting room. To this extent, although I remain unconvinced by the notion of an innate envy, in my clinical work I have nevertheless found invaluable Klein's ideas on the destructive impact of envy on object relations, on how the self defends against awareness of envy, and on how awareness of dependence on the good object can arouse a wish to spoil the goodness of the object. While envy manifests itself in different ways, Klein helps us to understand how the envious spoiling of the good object functions as a defence against psychic pain: the pain of separation, of loss, of longing, and of awareness of envy itself.

In this chapter I am concerned with envy arising from an actual experience of deprivation. Just as Klein describes it in the case of primary envy, an experience of deprivation may also result in attacks on the good object—that is, even when the object is not being depriving—as a way of defending against need and dependency on the object.

The source of envy

For most of those young girls who become mothers during adolescence, this represents a point of acute crisis. Internally, motherhood adds a layer of complexity to the psychic process of adolescence, which typically sets in motion an unsettling review of personal identity. The young person must now integrate into her sense of who she is the reality of the mature sexual body (Laufer & Laufer, 1984). This is inextricably tied with the resurgence of primitive anxieties about dependency and separation from parental figures and of oedipal conflicts. Adolescent mothers experience these primitive anxieties all the more urgently if, as is often the case, the earliest relationship with their own mother was in some way disturbed (see, e.g., Madigan, Moran, & Pederson, 2006; Pines, 1988).

A mother who enjoys feeding her baby helps the baby to move away from envy towards gratitude. Just as she freely offers her breast, so she freely offers her mind, too. She provides psychic nourishment—it is a breast with a mind (see Bion, 1962a; Winnicott, 1954). A mother who does not enjoy "feeding" is therefore experienced as also withholding her mind. This may lead to the internalization of an object felt to be unreceptive to the self's projections and therefore felt to be incapable of transforming psychic pain.

I would like to suggest that if the adolescent girl has internalized a maternal object that did not enjoy "feeding", then the losses and anxieties associated with becoming a mother during adolescence are more likely to mobilize internally an experience of deprivation that cannot be reflected upon. As she turns to her internalized mother for understanding, this young mother meets an object that is not felt to be generous and capable of sustaining the self at a time of significant crisis. Her own experiences as a daughter, and now as a mother, become very confused in her own mind. She literally cannot "keep in mind" and bear either her own or the baby's experience of deprivation and the envy that this may elicit in both of them. An internal climate of recrimination and grievance may then take root.

The troubled young mother's difficulties are indeed often manifest in her identification with the baby rather than with the wish to become a mother herself (Pines, 1988). The representation of her baby in her mind is thus typically distorted (see, for example, Slade et al., 2005). In my experience the quality and perniciousness of the envy mobilized in the young mother towards her baby depends on whether the baby is represented in her mind as a rival robbing her of her adolescent freedom and opportunities *or* as a withholding, depriving mother who keeps all nourishment for herself.

If the baby is experienced more as a rival who deprives the young mother of her felt "adolescent" entitlement, I am suggesting that envy of the baby takes on a less pernicious course. This is largely because the young mother in this scenario has some sense of herself and of having a mind of her own, even if projective processes still hold sway, as is the case for most adolescents as they struggle to discover who they are. Becoming a mother impacts, of course, on the conflicts around separation and on the oedipal anxieties that are inevitably revisited during adolescence, but this young girl is nevertheless approaching the challenges of early motherhood with a more integrated experience of herself. Crucially, she has some *desire* to separate from her primary objects, however ambivalent she may also feel about this.

As she feeds her baby, this young mother, I am therefore suggesting, relates to her breast as a "sexual breast". It is a symbol of her desire to develop her own emergent, separate identity. Indeed, the typical "complaint" voiced by this young mother is that the baby "gets in the way of having a life". The baby is felt as depriving the mother of her entitlement to the developmentally appropriate need to experiment and "play" so as to find out who she is. Because she feels deprived of "opportunities", this can then interfere with her ability to take pleasure in her baby and in his pleasure and opportunities. Significant problems can ensue for both mother and baby. This is, nevertheless, quite different to experiencing the baby as getting in the way of the very psychic survival of the self, which is the internal experience I am primarily concerned with in this chapter.

Where the core anxiety in the young mother is about psychic survival and fragmentation of the self, my impression is that the envy aroused in her by the baby takes on a more destructive course. Here, the envious attack is aimed at obliterating awareness in herself of longing, dependency, and separation. She feels deprived of a nourishing, loving breast, but her own longing for the breast becomes converted into hatred. In this scenario, I am therefore suggesting that the young mother, whose experience of herself is as a deprived baby, envies the nourishing breast the baby depends on. In her mind, the baby is unashamedly "taking". She hates him because he is felt to be oblivious to what *she* needs. In other words, the baby is not a baby in this mother's mind; rather, the baby represents a depriving maternal object who has no awareness of her baby's needs. This young mother can therefore all too readily experience the baby as a hostile presence in her life. It is not just that the baby takes something away from her; rather, the baby torments her. In the transference, it becomes possible to discern how the aim of the envious attack on the good object is to eradicate *her* longing for the nourishing, loving breast. (The mother's intolerance of the baby's access to good things may then be managed by establishing a relationship of ownership towards him. This thwarts the baby's attempts to separate from her. Instead, the baby is bound to her through obligation because she feels she has done so much for him. From the baby's perspective, I am suggesting that these are the foundations for an internal world dominated by an economy of ownership, debt, and obligation.)

In two of the cases I worked with more extensively it became clearer in the transference that these young mothers envied a particular state of mind attributed to the baby/mother. Its main feature is an absence of any awareness of painful thoughts or feelings—a kind of psychic Nirvana where it is the "(m)other" who has to absorb all psychic pain leaving the baby, quite literally, *care-free* to enjoy his feed. (I have chosen the expression "care-free" because it has come up a few times in my work with young mothers where they have used it to refer to their perception of the baby's enviable state of mind.) The "care-free" state of mind attributed to the baby/mother stands in total contrast to the young mother's experience of her own mind. Her mind now feels intruded upon by the baby's needs and by the disturbing feelings and thoughts that are stirred by the baby. Klein captures well the demand placed on the mother by the baby who feels that "it is up to her to prevent all pain and evil from internal and external sources" (1957: 185). The baby thus seeks relief from his own destructive impulses and his anxieties without any concern for the object. But the young mother's own deprived state of mind makes it less likely that she will be able to receive the baby's projections. This undermines the possibility for the baby's experience to be "kept in mind" by her.

The histories of these two young mothers suggest that their own mothers' difficulties had prematurely impinged on the earliest experience of dependency on an object who could digest disturbing states of mind. They powerfully conveyed through the transference an expectation that my mind would be unreceptive to their projections. I was often experienced as selfishly withholding my psychic space, which was felt to be unburdened by painful experiences. One of the patients often described me as "mean". She was convinced that I had "the answers" because my life seemed to her to be "cosy", but that instead of relieving her of her pain, I simply left her alone to work things out for herself. On one occasion, when I had to cancel a session at very short notice, this patient was convinced that I was going to have a last-minute holiday. It proved impossible for her to even entertain the thought that I might be ill or have to attend to some serious matter. I was often therefore a depriving, narcissistic mother who was, moreover, experienced as provocatively flaunting her riches. This more provocative quality of the object was a striking feature in both cases: I was felt to be cruelly exposing what they lacked while I enjoyed privileged access to good things, in particular my unburdened mind. These young mothers were both at the mercy of an object felt to be narcissistically wrapped up in itself and in identification with it—as was evident in their own mothering.

The comforts of hatred

> The infant receives milk and other creature comforts from the breast. . . . Suppose his initiative is obstructed by fear of aggression, his own or another's. If the emotion is strong enough it inhibits the infant's impulse to obtain sustenance. Love in the infant or mother or both increases rather than decreases the obstruction partly because love is inseparable from envy of the object so loved. . . . The part played by love may escape notice because envy, rivalry and hate obscure it, although hate would not exist if love were not present [Bion, 1962a, p. 10]

Ms E

Bion's words were often in my mind as I worked with Ms E, whom I first met aged 21. The needed, nourishing breast tormented her. Faced with the pain of longing for the object's psychic nourishment and love, hatred of the object provided a kind of comfort. Here the envious spoiling of the object was a defence against the pain of loving and the dependency this exposed. It killed two birds with one stone, as it were: the envied object and the self who longed for the object (Segal, 1993). This process became the focus in my work with her.

Ms E had become pregnant at the age of 16. She was referred because of depression and difficulties in managing her son. From a clinical point of view, however, the most important feature of her presentation was her narcissistic personality. She was a bright and, in many respects, likeable young woman. By the end of the four years of treatment she had made some limited, but encouraging progress in her capacity to be more receptive to her son's needs.

Ms E had been on drugs at a party when she had unprotected sex and became pregnant. Although not a heavy drug user, she regularly smoked cannabis, as a way of "not thinking", as she put it. Her parents were quite wealthy and had supported her financially, adopting a seemingly liberal attitude towards the pregnancy. Ms E had nevertheless been suspicious of her mother's encouragement to proceed with the pregnancy at a time when it was clear that this would severely disrupt her studies and social life. She felt that her mother had envied her freedom and popularity with friends, especially since her mother had become quite ill around this time.

As our work unfolded, it became clearer that Ms E had always experienced her mother as exciting, provocative, and unavailable. Ms E's mother had just turned 19 when she was born. The picture that emerged was of a narcissistic woman who, Ms E felt, had resented getting pregnant. She had not had any more children, which had confirmed Ms E's belief that the mother had not really wanted her. The father had remained a hazy figure throughout her life: the provider of money but not much else, as far as she was concerned. Ms E shopped excessively, using material acquisition as a way of deflecting her need for the object's love. It was difficult for her at first to even acknowledge that her parents had given her the money for shopping and for her analysis, if nothing else. Instead, Ms E behaved as if this was "owed" to her, thereby bypassing an experience of being in any way dependent on them.

As a child, Ms E felt she had always got in the way of her mother's work and her active and seemingly very exciting social life. She was left in the care of nannies for extended periods of time. This was the basis of her main accusation that her mother "wanted it all". It is, of course, impossible to know the actual quality of the mothering received by Ms E. I nevertheless gained the impression in the transference that she related primarily to an object felt to be wrapped up in itself and in some way denigrating towards her. I came to understand that Ms E had not had an opportunity to internalize an experience of a maternal object freely offering her space in her own mind. This was at the root of her very entrenched grievance towards her mother.

Her son was experienced as spoiling the good things in her life. Ms E ascribed malignant intentionality to his behaviour. For example, she once said to me that he had broken something in the flat "on purpose, to get at me because he knows I like it". She perceived him to be "without a care" or "always playing". She experienced this as if he were purposefully flaunting his freedom, and this aroused her envy as she felt burdened by this thing she called "responsibility". Over time we came to understand that "responsibility" meant for her the burden of "thinking and feeling" for both of them. She envied therefore what she perceived to be his privileged psychic space unburdened by painful thinking or feeling. Of course, in reality, this little boy was very disturbed and burdened.

At some level Ms E's destructiveness towards her baby elicited profound guilt in her. But she could not turn to an internal object that could bear to know her and forgive her for what she had done to the baby. She had no choice, as it were, but to continue envying and hating her son, who was felt to be the one draining her of all her resources. Grievance defended against the guilt about her own destructiveness.

Ms E projected her view of her own depriving, narcissistic mother into her son, and into me in the transference. She often ascribed a "care"-free, narcissistic, unthinking state of mind to me. She was then exposed internally to the presence of a "selfish", uncaring object who was felt to keep all good things for itself. This typically elicited a wish to rubbish or somehow spoil what I offered her or what she perceived to be good things in my life, as I hope to illustrate with a few sessions from the second and fourth year respectively of her analysis.

Year 2

In the Wednesday session Ms E said that she felt very angry with her son because he asked too much of her when he had already taken all that she had. She accused him of being selfish and "always wanting more toys, more of everything", she said. She brought a dream in which she answered a ring at her door, and it was the porter, handing her a parcel. She was then silent. I broke the silence and asked her if she could remember any more or had any thoughts about it, and she replied emphatically that there was nothing more. She sounded irritated with me, and I felt reprimanded for having asked for associations.

Ms E added that she could not "afford the luxury of analysing dreams". She said that she had too much on her mind to "play around at being Freud", and anyway her life was still a mess thanks to me (she was referring here to her repeated accusation that I did not offer her enough practical help with her son). I said that instead of helping her when she felt so besieged by her son's needs, she felt that I had handed back to her a parcel full of the feelings she wanted to get rid of while I kept a "luxury", fun parcel for myself.

In the Thursday session (the last session of the week for her), Ms E sounded irritable. She told me that one of the school teachers had praised her son over a task Ms E could never manage herself to get him to do (and with which this teacher had patiently helped this little boy over many months). She said that she had concerns about this particular teacher because she was often taking time off due to vague illness, and her class then had to be run by an assistant teacher. She felt that they should not employ unreliable teachers. This was why she had decided to change schools, because she did not have to put up with "their attitudes". She went on to say that she felt that as the school was a state school, the staff were probably envious of her more privileged background.

She then told me that she had been on the phone all day trying to get information about a breast enhancement. She said that one of her friends "had her breasts done" recently, and she was now seriously considering this option for herself. She spoke to me about her hatred of her own breasts, which had been "sagging" since she stopped breastfeeding. (She had only breast-fed her son for three weeks). She had been thinking about breastfeeding on the way to the session after she had seen a woman on a bench in the park breast-feeding her baby: "There will be nothing left of them [the breasts] once he [the baby] has finished with them", she said. She then added dismissively: "My friends were having the time of their lives when my son was born, and I was expressing milk. What fun! I gave up on this. Too much hassle . . . and the bottle is good enough anyway. He's such a little fatso [her term for overweight], so clearly it did him no harm." Her voice had a harshness to it that I had noticed on other occasions.

Ms E went on to talk about how her friend's breast enhancement had not been such a success: "They look fake", she added somewhat disparagingly. (This was a friend who had been quite consistently supportive of her.) Her mood then flattened, and she was silent for a while. I felt redundant in the session, a bit like the teacher and school who had been sacked by her.

She eventually resumed talking to tell me that her weekend was looking dreary because she would have no help with her son, as her parents would be away. She mocked her mother's tendency to "over-fill" her suitcase even when she was just going away for two days: "She always thinks she's going to see the Queen", she added. She said she had offered to pack her case because she wanted to spare her looking ridiculous.

Ms E went on to say that she was fed up with everything and that despite her efforts to fit in analysis while she was also trying to resume her education *and* having to look after her son, she was still feeling stuck and unhappy. I was aware of feeling somewhat drained by her repeated accusations of being useless to her. Like her, I felt in need of some kind of breast enhancement. I said that she was surrounded by "chubby, over-full people", but that she felt drained of good things for herself. Ms E said she hated analysis because it was "all talk", and what she needed was practical help. She thought that talking about feelings was overrated. She had recently read a review about a self-help book, and she thought it was very good because it gave tips on how to manage. This is what she wanted, and she said that maybe I should read it. She then angrily said that therapists should be more upfront about the fact that they never give actual help: instead, they just talk about feelings. I said that she seemed to feel that my mind was full of useless ideas about feelings and that she now wanted to pack my mind with exactly what she thought should be in there about her for me to take away over the weekend. Ms E laughed. She said that I had a way of putting things that made her laugh. I said that she hated the experience of actually feeling that what I offered her was of help; instead, it was more bearable to turn me into someone with "fake" breasts she could laugh at—not a real, helpful person she might actually miss.

Ms E's eyes filled with tears, and she was silent for a long time. She eventually broke the silence and said that she was upset because she felt that she was a bad mother and that she hated having to think about that, that she would rather be like her friend, who was "without a care" and only had to think about where to go on holiday. Her tone then switched back into harshness and she called this friend "a stupid cow" because she had no idea about real life and, anyway, she just looked down on others. I said that she had managed to connect with an upset feeling inside when she saw herself as a "bad" mother and was able to tell me about it, but it quickly felt too painful. As soon as she connected with this feeling she hated me for making her think about these things, especially because I then went off for the weekend without any painful thoughts in my own mind. It was this unthinking, stupid cow of an analyst who was now looking down on her struggling with her feeling of being a bad mother.

Ms E said: "Even the teacher is better than me at helping my son. I know she disapproves of me. They all do at the school. They all think: "Rich kid gets pregnant . . . serves her right." She felt that everyone saw it as her mistake and that she had to pay for it. She said that her son had been a mistake she would have to live with for the rest of her life. "He's got it easy", she added, "Now he has me to do everything for him. He doesn't even have to think about brushing his teeth, and then, when he's older, because he's a boy, if he gets a girl pregnant he can just walk away, just like his father did." She then shook her head and angrily repeated: "It's all crap, it's all crap anyway". She told me that she had been trying not to smoke (cannabis) but that she was going to get some because that was the only way she could feel at peace. She was planning to drop her son off at a friend's house and then she would just "get out of my mind".

I said that she feared that I disapproved of how difficult it had been for her to take pleasure in her son's recent achievement. It pained her that he could allow himself to be helped, but she could not. I said that she wanted to walk away from all this right now in the session and not have to think about anything. I added that this seemed like the only option open to her, because she believed I also wanted to walk away now that I was faced with her feeling that what I offered her was "all crap". We were near the end of the session: Ms E simply shrugged her shoulders and said that there was "a lot to be said for drugs". She was then silent until the end.

Discussion

In the Wednesday session Ms E starts by telling me of her experience of feeling scooped out by her son's demands and then by me asking her to think about the dream. On reflection, I had intervened too quickly and unthinkingly, perhaps enacting the projective identification into me of this demanding, greedy child/mother who cannot think about *her* experience. She sees me only as interested in more good things for myself (her son, she tells me, always wants "more toys, more of everything"). She feels I ask *her* to provide me with analytic material for me to "play" with, but I give her nothing, leaving her to sort out the contents of her own mind while I have the "luxury" of playing at being Freud. By now in the work this was a familiar transference scenario, whereby she experienced me as the one with no worries and no capacity to think about her. Like her mother, I was felt by her to always be in some other, more exciting, "luxurious" mental space, where there was no space to think about her pain. Breaks were typically experienced by her as me cruelly forcing her to look at all the good things I had. By giving me her dream, she had wanted me to take away with me over the weekend a parcel full of her painful thoughts/feelings, but, instead, I became intrusive in her experience.

By the Thursday session Ms E is feeling very besieged. She finds it impossible to enjoy her son's achievement and the fact that he is able to allow his teacher to help him. This helpful teacher becomes the target for the envious attack: she is unreliable and has to be sacked. Any envy is firmly located in the staff, who, she feels, envy her privileged background. The envious attack masks the pain of knowing that she actively spoils this good experience for her son. It is painful for her to acknowledge the teacher's help, because this success horribly reflects back to Ms E a sense of her own "badness".

Ms E's experience of feeling deprived is acute in this session, most probably because she is also facing the weekend break. I think she longs for me to feed her, but this longing gets perverted: her envious undermining of me is her triumph over her desire. She tries to soothe herself through her thoughts about breast enhancement, thereby letting me know that she can give herself something without needing to depend on me. I am, in any case, felt by her to be unreliable, like the teacher who goes off sick, and all I offer is "fake" breasts anyway. Like her mother, I am narcissistically wrapped up in myself ("The Queen") and she has turned me into a useless object of ridicule that needs her help. The internal representation of the maternal object as "Queen" also conveyed Ms E's experience of her mother as cruelly parading the riches withheld from her. I think that it was this more narcissistic quality of the object that fuelled the envious retaliation.

Ms E is eventually able to respond to my interpretation about how she hates recognizing any attachment or dependency on me and becomes distressed as she then sees herself as the bad mother. She manages to briefly stay with this feeling, which, I think, was genuine. But it then proves too much to bear, and she quickly retreats into a denigrating stance: I become a stupid, unthinking cow "without a care". This is the state of mind she wants for herself (and that she lets me know she *will* get for herself later by smoking cannabis). In her experience I am like her son at this moment who, she says, "doesn't even have to think about brushing his teeth", while I leave her to think about being a bad mother. Crucially, at this point, I think it becomes clearer that her inability to allow space for a more feeling and thoughtful her is disrupted by the ascendance, again, of an experience of me not only as unable to feed her, but also as someone who would denigrate and shame her when at her most vulnerable. I think that Ms E was in identification with this denigrating quality in her mother, and she frequently experienced me in this way through projective identification.

Year 4

I would now like to present a brief excerpt from a session fifteen months later, when Ms E was coming only three times per week. By then she knew that I was pregnant. Before the announcement of my pregnancy, she had in fact already decided to end the analysis, because she was moving out of London. Although my pregnancy therefore was not the trigger for the ending, it did nevertheless mean that we would be ending three months before we had in fact agreed to end. This was the first session of the week for her, three weeks after the announcement of my pregnancy. The week before I felt that we had made some meaningful contact.

Ms E began by telling me that she had been listening to the radio while having breakfast, and there had been a news item on child abuse. She was very critical of paedophiles and thought that there was no excuse for behaving in such a way towards children. As far as she was concerned, such people should be locked up forever—and, actually, the more she thought about it, she came to the conclusion that the death penalty should be brought in for those who committed the most serious offences. She went into quite a tirade about this. I eventually said that someone stood accused in her mind and had to be very severely punished.

Ms E paused for a while, became tearful, and then said that she had overstepped the mark the previous night with her son. She had shouted and sworn at him and then slammed the door behind her. He had been very upset. She regretted it, but at the same time she was furious because he had torn up one of her photo albums—a particularly important one, because it had photos of her days at secondary school, and she liked to look back on this time. I said that there was perhaps a way in which my going off on maternity leave and cutting short the ending of our work felt like me perpetrating a heinous crime against her—like me tearing up the album of our work together, so that she was left with nothing good to hold on to. I said that she experienced this as spiteful, as me spoiling something important to her by effectively putting my needs before hers.

Ms E said that she knew I had to stop. She herself felt ready to stop, and in fact thought that she could have stopped much sooner, as we were now "just covering old ground". She was silent for a while and then told me that she had a very bad dream two nights ago. She was not sure she should tell me about it, "because it might come true".

Eventually she told me that in the dream *I had given birth to a baby with Down's syndrome.* She clearly felt uncomfortable elaborating. She became very restless on the couch, and it took a long time for her to tell me that because of my age she thought it was more likely that I would give birth to a disabled baby. She imagined that I would find it hard working with someone like her at a time like this in my own life. It was nothing personal, but that's how life was—the older you got, the greater the chances of disability. She imagined that I would not want such thoughts in my mind. She thought I had looked so happy since I became pregnant—"glowing and all that", she added. She said she could not bear to look after a disabled child. She hated herself for feeling this, because she knew it was "wrong", but she felt repelled by disability: "I know people say babies with Down's syndrome are friendly, but I find them ugly." I said that she feared that I could not bear to look with her at her "ugly" feelings towards me. Instead, I would be repelled by the her who gives me a damaged baby. I said that she feared that I would neither understand her nor forgive her for this, but would sentence her to the death penalty instead.

Discussion

By the time this session took place, Ms E was more connected overall with destructive aspects of herself. She could think more about her grievance towards her mother and her son, and by now she was more supportive of the therapeutic help he was also receiving.

Ms E starts the session undermining the good work of the previous week by relegating it to a redundant "covering old ground". The dream is an envious attack on my ability to give life to a healthy baby. It also reflects her pain about losing me in the form of retaliation for the crime I perpetrate against her. My crime is not just that I leave her prematurely, but that I leave her so as to feed another baby when she is still so hungry. The experience of her own hunger for the breast and the phantasy of the baby inside me who will in reality have the breast triggers the wish to spoil, and so she omnipotently gives me a disabled baby. Ms E did feel envious of what she perceived to be my happiness about my baby, and this gets projected into me when she voices how *I* will be envious of her youth.

I will not enter into further detail about the session. I simply want to draw attention to the heightened anxiety at the point at which she starts to tell about the dream. One could understand this anxiety in different ways. I thought that it was connected to her experience of herself as spoiling something good for me and her fear about my response. Envy creates a fear of retaliation, which then reignites the destructive cycle. Ms E anticipates an unreceptive mind that not only cannot bear to dwell on "ugly" feelings, but will actually punish her very brutally for having such feelings: I will execute her. The anticipated ejection from the other's mind is therefore experienced as brutal violence against the self and is terrifying.

Concluding thoughts

There are many possible readings of a work as rich in ideas as *Envy and Gratitude*. For me, Klein's work is fundamentally about the reality of the pain of loving and how envious spoiling is an attempt to obliterate any awareness of the anxieties that *will* arise when we can be vulnerable enough to love and accept our dependency on the other.

My work with young mothers and their children has helped me to appreciate that feeling "known" and forgiven by the object for one's destructiveness, as Klein evocatively draws it, fosters a capacity for loving. It promotes the most profound sense of gratitude towards our objects. It helps us to internalize a generous object that offers its mind freely and can therefore tolerate knowing about both the good and bad aspects of the self and other. Disturbances in the earliest relationship with the mother undermine the possibility for such an internalization. In turn, as with Ms E, this can place the young mother and her baby at the mercy of a destructive cycle of envious retaliation.

7

Envy in Western society: today and tomorrow

Florence Guignard

Although jealousy evokes primal phantasies—and the primal scene in particular—envy can be represented only in a solitary and somewhat malevolent way. The metaphors it involves are violent, often focusing on somatic states: "He's drooling at the mouth; she's green with envy, I'm dying to have this."

The jealous person feels excluded not only from any (external) contact with the other person, but also from the company of the latter's internal objects. The envious individual, on the other hand, cuts himself off by attacking the capacity for love that the envied person has, because the idea of being in contact with drives and affects belonging to someone else is in itself abhorrent.

Melanie Klein's (1957) wide-ranging exploration of envy gave it the status of a true psychoanalytic concept. She discussed the phenomenon not only in terms of the envy that men experience as regards femininity and maternity, but also with respect to penis envy in women.

In this chapter I focus on the intergenerational impact of envy on the establishment of gender identity in children. In particular, I want to explore the implications for our understanding of envy of the disappearance, in the West, of the latency period. This has inevitably had an impact on the structure of the ego because, I am suggesting, envy is now no longer managed through post-oedipal repression.

The envied object

Envy nibbles away at the joys of life—one's own as well as those of the other person. Whenever envious individuals discover the existence and the beauty of the envied person's capacity to engage with their cathected objects, that capacity is attacked—whether those cathexes concern a human being (including the envious person), a place, a work of art, a memory, or an idea. Envy has a real gift for detecting the nature of drive relationships and strikes at them by using the very entropy of the drive involved.

Envy of the breast's ability to nourish is followed by envy of the maternal capacity to derive sexual pleasure from the father's penis and by envy of the ability to procreate. The deadly attacks that are levelled against these potentialities lead to a certain number of consequences for the infant's development:

- an increase in the persecutory aspects of unconscious guilt;
- an increasingly pathological expansion of projective identification in an attempt to get rid of that intolerable guilt;
- in parallel to this, splitting takes on a more directly pathological form, to the extent that internal and external, good and bad experiences may become confused;
- a deterioration in the quality of communication between the infant and the mother's mind;
- a deficiency in introjective mechanisms because of the fear that the envied and attacked object might be re-introjected;
- and, as a result of all this, a significant risk of future disruption in the development of thinking and of symbolization.

The intrusiveness that is a hallmark of envy weakens the process of primary identification linked to the acquisition of gender identity. The individual's entire sense of identity thus comes under threat, particularly as regards working through the depressive position and the various stages of the oedipal configuration.

Given the importance of splitting mechanisms, some aspects of the envious person's personality may well have a more healthy development. The envious part, however, attacks the relationship of love for and trust in a good object; which tries to develop in this healthier part. That is one of the main reasons for the failure of psychoanalytic treatment: the creativity of the analytic couple is so envied that the patient, unable to introject it, becomes dried-up and barren.

The economics of guilt will also be affected by the secret attacks made by envy. Here, unconscious guilt is fundamentally persecutory and not depressive in nature; it gradually reaches an intolerable degree of pathological importance and intensity, such that the envious persons cannot but try to do away with either the good parts of his or her self or any traces of the crime committed.

Envy and group mentality

Bion's innovative idea of group mentality (Bion, 1948) enables us to add another parameter to the exploration of the concept of envy. I have elsewhere (Guignard, 1994, 1997) emphasized the permeability of the frontier that separates, in a person's mind, paranoid functioning from its group-related counterpart. In my opinion, the pathology of splitting from which an envious person suffers will increase that permeability. Given the absence of any basic trust, be it in the criteria of their ego-ideal or in their perception and assessment of external reality, such persons will make considerable use of mechanisms that are essentially those of group mentality when dealing with any major affect-based relationship. Group mentality provides them with ready-made and *a priori* solutions, so that it becomes unnecessary to think about the relationship in any real sense of the term—a process based on the psychic experience of oedipal development. It is precisely in this oedipal sphere of their mental functioning that their own group mentality takes over from their ability to think things through. The whole economic equilibrium of idealization mechanisms will be distorted; and this, in turn, will ruin the fundamental process of transforming their infantile ideal ego into a good-quality post-oedipal ego ideal—that is, such persons will envy their primitive idealized objects in a paranoid–schizoid way and thus follow a destructive path in their relationships with real objects.

The painful destiny of those who are envied

Adults

The fact that envy becomes organized very early means that it is a major component of narcissism, such that traces of it can be found in all narcissistic patients who make life really difficult for their envied objects. It is for this reason that the narcissism of someone who is envied is put to the test, especially when there is a close relationship between that person and the envious individual. Trapped between the love the person has for the other person and the fear of being attacked by that same person, individual who are envied have difficulty in working through their own mourning process as regards loss of the object and loss of infantile omnipotence. The projective features of envy are such that the person envied will, in addition, have to carry the burden of the envious individual's excessive unconscious guilt.

If the envied person intends to protect the relationship with the envious individual, defensive measures will be required on three different levels:

- idealizing the envious person, with the aim of repressing the envy situation;
- taking some measure of avoidance in the relationship with the envious person;
- finding some way of maintaining a capacity for libidinal cathexis and of keeping other love objects alive internally, which will tend to reinforce splitting mechanisms in order to reduce the constraints which secrecy imposes on conscious functioning.

In the course of a psychoanalysis, narcissistic and envious patients' analysts will have to deal with quite specific conflict situations as regards their own *Infantile* dimension (Guignard, 1996). In the transference, the analyst is the envied object, a position that lies somewhere between the Charybdis of the temptation to repair and the Scylla of hatred in the countertransference, given the envious patient's attacks against the analyst's sense of identity.

Children

A mother may sometimes feel envious towards her own child. In such cases, the consequences for the latter's psychological development will be considerable. Since it is vital to maintain the relationship with the primary object, the infant will have no option but to comply. In a two-pronged defensive movement—aimed against introjection of the mother's envy and against its own desires—the child will make use of all the resources that splitting, denial, idealization, and narcissistic identification (both projective and mimetic with respect to the envious mother) have to offer—so much so that the child, by necessity and by proxy, will become envious. A collusive alliance is thus set up, both with the real envious mother and with the envious internalized primary object. The part of the child's ego that has thus become envious will prohibit any other object relation, even one that merely appears to be possible, and this will, of course, have a major impact on the child's oedipal development and capacity for symbolization. Sometimes children in such circumstances manage to use a defensive form of splitting quite adequately, thereby preserving for themselves some area of their mind, which has to remain secret, thanks to relationships with other growth-promoting objects. Here again any progress in development has also to remain secret for as long as possible.

Because of the child's love for the envious mother, both internal and external, its basic narcissism will be characterized by extreme fragility, due to powerful feelings of guilt arising from three different sources: the guilt that is projected by the real mother who is both loved and envious; that communicated by the child's envious internal maternal object; and that arising from the feeling of betraying both the real and the internal mother figure if the child cathects any other person. The child's depressive tendencies will further increase because of the conflict between disappointment with respect to the primary object experienced at such an early stage and a defensive idealization that has constantly to be shored up in order to preserve the primary relationship with that object. The outcome will be a relationship of phobia that is only partly hidden behind a precariously balanced "as-if" personality; such patients tend to run away from analytic treatment as soon as it calls that configuration into question.

When the pathology of envy strikes one generation, the generation that follows on from it will be so fragile narcissistically that it will transmit paradoxical messages to subsequent generations.

Envy and gender identity

The projective nature of envy, which Klein emphasized, enabled Freud, a man, to identify penis envy, and Klein, a woman, to discover envy of the breast. It is certainly not immaterial, in my view, that both of these major figures were particularly sensitive to their internal object of gender identity. It is well known that Freud found it difficult to acknowledge his maternal role in the transference (Doolittle, 1977) and that he said of femininity that it was for him a "dark continent" (Freud, 1926e, p. 212). Elsewhere (Guignard, 1996), I have shown that the scandal that was the discovery of infantile sexuality continues to give rise to powerful defensive manoeuvres that are expressed *via* the unconscious infiltration of the adult's infantile sexual theories—be they educational in parents or metapsychological in psychoanalysts.

As regards the various issues involved in envy, I think we have to go back to the three-phase situation introduced by Klein (1932) in her conceptualization of the early stages of the Oedipus complex, when she emphasized the organizing role played by the genital drives from about the middle of the first year of life.

Envy destabilizes the basic narcissism both of the envious person and—to a lesser extent but nonetheless significantly—of the person who is envied. Naturally enough, this destabilization focuses on the integration of bisexuality within the individual's sexual identity, since it attacks the process of identification. Whenever the basic gender identity is built on envy of the other gender's characteristics, psychic bisexuality will develop in an unbalanced way.

Klein (1957) understood envy as the oral-sadistic and anal-sadistic expression of destructive impulses, which operate from the very beginnings of life and which have a constitutional basis. That basis immediately creates a conflict between the libido and the death drive. The infant's biological sex plays a decisive role in the way in which that conflict situation is structured. Depending on whether the infant is a boy or a girl, these drive-related impulses—the manifestations of which depend on the infant's gender—will be treated differently in terms of the oedipal characteristics of the mother's reverie (Bion, 1962b). The importance of the adult's unconscious cathexis of the infant's genitals will modify the repression the child brings to bear on the mental perception of the early genital drives in object relations and in identification.

Envy of the primary maternal dimension, envy of the primary feminine dimension

In a previous paper (Guignard, 1995), I differentiated the sphere of the "primary maternal dimension" from that of the "primary feminine dimension". The "primary maternal dimension" is concerned with the mother's capacity to relieve the infant's painful projective identifications. As such, it is the first dimension of the infant's object relations and identifications. The "primary feminine dimension" is the next step in the infant's development. This occurs at the time of the "primary feminine phase" (at around four to six months of age), as described by Melanie Klein (1932). I want to emphasize here not only the infant's disappointment when he discovers the existence and the cathexis of the father by the mother, but also how the mother's sexuality is experienced as a "scandal" as the "maternal mother" is now felt to be totally out of the baby's reach.

I would like now to examine envy in terms of these two parameters of early infantile development.

The extension that Bion (1962b) gave to Klein's concept of projective identification (Klein, 1946) led him to conceptualize the mother's capacity for reverie as the capacity for thinking about the sense impressions (beta-elements) projected into her by the infant's primary anxiety; she then detoxifies these and sends them back to her infant in a form that enables them to become thinkable (alpha-elements) and be used for development. The intra- and inter-psychic space in which this communication takes place is what I call the "primary maternal sphere".

In *The Psycho-Analysis of Children*, Klein (1932) described the characteristics of the primary feminine dimension that is common to children of both sexes; this phase occurs towards the fourth month of life, triggered by an increase in the infant's genital drives. Klein described the features of this phase thus:

- discovery of the mother's desire for the father (whole object) and for his penis (part-object);
- the infant identifies with this feminine desire in the mother;
- hence an increase in the capacity for introjection and, as a result, in the infant's interest in the surrounding world.

Klein went on to describe the psychopathological states linked to difficulties encountered during this phase—in particular, excessive passivity and a fixation point for male homosexuality. It should be noted that this phase corresponds exactly to what, some three years later, Klein would describe as the depressive position (Klein, 1935).

I have attempted to examine more thoroughly the parameters of this phase in my description of what I call the "primary feminine sphere". In present-day Western society, in which sexual activity is seen more and more as quite distinct from the reproductive function, identification with the mother's maternal dimension is quite different from identification with her feminine dimension. I have observed, in girls and in women just as much as in boys and in men, the tremendous unconscious impact of the scandal that is the mother's sexuality—no doubt because, in our present day and age, that sexuality is much less hidebound than it was in Freud's—and even in Klein's—time.

The fate of the identification with, on the one hand, the mother's *maternal* dimension and, on the other, her *feminine* dimension (Guignard, 2002c) is crucial. I have observed that both oedipal rivalry with the mother's feminine dimension and the superficial identification with her maternal aspect are closely related to preconscious functioning. There remains, however, in all girls and women a deeply rooted splitting-and-denial as regards the causal relationship that governs these two phenomena. It is as though the social acceptance in present-day Western society of women's sexual freedom had no effect whatsoever on the unconscious feeling of scandal linked to the mother's sexuality. This psychological situation is not to any real extent modified by the advent of puberty and adolescence. The acknowledgement that the mother should have a sexual life—like it or not—concerns the oedipal conflict situation; however, her right to possess her own reproductive organs evokes in every daughter a much deeper sensitivity that brings to mind the splendid term "memories in feelings" devised by Klein.

Over and beyond any jealousy as regards their mother giving birth again, these young women consider anything that concerns her reproductive organs almost as an attack on them personally: uterine pathology, hysterectomy, and so on. Deeper analysis reveals the continuation of the fantasy of possessing the maternal uterus, linked to one of the primal phantasies described by Freud: returning into the mother's womb (Freud, 1933a [1932], p. 87). The result is a lack of differentiation between their own womb and that of their mother—with which these girls and young women are in a state of highly intrusive projective identification. The experience of motherhood may, in the best of cases, modify this split-off unconscious feeling. I have, nonetheless, had a patient who required, in the course of her analysis, to go through one pregnancy after another before she could succeed in processing her painful separation with the maternal womb projected onto me.

As regards envy, we could say that oedipal rivalry is concerned with the superficial aspect of the primary maternal and the primary feminine dimensions, as long as the functional link between them can be avoided. Since envy attacks creativity more than anything else, it will emerge whenever the fantasy of possessing the mother's womb can no longer hold—that is, when the uterus is seen to be linked to the vagina, the organ of sexual pleasure. For example, a young woman came into analysis while she was pregnant with her first child. She was extremely envious of me and aggressively resentful of any separation. This invariably aroused the fantasy of "the baby of the week-end", and so her rivalry with my own capacity to give birth—to real babies and to my own thoughts. Her repeated pregnancies were an attempt to keep at bay the envious feelings aroused by her developing awareness of the relationship between my manifest creativity and my fantasied sexuality.

Envy attempts to restore and strengthen the split between the organ of sexual satisfaction and that of reproduction in order to deny that they are linked in any way. That is what I have called the "scandal of the mother's sexuality". To the infant mind, that reality is a contradiction in terms. It is obvious that boys and men are not exempt from the primal phantasy of returning into the mother's womb, nor can they evade the problematic issues surrounding their envy of maternal creativity. Their gender identity, however, does not oblige them to face up to the *biological* necessity to search for a compromise solution, as is the case for girls and women.

For several years now I have been conducting a research seminar in partnership with a male analyst, during which I have observed that there are considerable differences in the way male and female analysts listen to the material presented to the seminar group, depending on the gender configuration of the analytic couple (Guignard, 2001).

To summarize the main points considered from the perspective of envy and its relation to the primary maternal and primary feminine dimensions, I would say that since the primary maternal dimension is intimately linked to the analytic function of reverie, male and female analysts use that dimension as a "third force" in situations in which envy threatens to take over from oedipal sexual issues involving rivalry and jealousy. This technical solution tends to encourage a countertransference splitting-and-denial in the analyst in an attempt to avoid and defend against the corrosive problems posed by envy.

It is here that strategies differ, both in male/female patients and in male/female analysts, depending on the make-up of the analytic couple. Let me give some examples:

- Often a female patient's erotic transference to a male analyst will be apprehended and dealt with by the other male analysts in the group via their maternal reverie, while the female analysts in the group immediately grasp the dominant erotic aspect. This technical detour has the advantage of offering a protective shield against excitation in the face of an erotomaniac danger which, as we know, is always underpinned by a negative transference (Freud, 1912b) but represents the same a blind spot (Guignard, 2002a) in the male analyst's countertransference that could lead to a failure to analyse the scandal of the mother's sexuality.
- Male analysts have no difficulty in identifying penis envy in women patients, but they do find it harder than female analysts to identify envy of the breast's creativity. Their countertransference is blinded—another blind spot—by the importance of the phallic aspect of their gender identity, which protects them against their own envy of the breast.
- Female analysts often try to protect themselves against the erotic transference of a male patient by focusing on the paternal aspects

of the transference. The risk here is that they fail to take up the envy of maternal creativity that is one component of male homosexuality.

- With female patients, female analysts are often more at ease in interpreting oedipal rivalry—in both its maternal and feminine dimensions—than when they have to deal with the envious dimension of the transference relationship. Given, on the one hand, the prevalence of disorders of symbolization in envious patients and, on the other, the fragility of the paternal third-party imago in the psychoanalytic relationship between female analyst and an envious female patient, the risk of a depressive breakdown in the patient means that the range of possible interpretations is much narrower.

To put it briefly, where analyst and patient are of the same sex, the issues that arise seem to be much more complicated than when one of them is male and the other female.

Present-day changes in Western society

If we psychoanalysts are not to leave our technique and theories in limbo, we shall have to examine closely the profound changes that have been taking place in Western society and that impact on our understanding of envy.

a. For more than thirty years now, the group mentality of Western society has been under the influence of a powerful demand to liberate the individual—especially women, who now have a powerful voice and a major role to play in the organization of society. It will take time, however, before that external evolution finds itself in harmony with the principles that continue to govern the human mind and its workings (Freud, 1911b). The sensitive issues concern above all the de-structuring of family life, with the almost complete disappearance of the extended family, the widespread incidence of divorce, and the emergence of "new-style" families of the reconstituted, homosexual, or single-parent variety.

It is still too early to assess the long-term consequences in young children of what might turn out to be an "uncoupling" of the primacy of the oedipal structure.

b. In addition to the changes in family structure, another significant change concerns the latency period, which has been gradually vanishing over the past ten years. Nowadays, whatever their social background, most 6–12-year-old children who live in urban areas resemble the adolescents of nearly 10 or 15 years ago. Given their obvious interest in sexuality, their behaviour, and the way they talk so freely to adults, whom they imitate as much as they can, hyper-maturity—or pseudo-maturity—is becoming ever more widespread, to the extent that it is almost the norm: from a psychopathological point of view, it therefore loses all meaning.

Psychoanalytic theory is thus faced with an impasse. Freud's model of infantile neurosis and that of the transference neurosis that follows on from it are based on the two-stage development of infantile sexuality, separated by a latency period (Freud, 1905d). If the latency period disappears, it takes with it the Freudian definition of the concept of "deferred action" [*Nachträglichkeit*], the cornerstone of the theory of repression. The acknowledgement of the difference between the sexes and between generations, consequent upon the construction of an Ideal superego *via* identification with the parental couple and with representatives of preceding generations, was considered to be a landmark for the developing mental structure of the individual. It was the identificatory bridge to the parents as guarantors of the supremacy of the reality principle over the pleasure/unpleasure principle. Puberty occurred when the ground was already "cultivated", in every sense of the word, thereby limiting the deferred-action effects of the adolescent's identity crisis.

The absence of a latency period is likely to deeply disorganize the balance between the forces of the primary defences—splitting, denial, idealization, and projective identification—and those of the post-oedipal defences—mainly secondary repression. It is likely that, from now on, envy that develops in the earliest phases of life will appear unmodified and unrepressed and will play a greater destructive part in the organization of the personality.

From the point of view of gender identity, we observe a lessening of the characteristics of each gender at a behavioural level, but from a psychodynamic point of view this does not prevent the influence of the "bedrock" (Freud, 1937c) on envy of the other gender. More specifically, when envy attacks the first step of integration of libido with the death instinct, we might expect that the sadistic impulses will be more widespread, in a less elaborated form, than was the case in Freud's time, a century ago. This is likely to be particularly apparent during adolescence.

c. The impact of virtual reality on psychic functioning also deserves consideration. The globalization of virtual communication compels individuals to face up to new kinds of anxiety and to the danger that group mentality may take precedence over thinking for oneself. In particular, the Internet makes it easier to be in contact with people outside one's usual domain, no matter the geographical distance. This extraordinary instrument of knowledge and communication, which has enabled incomparable progress to be made in the field of science and technology, modifies in an entirely new way the feeling of isolation characteristic of each member of the human species; as a result, one's relationship with oneself and the way in which one's internal mental life is cathected are also modified. The Internet facilitates immediate virtual communication in which the difference between the sexes and between generations no longer plays its traditional role—one that, for psychoanalysts, is decisive for the resolution of the Oedipus complex. Virtual reality has a completely different relationship to the pleasure/unpleasure principle and to the reality principle from that of fantasy, because it offers an illusion of what is real, thus circumventing the need to process mentally the links and transformations on which is based a positive relationship between the internal mental world and external reality. On the perception ↔ representation axis, a society in which virtual reality is so prevalent locates the cursor much closer to perception than to representation: it forces on the spectator's perception a much bigger quantity of predigested representations, whose relationship to the real world is more or less subtly out of phase, so that the vanishing point that it proposes when perceived reality is too painful becomes all the more attractive.

Virtual reality favours a highly specific form of thinking strategy—and a master strategist keeps all feelings on a tight leash. The kind of communication proposed by virtual reality has more to do with cathecting knowledge and performance than with emotions and the development of thinking that results from these. From the point of view of the internal mental world, the pre-digested images of virtual reality are pseudo-representations of pseudo-objects; their relationship to the individual's internal objects are obscure and, when all is said and done, of little importance. As a result, there is no need to develop any internal communication, since the part inner discourse plays in exploring the relationship with one's internal objects is similarly diminished.

The fate in our patients of the link between symbolization—a tripartite relationship (Segal, 1957)—and the artificial intelligence of virtual reality—a two-term relationship—deserves exploration. This would no doubt help us identify how envy is portrayed in these new developments as it concerns the sense of identity and creativity in mankind.

Conclusion: Envy and the practice of psychoanalysis in tomorrow's world

From a dynamic and economic point of view, now that the latency period has all but disappeared, the model of the neuroses is no longer at the centre of psychoanalytic theory. There is, in particular, an unrestrained arousing of infantile genitality characterized by imitation of adult sexuality—this is a direct expression of the denial of the difference between generations. Children no longer have any childhood: their depressive feelings are evacuated as excitations that tend towards burn-out or suicidal breakdown.

From a topographical and structural point of view, oedipal elements are no longer structured as an Oedipus complex, just as those aspects that have to do with castration are not organized into a proper castration complex. Consequently, no adult genital mental organization is set up in late adolescence or at the beginning of adult sexual life. It is replaced by the continuation of phallic and group values: the pursuit of some exploit or other, in a voyeuristic/exhibitionistic mind-set.

As the latency period vanishes, the earliest components of the mind—and, more specifically, envy—are likely to remain active and are not transformed by secondary repression. I have been suggesting that this has widespread consequences upon today's and tomorrow's young adults, especially in terms of the impact of a lack of integration of primary sadism and of the so-called post-oedipal acceptance of the difference of gender and generations. As psychoanalysts, we shall have to take into consideration the impact of envy, untransformed and unrepressed, upon the object relations and identifications of the generations to come, and the modifications to gender identity that derive from these new configurations of psychic bisexuality.

With her concept of envy, Klein gave us much more than a better understanding of the psychopathology of early relationships. *Envy and Gratitude* is the cornerstone of the many studies she made of the fundamental role played by the binding of the drives in primary sadism (Guignard, 2002b). For present and future generations, this work draws a clear distinction between real integration of the drives and mimicry, and between real psychic development towards a genital state of mind and the use of adult sexuality in the service of power and narcissistic satisfaction.

8

He thinks himself impaired: the pathologically envious personality

Ronald Britton

Envy and Gratitude was written in the last decade of Melanie Klein's life. It is mainly based on the analysis of adults but has a background in her earlier analytic work with children, notably Erna, the 6-year-old subject of her 1924 paper, who said: "There is something about life that I do not like" (p. 35); she wrote this paper when she was in analysis with Abraham, with whom she had also been in supervision. When she turns to the subject of envy forty years later, she acknowledges his work as being inspirational; however, she does not mention his 1919 paper on the difficulties in the analysis of individuals with narcissistic disorders, which clearly influenced Rosenfeld. Abraham described how such patients:

> abandon the position of patient and lose sight of the purpose of their analysis. In particular, they desire to surpass their physician and to depreciate his psychoanalytic talents and achievements. . . . The presence of an element of envy is unmistakeable in all this. [Abraham, 1919, pp. 306–307]

In *Envy and Gratitude* Klein combined her analysis of the clinical phenomena of envy and its obstruction of gratitude with her theories of the part it plays in infantile development. She allocated envy to the earliest paranoid–schizoid stage, where, she thought, it complicated the establishment of a good object and the necessary primal splitting between good and bad experience. In the ensuing contentious debate such was the intensity of argument about infantile development that the clinical phenomenology of envy was not adequately addressed. It became, together with the death/destructive instinct, a partisan issue. The part of Freud, his emphasis on innate destructiveness, which had proved unacceptable to some of his followers, was now located in Klein's theorizing, and in a similar way Abraham's emphasis on envy as central to destructive narcissism was attributed to her and her followers. Envy became anathema for some and talismanic for others.

According to James Gammill, who was in supervision with Melanie Klein at that time, she found the reaction of both disconcerting. She complained that several people had brought material where they had interpreted envy when there was no evidence for it, "You know", she said, "I don't know if my work will be destroyed by my most fervent followers or my worst enemies! It has been that way each time I have written an important paper which brought in new concepts. Some have broken off with me because of the new concepts; others want to believe that the new concept will deal with and explain everything" (Gammill, 1989).

For these reasons, even though the concept was used by Rosenfeld and Bion, the developmental theory of envy was not further "unpacked" and its origins not further explored: it was accepted by some (Kleinians) or rebutted by others (anti-Kleinians). Hanna Segal's clear re-statement of Klein's formulation was taken as Kleinian orthodoxy; she contrasted it with greed, which she saw as libidinal (Segal, 1964).

What do we mean by envy?

The word "envy" in English has two roots, one from the old French *envie* to mean desire in the sense of admiration, and from the Latin *invidia*, meaning malice, ill will (OED). It is in the former sense that is sometimes used in casual conversation, and one finds it in nineteenth-century novels, such as those of Jane Austen or Anthony Trollope, when characters speak lightly of envying others in order to convey admiration, here it is clearly meant to be not the prelude to an attack but a mark of recognition. But more often, from Classic to early English literature, from the Renaissance to modern writing, it means displeasure and ill will prompted by the success of others.

A feeling of envy may be the price we pay for the recognition of another's qualities or abilities that we do not possess but to which we aspire. It is a twinge of pain in the midst of a surge of admiration. Like love, anxiety, loss, and guilt, envy, and fear of envy, is ubiquitous. So we would expect it, like them, to flicker through the daily sessions of analysis, reported, remembered, and relived: it does just that. But in a minority of people it dominates the analytic scene and their mental life. This is what I mean by pathological envy and the personality disorder of which it is a part.

Theologians of various religions, Jewish, Christian, and Muslim, have accorded more central importance to envy as a source of destructiveness than many analysts, and the definition in a Catholic Catechism for student priests gives as good a clinical description as one could find:

> Envy is a feeling of sadness, uneasiness, or discontent excited at the sight of another's superiority or success: whether in the spiritual or in the temporal order; and this because we fancy our own merit to be lessened thereby.
>
> Envy is not only contrary to charity, but leads to rash judgement, calumny, detraction, hatred and to rejoicing at another's ill-fortune. [Hart, 1916, pp. 364–365]

It is included among the seven deadly sins, "so called because they are the sources from which so many sins take their rise" (Hart, 1916, p. 364). They are the "passions" and the comment is made that "every man . . . has within him some particular passion stronger than the rest"—a "ruling passion"—and it is modifying or containing this that is the "chief work of the spiritual life" (p. 364).

This speaks to something that is important for analysts to keep in mind: that a person afflicted with an envious nature is not only a potential aggressor, but also a victim of his own disposition. Such a sympathetic attitude permeates Melanie Klein's account of all her envious patients, whether they were like her child patient Erna in her 1924 paper or her adult patients, as described in her 1957 work.

In *Envy and Gratitude* Klein quotes the *Wisdom of Solomon* (which was probably written in the first century in Greek by a Hellenistic Jew in Egypt; it is in the Greek version of the Old Testament, the

Apocrypha of the Protestant Bible and the deuterocanonical writings of the Catholic Church). She uses this to make the point that through envy evil entered the world in the form of the Devil:

> For God created man to be immortal, and made him to be an image of his own eternity. [*Wisdom of Solomon,* Ch. 2, v. 23]
>
> Nevertheless through envy of the devil came death into the world: and they that do hold of his side do find it. [Ch 2, v. 23]

We could reverse this to say that through the awareness of death, of the finite nature of things, and of the limitations of the self, envy came into the world. In a state of narcissistic omnipotence these finite limitations and qualities are denied. Envy is thus forestalled, but this can only be sustained by the annihilation of experience, resulting in individual or collective psychosis or the incarceration of belief in immortality and immunity to natural causes in a religious system. When development exposes and experience penetrates the self's "supernatural" immunity of un-breached narcissism, may be attributed to someone else, who is then the object of envious hatred. Within this complex the imputably privileged, enviable person, created in part by projective identification, is felt to possess attributes that the envious person thinks should rightly be his: thus *he feels himself impaired.*

This is the origin of envy that Milton describes in *Paradise Lost* as the cause of Lucifer's fall, which creates hell, bringing evil into the world and resulting in the subsequent fall of mankind:

> Satan, so call him now, his former name
> Is heard no more in heav'n; he of the first,
> If not the first Archangels great in power,
> In favour and pre-eminence, yet fraught
> With envy against the Son of God, that day
> Honoured by his great Father, and proclaimed
> Messiah king anointed, could not bear
> Through pride that sight, and thought himself
> Impaired.
>
> [Milton, *Paradise Lost, Book V,* v. 658–665 (1975, p. 131)]

Before discussing what light this might throw on the origins of pathological envy in psychoanalytic terms, I would like to illustrate its manifestations and its connections with pride and despair through a superb literary example. (Using a comparable clinical case study would be too great a breach of confidence, but I have met similar cases both in practice and, even more often, in supervision.) The fictional character is Trollope's Rev. Mr Crawley: a brilliantly drawn portrait that links the triad of pride, despair, and envy (again, I have met in practice cases similar to his.)

The Rev. Mr Crawley first appears as an arresting character in a sub-plot in *Framley Parsonage* (1861); he becomes the centre of the main drama in a later novel, *The Last Chronicle of Barset* (1866). When we first meet him in *Framley Parsonage,* Trollope tells us:

> Mr Crawley was a strict man—a strict, stern, unpleasant man, and one who feared God and his own conscience . . . he was now some forty years of age [Trollope, 1861, p. 139]

Mr Crawley had been Curate of Hogglestock, a poor parish, for five years; prior to that he and his wife had spent ten miserable, impoverished years while he was a curate in North Cornwall. They both came from genteel backgrounds, and he was a notable scholar. Their poverty bore physically hard on both of them and their children, but it bore down even harder on his mind. The description of Mr Crawley at this time evokes thoughts of Job—as I think they are intended to—and also, to anyone familiar with it, the clinical picture of melancholia:

> He was prostrate—prostrate in soul and spirit. Then he would complain with a bitter voice, crying out that the world was too hard for him, that his back was broken with his burden, that his God had deserted him. . . . He would sit there unwashed, with his unshorn face resting on his hand, with an old dressing gown hanging loose about him, hardly tasting food, seldom speaking, striving to pray, but striving so frequently in vain. [Trollope, 1861, p. 141]

Poverty inflated his envy beyond endurance, leading him to hate everyone he saw as superior and to loathe himself for his self-indictment of inferiority. Their penury was not self-chosen, but it was compounded by Mr Crawley's proud boast that he would ask aid from no man. His reluctance on this score went further and became an obstacle to any life-saving pecuniary assistance that was in fact forthcoming. For Mr Crawford had a good friend of his youth who at this time was not rich but could have given sufficient to make a great deal of difference.

The friend was Dr Arabin, whose acceptability to Mr Crawley, as a source of help, decreased as his good fortune increased. As

Dr Arabin achieved promotion in the Church and a marriage that brought him money, so his welcome as a friend diminished until Mr Crawley could not bear the sight of him. Nevertheless it was Dr Arabin who engineered a rescue for the Crawleys that placed them in the still relatively poor but crucially better situation of the Curacy of Hogglestock, and their debts were paid surreptitiously.

It is crucial in understanding this story to know that Mr Crawley regarded himself as the intellectual and moral superior of his best friend, and always had done, since their student days. His friend's good fortune therefore was experienced as an injustice, but what heaped coals of fire on his head was his friend's and his friend's wife's generosity.

Given what we know of his poverty-wounded pride and his stiff-necked rectitude from the first book, his fate in *"The Last Chronicle of Barset"* seems like the worst imaginable. He becomes the source of a mystery and a scandal when he used another person's cheque to pay an overdue bill to a tradesman. Mr Crawford cannot remember how he acquired this cheque and is consequently charged with theft. He is tormented by uncertainty: "Yes, he said, Yes, that is the question. Where did it come from? . . . It is because I cannot tell you where it came from that I ought to be—either in Bedlam, as a madman, or in the county gaol as a thief." Those who respect him do not suspect him but worry about his sanity; those who dislike him condemn him as a thief. Mr Crawley's self-indictment remains poised between the two (Trollope, 1866).

As events unfold, more of Mr Crawley's psychic reality is exposed. There are moments when he is released from his self-incarcerated prison of persecutory thoughts and envious feelings, and at such times we see what a many-splendoured thing his self-righteous pride can be. One small instance had introduced this in *Framley Parsonage*, when, as a rigorously austere clergyman, he was asked by Lady Lufton to give spiritual correction to her comfortable, likeable, easy-going Vicar, who, she feared, might be becoming too sociable. There is no diffidence or deference in Mr Crawley in this context, and no sign of envy: the reprobate Vicar is first shown the errors of his ways and then the helping hand of salvation is extended to the anticipated penitent with the generosity of grandiosity. Trollope does not have any comment to make but lets us sample his character's demeanour and behaviour as if we were there. *We are left, however, with the knowledge that this is a man who only feels well when he feels superior.*

This can be seen in a much bigger way in the story of the mystery of the cheque. His Bishop, under undue pressure from his sanctimonious wife, suspends Mr Crawley from his parish duties before he has been found formally guilty. This is technically a misjudgement of Church Law. Mr Crawley is immediately confident that he has been wronged and is empowered, re-energized, and ready for confrontation. Bishop Proudie—under orders from Mrs Proudie, the shameless power behind the Ecclesiastical throne—has exceeded his authority and tried to relieve Mr Crawley of his clerical duties before his trial: something that only a properly constituted Church Commission could do. He confronts the guilty pair, speaking to the Bishop with formal deference and official humility while completely ignoring Mrs Proudie, finally telling her, in effect, that she should keep to her inferior station as a wife and remain silent. He is the only man in Barsetshire who finally squashes Mrs Proudie, armoured as he is in rectitude, and he proudly exposes the Bishop's error and Mrs Proudie's presumption.

In contrast to this bravura performance, when Mr Crawley is wrongly accused of stealing the cheque, he is disabled. He cannot remember how he acquired it, he cannot assure himself he is guiltless, and if it were left to him, he would make no effort to defend himself or protect his family. He is finally saved by the return from overseas of his old friend Dr Arabin and Mrs Arabin, who can account for his possession of the cheque. She it was who had placed the 20-pound cheque, as an extra, in an envelope already containing 50 pounds that her husband was about to give to a very reluctant but desperate Mr Crawley. This was the transaction of which Mr Crawley had no recollection, by which he had received with such mortification 50 pounds in cash and an even less acceptable gift from a woman, Mrs Arabin—money that paid for his family's food. Trollope later wrote, "I cannot make myself believe that even such a man as Mr Crawley could have forgotten how he got it. . . ." (Trollope, 1883, p. 274).

Here I think psychoanalysis can offer posthumous help to the author. Trollope, though he was a pre-Freudian author, was not afraid of the word "unconscious". He quite often applied it to attitudes, perceptions, motivation, and emotional reaction. But he did not link it with Mr Crawley's amnesia. We can, I think, apply to Mr Crawley an unconscious sense of guilt by which he becomes one of those Freud described as criminal from an unconscious sense of guilt: those who elicit punishment for one offence to deal with another of which they are unconscious. I am suggesting that Mr Crawley's amnesia, which leads him to expose himself to an inevitable accusation, is the product of a guilty mind. The real source of his guilty feelings remains as unconscious to him as the evidence of his actual innocence. His use of the cheque for material relief, while he maintained a resentful refusal to acknowledge the gift and its source, was a form of theft.

His friend's gift that relieved his financial distress was experienced as a humiliating reminder of the difference in their fortunes and thus was a source of grievance and exacerbation of his hatred. He felt entitled to be as wealthy, if not more so, than his old friend, the Dean, and his ruminative, sustained grievance was like a continued assault on his friend's good nature. This, in turn, generated guilt and exposed him to the ferocity of his own moral judgements. In order to expiate this he is prepared to suffer injustice. The alternative to his self-inflicted punishment would be facing awareness of the depth of his envy-driven ingratitude: this, he believes, would drive him mad.

There are other even more enviable characteristics of Dr Arabin that madden Mr Crawley: one is his tolerance, and another his relative freedom from envy. Mr Arabin happily admits that Mr Crawley is the greater scholar. This is something that would have been completely beyond Crawley himself, but something, we are quietly led to believe by Trollope, that he recognizes in his friend. So he wrongs his friend and defaces his image when he imagines him to be self-indulgently triumphant, but he faces guilt if he restores his friend's image by recognizing his modesty and generosity. Mr Crawley has an unforgiving superego, and when he recognizes that he has wronged his friend, he is assailed by an accusation of sin beyond redemption. This makes for an even greater feeling of unworthiness and paves the way for further envious attacks on those perceived as more virtuous.

This cycle is one familiar in the analyses of some depressive patients. It is also one attributed to Satan by Milton in *Book IV* of *Paradise Lost.* Satan arrives at the beginning of *Book IV* planning revenge on God by tempting the primal couple to betray their creator; fuelled by his rage he is hell-bent on revenge and insulated by his indignation from doubt, dread or pity: he is not simply in a rage, he is outraged. However, at the moment of giving birth to the vengeful project of his boiling feelings, he is momentarily overcome with remorse:

> . . . like a devilish engine back recoils
> Upon himself; horror and doubt distract
> His troubled thoughts, and from the bottom stir
> The hell within him, for within him hell
> He brings, and round about him, nor from hell
> One step no more than from himself can fly
> By change of place . . .
> [Milton, *Paradise Lost, Book IV*, v. 17–22 (1975, p. 85)]

Satan recoils upon himself: in our language he ceases to project and finds that hell is within himself and is not his unjustly imposed prison. Milton also, like his character Satan, has "back recoiled" upon himself in the sense that he has looked inwards into his own human nature to find an explanation for Satan's continuing destructiveness. He does so in the vicissitudes and complexities of a depressive position, compounded by despair and unbearable envy. He makes Satan human, and in this short passage makes clear why this particular human cannot work through the depressive position and is left with a choice between melancholia or the role of the destructive narcissist.

Satan cannot bear the thought that if he repents and is forgiven, he will once again feel provoked by envy into a rebellious attack. He cannot imagine that he will be able to contain his feelings and integrate them with his acknowledged admiration and gratitude,

> . . . now conscience wakes despair
> That slumbered, wakes the bitter memory
> Of what he was, what is, and what must be
> Worse; of worse deeds worse sufferings must ensue.
> [Milton, *Paradise Lost, Book IV*, v. 23–26 (1975, pp. 122–126)]

The origins of pathological envy

In order to explore further the link between narcissism and envy, I would like to look more closely at Milton's account and to use it to suggest a possible relationship between the superego, the ego-ideal, and the ideal ego that gives rise to envy. Like Lacan (1977, p. 257), I see the ideal ego and the ego-ideal as different—in his terms, the one coming from the "imaginary register", the ideal ego, and the other from the "symbolic register", the ego-ideal, that is "already there" (Vanier, 2000). Charles Hanly (1984) suggests that it is useful to retain the term ideal ego and to differentiate it from the ego-ideal. The latter, he says, is aspirational, "a state of becoming", whereas the former [ideal ego] is an illusional, perfect self. I would agree with this, and I believe that the aspirational ego-ideal is the successor to the ideal child that once existed in the parent's mind.

Satan (ideal ego) feels deposed when God (superego) proclaims that his Son (Christ) is the Messiah (ego-ideal) and not he, as he assumed. He not only was jealous, "he thought himself impaired" and thus was "Fraught with envy". Crucial to this is the revelation by God, in line with the doctrine of the Trinity, that the Son was of the same divine substance as the Father and had therefore never been created—that is, he, unlike the Angels, was not a creature but, like God the Father, had always existed.

> "Satan, . . .
> . . . fraught
> With envy against the Son of God, that day
> Honoured by his great Father, and proclaimed
> Messiah king anointed, could not bear
> Through pride that sight, and thought himself Impaired."
> [Milton, *Paradise Lost, Book V*, v. 658–665 (1975, p. 131)]

Christ is revealed to be of the same substance as God—that is, to be *an eternally pre-existing thought in the mind of God therefore divine*, "the Word", "begotten not made", unlike the Angels, including Satan, who were created *at some point in time* by God.

Satan's claim in rebellion against God's pronouncement is, therefore, to deny this and assert that he and his fellow Angels were not created, and therefore are not contingent and not dependent. He said:

> We know no time when we were not as now;
> Know none before us, self-begot, self-raised
> By our own quick'ning power.
> [Milton, *Paradise Lost, Book V*, v. 859–861 (1975, p. 136)]

At this crucial moment of revelation Satan discovers his ideal ego, his narcissistic self, is not the same as God's ego-ideal, God's filial ideal.

The moment that gives birth to envy and hurt pride is the revelation of the gap between the ideal ego—that is, the idealized self—and the ego ideal as a pre-existing idea of perfection. In Bion's terms a pre-concept and in Lacan's terminology part of the symbolic order, the "already there" would, in Lacan's terms, be at the "mirror stage", when there is a potential realization that the ideal ego of the imaginary register is not the ego ideal of the symbolic order (Lacan, 1977). In Klein's terms it would be the depressive position when the separate existence of the self and object begins to emerge and the differentiation begins between the imaginary relationship and the experiential relationship.

It is the revelation that the source of life is outside, pre-exists the existence of the self, is not of the same substance, and is the essential part of an asymmetrical relationship: the parental ideal figure can be worshipped but does not worship in return. It is the discovery that the parent's projected ideal child was not born out of experience of the idealized self but on an internal, pre-existing pre-concept in the parental mind.

As I have written elsewhere, I consider envy to be not an atom but a molecule: not an element of the personality but a compound (Britton, 2003). It arises, I believe, from the conjunction of a number of factors: the recognition of the separateness of self and object; the disappointed wish to have the same nature as the loved object and for worship to be reciprocal—in other words, the disillusion that comes with the realization that idealization of the self does not make one the ego-ideal. I think envy arises where there is a persistence of the belief that *someone* possesses this lost identity, that *someone else* may be the ego-ideal existing in mutual worship with the superego. This might for some children—in Erna's case for example (Klein, 1924, p. 46)—come to be seen as the parental relationship. One of 6-year-old Erna's dramatized stories is not unlike *Paradise Lost*:

> a teacher and a mistress were giving the children lessons in manners . . . suddenly they attacked the teacher and mistress, trampled them underfoot and killed and roasted them. They had now become devils, and gloated over the torments of their victims. But all at once the teacher and mistress were in heaven and the former devils had turned into angels, who . . . knew nothing about ever having been devils. . . . God the Father, the former teacher, began kissing and embracing the woman passionately, the angels worshipped them and all was well again. [Klein, 1924, pp. 36–37]

In this sense envy arises as a three-person relationship, as do all the object relations of the depressive position. Melanie Klein considered envy to be dyadic, and Hannah Segal regarded it as a manifestation of the "death instinct" in the paranoid–schizoid position. I am suggesting that envy is a compound that can be formed at the point of entry into the depressive position. If in addition to the elements that compose it, as mentioned above, a powerful quota of innate hostility is added, this creates a potentially pathological envious complex. It is this element, the destructive instinct, that operates in the paranoid–schizoid position, complicating the relationship to the primary object and, if carried forward into the depressive position, gives envious experience a diabolical dimension.

If envy is a compound, it may come into existence at any stage when its elements combine and disappear when they dissolve. It may therefore come and go in life and in analysis. I believe, this to be the case in most people's lives and what we find in most analyses. However in some there remains like an insoluble compound within the personality an envious complex influencing and colouring all psychic eventualities and circumstances. I think it is the presence in significant amounts of what Hanna Segal would call the "death instinct" and I prefer to refer to as the destructive instinct, initially outwardly directed. I have gone further with this and described it as a xenocidal impulse, "an innate libido-phobic, anti-object relational propensity that seeks to obliterate that which is intrudes on the self and is not self" (Britton, 2003, p. 126). As Bion suggested in his paper "Attacks on Linking", this destructive impulse may also be directed to the internal connection to the object and even the perceptual apparatus that links the self to it (Bion, 1959).

A dream from the analysis of a young woman whose analysis I supervised might illustrate this point.

> The patient suffered from a severe narcissistic disorder of a predominantly destructive kind. She found the analytic situation difficult to bear, and she made it even more unbearable for her analyst. Usually she wanted her analyst to listen only to her and to add nothing, raged against the journey to analysis and the timetable as representing humiliating submission, and denigrated the analyst both professionally and personally. At the same time she was very demanding and constantly pressed to be seen at times of her own choosing. When she found analysis helpful she was mortified and in due course felt envious of her analyst and then, painfully, of other imagined patients who might find the experience pleasurable. All this provoked murderous phantasies and

savage enactments, which had no small effect on the analyst's well-being. The dream I am quoting was in the middle period of the analysis.

Dream

The patient L is feeding a baby with a spoon—her mother is in the room—L is unsure whose baby it is. As she feeds, the spoon becomes a fork, and the fork takes the skin off from the baby's lips, who then eats it. She turns to her mother for help. Her mother says, you do it like this: she takes off bigger chunks of the baby's mouth with the fork and says this is what the baby eats.

The patient says there must be another way, so that the baby doesn't have to eat itself.—The baby's lips are very red and firmly shut and look like genitals. Then she realizes it isn't mother, it is X, a former girlfriend, and that they are not feeding a baby but having sex.

"In real life", said the patient, "I had a homosexual sexual relationship with M; M had the ideal body—I adored it—what I mean by ideal is that she had just the body I *imagined* my father would have wanted a woman to have".

This complex material vividly illustrates that a narcissistic alternative to feeding from an object is represented in the form of infantile self-cannibalism and its transformation into a narcissistic sexual relationship. In this latter the patient lays claim to the ideal ego (girlfriend with ideal body) being the same as the ego ideal (just the body my father would have wanted a woman to have).

This patient, like others afflicted with such an envious core to the personality, did indeed feel herself impaired by each and every success of others around her and was only gladdened by their misfortunes.

9

The repetition compulsion, envy, and the death instinct

John Steiner

Freud's attitude to the compulsion to repeat changed over the years. At first he was frustrated that patients repeated rather than remembered their history, but in what I have always considered to be sign of his genius, he recognized that the repetition was precisely what made therapeutic change possible. Because of the compulsion to repeat, patients were able—indeed they were compelled—to relive their experiences in the transference, and it was this which presented a new opportunity for understanding and change.

As he put it, "We admit it [the compulsion to repeat] into the transference. . . . [And in this way] we regularly succeed in giving all the symptoms of the illness a new transference meaning and in replacing [the patient's] ordinary neurosis by a 'transference-neurosis' of which he can be cured by the therapeutic work" (1914g, p. 154).

However, Freud gradually realized that the compulsion to repeat was also an expression of resistance to change, and he came to consider that the analysis of resistance was a central task for the analyst. Later he became convinced that the resistance to change was particularly unyielding in certain patients who seemed senselessly to persist in seeking outcomes that led only to unhappiness and suffering. He noted that, in these situations, patients cannot learn from experience and instead behave as if "pursued by a malignant fate or possessed by some 'daemonic' power" (Freud, 1920g, p. 21).

Freud was pessimistic abut the possibility of change in patients with a repetition compulsion, but I believe that further understanding of the factors involved allows us to consider that, as with other repetitions, its emergence in the transference gives the analyst a chance of understanding it and of "transforming it into a transference repetition which can be cured by therapeutic work". Of course central to this argument is the question of whether we can understand it, and, by placing the repetition compulsion "beyond the pleasure principle", I believe that Freud had in mind that it could not be understood in an ordinary way. I would argue that initially Freud did little more than give this area of human experience, which was beyond understanding, a "habitation and a name", using the term "death instinct" to delineate something that could not at that time be understood. However, even in his original paper (1920g), Freud had a great deal of interest to say about the nature of this mysterious force, including the idea that it was destructive of the meaning and structure that living organisms create.

"I drew the conclusion", he wrote, "that, besides the instinct to preserve living substance and to join it into ever larger units, there must exist another, contrary instinct seeking to dissolve those units and to bring them back to their primaeval, inorganic state (Freud, 1930a, p. 118).

I believe that it is possible to clarify the role of the death instinct in the repetition compulsion if we think of it primarily as an anti-life instinct representing a hatred and intolerance of all those things that stand for life and for creativity in particular (Feldman, 2000). The purpose of such an instinct remains difficult to understand, but the reality of its manifestations is impossible to avoid. When it is formulated as an anti-life instinct the relationship with envy becomes clearer, and the two may indeed turn out to be different aspects of the same thing.

In this chapter I consider the repetition compulsion to be a particularly unyielding type of resistance that arises from the patient's hatred and intolerance of anything new, and particularly of anything creative of which he is the beneficiary, and I relate this intolerance to the operation of envy and as a manifestation of the death instinct. These are difficult ideas, and initially Freud himself was uncomfortable with the idea of a death instinct, and he saw how unpalatable the idea was among many of his colleagues. Nevertheless, the death instinct retained a central importance for Freud, and it had an equal importance for Klein, who linked it to the operation of envy.

Just as they have trouble accepting the notion of a death instinct, many analysts find envy difficult to understand and accept, and although it is now over 50 years since the publication of *Envy and Gratitude*, we have not yet fully assimilated the ideas in that book nor come to terms with all of its findings. Klein saw the good aspects of the breast as representing the prototype of maternal goodness, patience, generosity, and creativity, and she argued that a good relation with it was vital if the infant was to establish a good internal object that can provide the foundation for development in the future (Klein, 1957). In her view, envy threatens to destroy this goodness and comes to be a major obstacle in the development of a healthy character and relationships.

Goodness, however, cannot exist in isolation, and I think it is clear that the good breast as a prototype of goodness is envisaged to be part of an object relationship, most basically that between mother and infant. Bion (1959) recognized this when he proposed that it was the link between objects that is most difficult to tolerate because it is this link that provokes such envy. The patient with a repetition compulsion cannot tolerate to be the recipient of goodness, which he experiences as a humiliation, and he repeatedly turns instead to possess the goodness through identification so that he is in a position to give rather than receive.

Freud considered the repetition compulsion once more in "Analysis Terminable and Interminable", where he described patients who hold onto their illness and give the impression they will never change, because of "a force that is defending itself by every possible means against recovery and which is absolutely resolved to hold on to illness and suffering" (Freud, 1937c, p. 242).

It is clear that he attributes this force to the death instinct and that he is describing again a phenomenon similar to that which he had portrayed earlier as a daemonic compulsion to repeat. Now, however, he adds a new observation that to me seems surprising and highly significant. He attributes the resistance to what he calls the "the repudiation of femininity", and at first sight it is not clear what an intolerance of femininity has to do with resistance or with the death instinct. For the woman, he argues, a discontent with her femininity leads her to want masculine attributes, expressed by a desire for a penis. For the male, the adoption of a feminine attitude makes him feel inferior and leads to a masculine protest. Freud describes how

> The decisive thing remains that the resistance prevents any change from taking place—that everything stays as it was. We often have the impression that with the wish for a penis and the masculine protest we have penetrated through all the psychological strata and have reached bedrock, and that thus our activities are at an end. [Freud, 1937c, pp. 252–253]

I believe that what Freud refers to as a "repudiation of femininity" is more appropriately thought of as an intolerance of a receptive dependence on good objects, which seems to present similar problems for both men and women and is, in fact, the position that infants of both sexes have to adopt in their earliest relationship to the mother and her breast. It is not simply then seen as feminine but also as infantile, and the relationship with a good object can lead not to pleasure, growth, development, and gratitude but to embarrassment and humiliation (Steiner, 2006). A marked preference for giving over receiving is what seems to underlie both penis envy and the masculine protest, and which I think Freud correctly identified as an important source of resistance to change.

Today it seems more correct to suggest that what these patients repudiate is a creative linking in which giving and receiving are complementary. The resistance to change in the repetition compulsion may then arise because of a hatred and intolerance of the link created in the analysis between the analyst and the patient. I think Betty Joseph is pointing to something similar when she suggests, in an early paper (Joseph, 1959), that the repetition compulsion is established to deal with anxieties of dependence. She argues that dependence itself implies the possibility of loving and valuing, and that this stirs up hatred and destructiveness since it reactivates envy in which the primary object, the breast, is envied, hated, and attacked. The tolerance of a receptive dependent relationship is a step towards the experiences of the depressive position, and the manic defence against such steps represents part of the defensive reaction that attacks creative links and prevents change.

Bion (1959) describes this kind of attack as arising from an ego-destructive superego, which functions either within the patient as an envious object attacking links in the external world or, more often, is split off and projected when it is felt to attack any creative links that the patient feels are potentially open to him. This leads to a fear of being envied, which functions as a strong inhibitory force preventing development and change (Britton, 2003).

In this context, penis envy is more properly thought of as a desire for an omnipotent phallus and has more to do with exercising power than with making links. Birksted-Breen (1996) has clarified this by distinguishing the omnipotent phallus from the penis as link, which, like the breast as link, must involve both a giver and a receiver for the link to be creative. An essential feature of the creative link is that it involves a relationship between a couple whose members are complementary, mutually dependent, and different. Between parent and child this involves a difference between generations; in a sexual couple, a difference of gender. This type of difference readily provokes feelings of superiority and inferiority, and, if these are extreme, shame and humiliation play an important part in the intolerance of creative links. Omnipotent solutions in which envy is denied through a narcissistic organization lead to the phantasy of an idealized phallus, and the problem of adopting a receptive position in relation to the good object is doubly difficult if it requires a relinquishment of a narcissistic superiority.

The basic defences that are used to master the anxieties of a receptive dependence involve a combination of splitting, projective identification, and introjection (Joseph, 1959), which are often combined to create complex narcissistic organizations (Rosenfeld, 1964, 1971). These organizations help the patient to deny separateness and difference and hence to avoid envy, since when the goodness of the object is idealized and possessed, there is nothing to be envious of because all the goodness is felt to be owned and controlled by the patient. I have argued that such narcissistic organizations provide a kind of hiding place or psychic retreat (Steiner, 1993) where self and object are so fused, often with one inside the other, that there is insufficient separateness for either to be properly viewed. This serves as a defence against the reality of object relations because this reality involves separate objects, each with their own individual characteristics. If the narcissistic organization collapses, separateness is experienced in what is felt as a sudden and brutal expulsion from an area of safety. However, if the patient makes progress and voluntarily begins to emerge from the psychic retreat, the resulting separateness is less sudden and brutal but may still be difficult to tolerate. In either case, the object can be observed more clearly, and if a dependence on its goodness becomes evident, it may once again lead to the emergence of envy.

I am suggesting that some of the problems created for both the patient and the analyst arise from a perception of goodness that provokes love and desire and inevitably gives rise to an awareness of difference. The discrepancy between self and the object gives rise to envy of the richer member of the pair, while the poorer member cannot make use of the available goodness because he is aware of a lack, which gives rise to feelings of humiliation. I have found that for the patient to feel contained and understood, the analyst has to recognize his propensity to feel humiliated when he feels he lacks good things and envied if he were to acquire them. The analyst's capacity to understand these obstacles in his patient is made easier if he can recognize that similar difficulties may prevent the analyst from seeing good things in his patient.

It sometimes happens that the patient will emphasize bad elements and keep good qualities hidden. The capacity of the analyst to accept the disturbing nature of what is projected, to understand it, and to tolerate the emotions that are produced may allow good elements to be revealed. If the projections are too disturbing, and if the analyst's own envy is provoked by developments in the patient, it may be the analyst who attacks the link and prevents the patient from getting through to him.

Clinical material: Mr Y

I believe that Freud's ideas about the death instinct and Klein's description of envy help us to orient our thinking in this area. I will use them to explore the resistance to change seen in a patient who had a striking compulsion to repeat. In spite of the fact that Mr Y vigorously pursued what he saw as desirable goals, they regularly and in what seemed entirely predictable ways ended in disappointment and often in humiliation. For example, following a frustrating setback, he told me, "It has happened a million times before, and it will happen a million times again." This seemed to be a warning to me that I would be able to do nothing to interrupt the repetition and that no change was going to be possible. He himself connected it with the singleness of purpose with which he felt driven to advance his career. If his work went well, he argued, everything else that he wanted would follow.

A striking feature of our interaction was his lack of response to any interpretation of transference. He seemed to deny the presence of any meaningful link between us and would calmly explain that my comments meant nothing to him. He could not understand what I meant, and even when he could follow, he had no reaction. Once when I interpreted his curiosity about my weekend, he said: "Do I know what you are doing on the weekend? No! Do I care? No!" The immediate and pressing need seemed to be to prevent me from having any significance for him.

A recurrent dream

After he missed four sessions because of a trip overseas, he reported a dream that was an instance of a recurring dream he had had since his college days. In this dream *he was having to sit his final exam, for which he was completely unprepared because he had been absent for most of the year.* On this occasion he was more upset by the fact that he realized that he was cut off from his friends. He said it was very upsetting. In that year he didn't even go into the bar and had become lonely and isolated. In the dream *someone asked him to raise money for a charity, and he had to say he just couldn't do it. Instead, he begged his wife not to leave him, and he was moved to tears when she said she loved him and would not leave.*

I had heard the first part of the recurrent dream several times before, but I noted that, on this occasion, he was not so concerned with examination failure as with the loss of his friends. I thought this shift of emphasis in the dream was connected with his fear that he had alienated me and lost my friendship through missing four sessions because his work took priority. However, I also thought that there was some relief that, like his wife in the dream, I was able to stay with him and was willing to continue my work. All my attempts to explore the dream were met with incredulity and led to his usual dismissals. He saw no connection between his dream and the missed sessions, and he denied that he had any fear of losing me nor any relief that my work continued. The repetitive nature of the dream seemed to be an instance of the repetition compulsion, but, especially since it was brought in the form of a dream, I thought it raised the possibility that we could work on it together. The blanket rejection of any meaning in my view of what had happened was, however, also an indication of the power and fixity of the repetition. When I suggested that his link to me had meaning and significance, I thought he saw me as demanding recognition from him and that, like the raising of money for charity in his dream, he was not up to it. He seemed to be feeling that he had too few resources to be charitable and it was this that made him feel so dependent on me and his wife in the dream.

Despite the apparently unyielding repetition, there seemed to me to be occasional indications that he was more able to recognize an interest and curiosity in himself, which the analysis fostered. After he went to Krakow for a business meeting, he mentioned that there was some Jewish blood in his family, which both parents seemed reluctant to talk about. A taxi driver in Krakow had mentioned that Auschwitz was only a short distance away, and later he found that two of his colleagues were going to visit Auschwitz after the meeting. He had agreed to return home quickly, and he felt some regret that he could not join them, even though he thought it would be too disturbing for him were he to actually do so. It seemed to me that there was a partial insight in his recognition of his need to leave the scene so promptly and to avoid any contact with the disturbing personal links with a concentration camp. There was also some curiosity about links to my background and my own capacity to face cruelty and horror.

Session One

Just before the Easter break he announced that his son and his wife were to have a baby. His children, his wife, and her family were delighted and excited, but his feelings were more mixed. He had to go along with the family enthusiasm, but it only made him feel terrible, and he seemed aware that his failure to respond represented something sinister and frightening in relation to the arrival of a new baby.

He began the last session before a two-week break reporting that his daughter-in-law had come out in a rash. He thought nothing of it, but when he mentioned it to his wife, she was concerned that it could be German Measles, and if that was the case, it was terribly serious.

He said he found it so extreme: "You can't be a little bit pregnant. She either has German measles and it is a terrible disaster, or not." I suggested that this is what he felt about himself too. Either everything is wonderful or, if I am able to reach something small and vulnerable within him, then it is a disaster. When he said you can't be a bit pregnant, he expressed his fear that if he allowed something good to grow within him, it would be irreversible and prove to be too difficult for us to protect from what he saw as murderous forces. However, I thought that, at the same time, he had brought this situation in the last session before the break, and I suggested that he *did* want to use the session to understand what the real danger was, to the baby and also to himself, and to give us a chance of facing it while I was still here.

He said he could not cope when his wife became anxious since she also implied that he does not notice things and does not care. I interpreted that he was not sure if he cared too little or too much. It all seemed to go from the rash having no significance to it being a disaster. I thought that just before a break he was also concerned to know if I cared or not. To this he replied that he could not see why I should care. He knows what will happen after the session. His daughter-in-law will have already gone to the GP to sound him out about the rash, and he is sure that everything will be alright. He can then phone his wife and reassure her.

I pointed out that he was establishing himself as the one who remained calm and sensible, assuming that in all likelihood everything would be alright. I was dismissed as making an unnecessary fuss, particularly when I suggested that he felt he needed me to support him and feared I could not do this through the break. He said that he could not afford to get too involved because he has to contend with the next two weeks, when I am away. I suggested that he felt that he had to justify being thick-skinned to protect himself from feeling too much, and that he felt it was too dangerous if, like the rash, something got through his armour.

At the same time it seemed clear that to have a grandchild was terribly important to him. He feared it would be too much of a commitment for him, and he was also afraid that his loving and caring would be mocked and ridiculed. If he allowed himself to care, then the idea of German measles and a possible abortion were terrifying.

Later that day he left a message on my answerphone to say that the doctor had confirmed that the rash was not serious. I thought he had become worried that, like his wife, I had taken the rash seriously and he wanted to relieve my anxiety. Examining the meaning of the rash seemed to have been something like the potential visit to Auschwitz, and he was terrified of the extreme feelings involved and needed to keep his distance.

Session Two

Two weeks later he returned after the break looking miserable and reported that things had gone wrong, exactly as he had predicted. Everything was great for two days, and then his wife became upset and blamed him for all their problems, anticipating that he would not be a caring father and grandfather. He complained that for the rest of the holiday he had to shop and cook the meals, and his anger flared up as he described that he had developed laryngitis and felt that no one gave him any consideration or care. Ironically, he added that the one bright spot was when his wife went out and spent much too much money on a new sofa that he did not think they needed. Then he added that he expected that I had a peaceful and very enjoyable break. He knows I will point out that this is his fantasy, but this is what he believes.

I interpreted that he thought that I managed to get away from the awful situation he was stuck with, and he reacted by saying: "Yes, and good for you. I certainly would if I could." But when I suggested that now I am back he wants me to accept responsibility for the state I left him in, he disagreed and rejected all the transference connections I tried to make. He argued that the events of his break were not my responsibility. Nor does he think they should be. He said he was anxious and uncomfortable with everyone, especially when they discussed the coming baby.

The session itself remained pretty repetitive, each of my attempts to connect his experience with my work being dismissed as unreasonable. When I interpreted that my couch was like the expensive sofa his wife bought, which he felt he did not need and yet which gave him some respite, he disagreed. He said that he greatly appreciated the analysis, which had helped him to stand up to his wife's distress better than he would otherwise have done.

I pointed out that nothing I said seemed to touch him, even though he did acknowledge he was caught in a repetitive situation that he had predicted but one that the analysis had done nothing to alter. He explained that he did not expect the analysis to help in that way. "Why should it? He saw no point in describing to me the details of what had happened, it was too repetitive and too boring.

I interpreted that he did get some satisfaction from a situation where his wife could be seen as the one who became upset, and the same seemed to be the case in the session, where he was calm and impassive, with no response to anything I said. I thought he expected me to be made anxious and frustrated when I was put in this position of repeated helplessness, and he got some satisfaction from it and from being able to cope with me when I was like that.

He did not reply to this comment but did explain a bit more about the rows that had erupted in the break. He said his wife had insisted that he always insulted her and looked down on her while he felt that her family looked down on him.

I suggested that the he felt that he was never going to be accepted by his wife's family or by me, since we looked down on him and on his career. In this way he could show his hatred and contempt and provoke us into trying to maintain our superiority by humiliating him. When I tried to make contact in today's session, he saw this only as my condescension, which he could not accept. He said he agreed that it was all about humiliation.

I interpreted that he did not believe that I could recognize his desperation and that, instead, I became superior, and he wanted to provoke me and to show me what it feels like to be humiliated.

Discussion

My interest in the repetition compulsion arose first because of the clinical problem we so often meet when patients seem to be stuck and unable to change, but also because I saw in it the possible convergence of several lines of enquiry that seemed to be of interest. First there was Freud's (1920g) own description of the compulsion to repeat, which, he believed, was not explicable in terms of a libidinal drive such as a desire for food or sex on which he had based so much of his psychology. Something different was required, and this led to a new principle based on the death instinct to account for a malevolent destructive force working against life and creativity.

Then came the recognition that if we consider the death instinct as primarily an anti-life instinct, we are dealing with a very similar area to that which Klein brought to our attention in her descriptions of envy. Certain attributes of the object provoke envy and drive the envious individual to attempt to eliminate this painful experience by attacks on the envied attribute with the aim of annihilating it and hence abolishing the envious experience. This desire to annihilate good objects is part of the unbearability of envy and leads to a number of defensive manoeuvres, as outlined by Klein and elaborated in detail by Rosenfeld and others. When the envious object is bound in a narcissistic organization, the destructiveness becomes less openly violent and more chronic. The patient then seems to be able to stop short of a total annihilation of the envied object and is content to remove its vitality and to strip it of meaning and creativity (Feldman, 2000; Joseph, 1982; Rosenfeld, 1964, 1971; Steiner, 1993)

A further concordance seems to me to arise if we consider more precisely just what it is that provokes envy. Klein (1957) considered that envy was provoked by the good aspects of the breast, which she saw as "the prototype of maternal goodness, inexhaustible patience and generosity, as well as of creativeness" (p. 180). However, I think it is clear that this view envisages the breast in a relationship; Bion (1959) recognized this when he proposed that it was the link between objects that is most envied. The envy of a small child watching his mother with a new infant is easy to recognize, but it seems even more important to appreciate that envy is often provoked when the other is the patient himself, sometimes represented by something new developing within him. Bion suggests that these links are stimulated by the verbal link between analyst and patient, which may provoke envy, and also by the link through projective identification from patient to analyst, which may be difficult for the analyst to accept and understand.

It seemed to me that it was the adoption of a receptive relationship to the goodness of the breast that proved to be so difficult for Mr Y, and it was precisely this relationship that was attacked by envy. Sometimes it seemed to be clearly the patient's envy that got in the way of receptivity, but sometimes it seemed to be the fear of a powerful attack from an envious object that was avoided by keeping the receptive stance hidden or blocked. If no new development was allowed, there was nothing that would provoke the attack.

The detailed descriptions given by Klein (1957) of the operation of envy, of the defences against it, and of the facts that give rise to it, enable the analyst to recognize it as a universal response to creative links and helps him to accept envy as something that has to be tolerated and lived with, despite its unbearable quality. The analyst's own propensity to split off and project envy is sometimes precisely what the patient experiences as a superiority that defensively imposes shame and humiliation on others, while making himself impervious and immune. I think it was this type of figure with which my patient identified as he struggled with a growing possibility of allowing himself to accept a receptive position in relation to my thoughts, ideas, and feelings. It seemed to me that it was this receptivity that was seen by my patient as feminine and inferior and was the most difficult experience for him to tolerate.

It was possible to recognize that Mr Y felt himself unable to allow a good experience to enter and develop something good inside him. His anxiety seemed to emerge in relation to the idea of having a grandchild and his recognition that you can't be a little bit pregnant. It seemed to me that he also knew that you can't have a little bit of an abortion, so that letting something grow was dangerous if it unleashed such terrible violence. He arranged then not to be concerned about his wife's rash and not to go to Auschwitz, although these issues were brought, I think in the hope that I would be able to allow such frightening thoughts into my mind and without being too disturbed by them. Perhaps this was an instance of what had to be communicated by projective identification and needed to be accepted by me.

The dismissive way Mr Y reacted to my interpretations was associated with a kind of indifference in which he remained calm while I struggled to get him to see something and, especially, to feel something. There was a superiority in his unresponsiveness that made it seem that I was the one who needed him and was pleading with him to allow an interpretation to have meaning. I felt obliged to tolerate and accept the provocative way he dismissed me, but I could feel that it was gradually making me angry and sometimes provoked me to criticize and attack him.

His exaggerated narcissistic pride led Mr Y to look down on others with great contempt but could also be turned on himself when he described his own shortcomings. There was a strong sado-masochistic quality to the expression of his views, and he got great enjoyment from finding colourful language—sometimes amusing but often very cruel—to show up the shortcomings of people he had to contend with. I thought he was relating to an envious ego-destructive superego and getting gratification both from being attacked and shamed and from shaming others. It was this sado-masochistic quality that I thought contributed to the compulsion to repeat and functioned to enliven and sustain him. It seemed essential for him to stop short of a total collapse and a total destruction of his objects, because he needed an object with whom to enact the repeated cycles of excitement and collapse, and of superiority and humiliation. Despite Mr Y's repeated crises, he was able to preserve his marriage; his businesses were repeatedly almost destroyed completely but were left with just sufficient resources for him to continue and begin to build them up again. The combination of attempts to destroy with attempts to protect his achievements seems to result in a prolonged cruelty rather than in a total destructiveness and produces what Joseph (1959) called that "particular balance between destructiveness and love" that sustains the repetition compulsion.

A sensitivity to shame and humiliation meant that my patient constantly felt looked down on and driven to reverse the humiliation by mocking and ridiculing his good objects, just when he had a chance of becoming understood and accepted. This meant that emerging from a psychic retreat was particularly difficult, since it exposed him to seeing and being seen, to envying and being envied. Separateness meant that he could see his objects more clearly and was confronted with their reality—both the good elements, which were envied, and the bad, which were feared. At the same time it enabled him to be seen, more clearly and more realistically, again with his good and bad qualities exposed. His envy was so immediately split off and denied that he constantly expected and often provoked a destructive attack on his good qualities.

A better understanding of the nature of envy and the defences that are mounted against its recognition and integration into the personality may help us to tolerate, understand, and contain these repetitive compulsions when they appear in our patients. By seeing them in this way, repetition compulsion can be recognized to be similar to all resistance to change and to be viewed as part of the ordinary difficulty of doing analysis. We owe a great deal of our understanding to Klein's detailed descriptions, which put envy on the map (Klein, 1957), and to a better understanding of the death instinct and the defences that are typically mounted against its emergence.

10

Romantic perversion: the role of envy in the creation of a timeless universe

Heinz Weiß

In this chapter I illustrate some of Mrs Klein's ideas on envy, splitting, and pathological projective identification, by describing the case of a 57-year-old female patient who created an unchanging romantic universe that appeared to serve as a defence against experiences of envy and separation. Within this universe, which was vividly lived out in the transference, everything seemed to be timeless, idealized, and erotized. I want to show how it provided a *psychic retreat* (Steiner, 1993) based on misconceptions, particularly concerning the reality of time, and how a powerful belief system was brought into play to maintain a state of *psychic unreality* (Britton, 1998). This situation often made me feel helpless and paralysed, presenting the analysis with considerable technical difficulties.

Klein's and Rosenfeld's ideas on envy, pathological splitting, and projective identification

In *Envy and Gratitude* Klein defines envy as an expression of destructive impulses that are operative from the beginning of life and represent the "most potent factor in undermining feelings of love and gratitude at their root" (Klein, 1957, p. 176). She underlines the role of envy in pathological splitting and projective identification and differentiates between normal and pathological splitting, the latter leading to the idea of an idealized and an "extremely bad" object. Klein writes:

> So deep and sharp a division reveals that destructive impulses, envy and persecutory anxiety are very strong and that idealisation serves mainly as a defence against these emotions. [1957, p. 192]

She clearly links the need for idealization with the power of destructive impulses and describes how "the idealised object is much less integrated in the ego than the good object" (p. 193). When the predominance of envy impedes identification with a good and whole object, "excessive projective identification, by which split-off parts of the self are projected into the object", can lead to a "strong confusion between the self and the object" (p. 192).

Later in her work she discusses the manifold defences against envy and examines their manifestations in the transference situation. Among these defences she mentions withdrawal and confusional states as well as the *greedy internalization of the idealized object* when its independent and separate existence cannot be tolerated. In this case "powerful and violent possessiveness" does not only counteract envy and gratitude, but may quickly turn the envied object again "into a destroyed persecutor" (p. 218).

Following Klein's ideas, Rosenfeld (1964) showed how invasive projective identification is often motivated by envy and an intolerance of separateness: as long as the patient can see the analyst's mind as an extension of his own grandiose self, he does not have to face the problems of envy, hatred, and dependency that arise from the acknowledgement of his separate existence.

Rosenfeld also pointed out that by means of narcissistic and perverse mechanisms the underlying destructiveness can become covered up as a longing for harmony, timelessness, and endless peace. He described these phenomena as "pathological fusions" between the life and the death instincts (Rosenfeld, 1971) and showed how they can be linked together to build up pathological organizations of the personality. Such states can be idealized and erotized, with a silent destructiveness being directed at both the perceived object and the perceiving self (Segal, 1993).

Romantic perversion and misconceptions of psychic reality

Such "misrepresentations" of psychic reality can be seen in themselves as expressions of pathological envy. In this sense Bion described –K as an activity that is directed against the acceptance of reality and dominated by a "hatred of any new development of the personality" (1962a, p. 98). In a similar way Money-Kyrle (1968) spoke of "misconceptions". He saw them as operating against the acknowledgement of three basic "facts of life", which he regarded as innately predetermined: (1) the recognition "of the breast as a supremely good object" on which the baby depends; (2) the recognition "of the parental intercourse as a supremely creative act" from which the infant is excluded; and, finally, (3) the recognition "of the inevitability of time and ultimately death" (Money-Kyrle, 1971, p. 443).

If these "facts of life" cannot be fully acknowledged, perverse arguments can be brought into play in order to distort them. This process can give rise to perverse misrepresentations in which reality is half-acknowledged and half-disavowed. Concerning Money-Kyrle's third fact of life, the recognition of the inevitability of time and ultimately death, it is the inevitability of limitations and loss that has to be faced. If this fundamental aspect of reality is only half-accepted, this may give rise to a fairy-tale-like world of idealizations in which evil is defeated, good things go on forever, and frustration does not really exist. Therefore, in addition to the narcissistic and sexual perversions, containing misrepresentations of Money-Kyrle's first and second "facts of life", Steiner (1993, p. 93) speaks of a third group as "romantic perversions of the reality of time".

Impasses and technical problems

In this chapter I illustrate how a near-delusional romantic system manifests itself in the transference, and especially how the analyst's interpretations are silently transformed and incorporated into the patient's sanitized universe. In the case of my patient, whom I will call Ms R, this was expressed by a strong longing for love, uniqueness, and infinity. While she consciously acknowledged the limitations of the analysis, another part of her seemed to undermine this knowledge.

Instead of facing reality, this patient used emotionally significant aspects of our encounter to shape a phantasy universe characterized by timelessness and by an absence of separation and conflict. In this world there existed neither mourning nor guilt. It represented a romantic island where the differences between good and bad, longing and pain, life and death appeared to be lifted—as in the phantasy of romantic death. As Klein describes, the obliteration of these differences is often an expression of excessive envy, but can also be "used defensively" (1957, p. 216) in order to masquerade envious experience. In my patient the underlying destructiveness seemed nevertheless quite obvious in the way in which emotional reality was denied, cruelty was projected and split off, and pressure was exerted on other persons to correspond to the very image the patient had created of them.

When this pressure failed, the idealized world collapsed, and the longed-for object turned into a cruel one. She would then submit to this object with the same addictive suffering, just as before she had clung to a romantic illusion. These two states of mind shared the way in which separateness was denied and either suffering or gratification would go on endlessly. In both of them, envy and destructiveness were not expressed openly, but disguised in an illusion of immortality, endless longing, or never-ending torment (Feldman, 2000). Or, to say it with Hegel (1812): they manifested themselves in "*schlechter Unendlichkeit*" (i.e. "bad infinity").

The patient's longing for love often made me feel paralysed. Like the computer virus that had spread under the name "*I love you*", the greedy, invasive properties of this "love" seemed to be expressed in the way they impaired my internal network, obstructing my freedom and my capacity for thought. Sometimes I felt trapped in a situation that seemed hopeless and designed to be re-enacted time and again. On other occasions, however, small movements were visible, and the patient would allow more contact with feelings of anger, sadness, and disappointment before withdrawing in a negative therapeutic reaction once again. In the following sections I want to give an impression of some of the movements and impasses that confronted us in the early stage of her analysis.

Clinical material

Ms R

Ms R, a social worker, had sought therapy after a depressive breakdown in her mid-fifties. She could not cope with the idea that her husband, who had left her and now lived with his new partner, was planning to divorce her. It soon became clear that for many years she had suffered humiliations in her marriage without complaining, and she kept hoping that one day her husband would return. However, alongside the version of her husband as cruel and humiliating, a romantic version of the relationship seemed to coexist in which certain memories and qualities, like the sound of his voice, took on great importance. Thus while looking after her 17-year-old daughter and responding to the demands of everyday life, internally she withdrew to a phantasy universe characterized by suffering and unfulfilled longings.

Biographical material revealed that this situation partly reflected the relationship with her father, a man engaged in many altruistic activities and aesthetic interests, who demanded obedience and who used to punish the children cruelly with a crop. The patient was the youngest of five siblings, and she spoke of him with a mixture of admiration and fear. As compared to her father, her mother, by whom she felt rejected, remained a distant but dependent figure in the background. Some of her most vivid memories concerned a religious boarding school where she had had to repress her homesickness and was often humiliated in the presence of other children.

All these details conveyed the impression that Ms R was governed by a cruel internal organization that forced her to idealize her suffering so as not to be abandoned. This was also reflected in another recollection from her childhood: she recalled a hiding place on her parents' farm to which she used to escape when she feared punishment or rejection. There she would bite into her arms and longingly suck the pain from her wounds. It was later on that we learned that the analytic situation reflected quite a similar *psychic retreat,* where she would inflict pain upon herself and indulge in unfulfilled longings.

Course of the analysis

When Ms R began therapy, she tried to establish her defensive organization by creating a romantic atmosphere where I was incorporated into her phantasy life. Coming to the sessions, which was quite a long drive for her, she would deny the effort of the journey but would instead describe the beauty of the landscape, or the colours of the season. She would give herself a much younger appearance and speak in a melodic, girlish voice, which sometimes turned into a sort of tormented sobbing.

As long as I was felt to comply with the romantic picture she had created of my person, the therapy seemed to represent a blissful "enclave" (O'Shaughnessy, 1992), characterized by the absence of disappointment, anger, or conflict. She then experienced my speaking as a "revelation of truth" and would sometimes even speak of "sugar sessions".

If, however, she felt that my interpretations undermined her picture of me, she would make me feel that I had done something improper, that I was trying to mock her and get rid of her. Then the atmosphere changed, and she would now submit to an object that would treat her in a merciless way. In those situations she evoked in me a guilty feeling of being cruelly sadistic towards her, as she would take in my interpretations with a painful hissing that seemed to be connected with her father's beatings. Mostly, however, the atmosphere of the sessions was romantic and timeless, and for this phantasy to be maintained the finite nature of the analysis had to be denied. The patient had expressed on several occasions her wish one day to die peacefully on the couch.

The issue of timelessness was the main focus, and for long periods it seemed to be the only theme of our therapeutic work. Often I felt that my interpretations were bypassed and really did not affect her. One of the mechanisms by which this was achieved was that the patient isolated a sensual element—for example, the sound of my voice—from the content of what I had said. Then all that I said sounded "like music".

However, if she listened to the content of what I was actually saying, the atmosphere changed, and I would again be heard "as this terrible voice of a prosecutor", full of reproach and accusation. So we would find ourselves in a situation in which there was either *love without words* or *words without love,* with only little space for thinking and constructive therapeutic work. There was some indication that, in the first case (love without words) the patient was relating to an idealized internal mother figure, and in the second case (words without love), she was submitting to a cruel father authority without allowing a relationship between her internal parents.

These problems were especially urgent when the patient felt confronted with the reality of time and loss. Once, before a break, she gave me an interesting book, illustrating the sinking of the *Titanic.* It seemed as if she was experiencing the reality of loss, like a collision with an iceberg. However, it was not quite clear whether the *Titanic* involved any idea of loss at all, because Ms R also seemed to be romantically involved in a shared death phantasy with Leonardo DiCaprio, the actor in the film.

Such phantasies came to the surface whenever the patient felt confronted with the harshness of reality, which she often found hard to bear. When she got a taste of separation—whether through her own thoughts, an interpretation, or the end of a session—she would retreat into masochism and imagine a romantic death on the couch, without separation or loss. Returning from those sessions, she would sometimes watch the sunset or listen to Schubert or Mozart arias, indulging in an atmosphere of endless peace where dying was experienced as a relief, and death appeared as a longed-for state.

Such a situation had evolved when we were approaching another break in the second year of her analysis. Again the patient had mentioned how much she enjoyed the sessions, but then she had noticed a fold in the cover of the couch and reacted jealously to the idea that the couch did not belong to her alone. She then related in some detail that her daughter found it difficult to express her feelings for a fellow pupil. In order to help her, she had created a situation in which they both simulated the movements with which the daughter could touch and caress the boy. When I connected that with her fear of the impending break, her reluctance to change, and her wish to cling on to a longed-for, "simulated" relationship with me, she started to weep, expressing her fear that I would throw her out and stop the analysis too early.

Material from a session

In the following session, the last but one before a break, the patient reported how bad she had felt after the previous day's session: like a goose that is being "stuffed". She then described in great detail some childhood memories from her parent's farm: how the geese had been forced to swallow food by keeping their mouths open, and how terribly they screamed. While the patient said this, she began to weep.

I said that she must have felt I'd been absolutely cruel in the last session.

She replied: "Yes, by reminding me of the break, the relationship with my daughter, and the relationship I wish to maintain with you. . . . I felt you were mocking me." She then went on to describe how her daughter had returned from school, feeling quite helpless about her love for her classmate, and she finished by mentioning her daughter's violin lessons.

I interpreted that I thought that after the session, she had transformed her anxiety and pain in connection with the break into a form of relationship in which the hatred and cruelty were experienced as coming from me, thinking that I was "stuffing" and mocking her.

She did not reply to this, but she went on to speak about a meeting of an Amnesty International group she had attended the day before, where they discussed the torturing of Libyan political prisoners. But although she generally supports the work of Amnesty International, she disliked the way some of her left-wing friends had mocked the former German Chancellor, Herr Kohl. . . .

She then got sidetracked even further onto yet another theme, saying that she would like to ask me for advice: "although I know you don't like to give me advice". She couldn't decide whether to keep and repair her old, damaged car or buy a newer, safer one, following the advice of several friends. In bringing up the theme of the car, she was alluding to a recent accident on her way home from the session in which another driver had damaged her car.

I attempted to connect this with the previous material, suggesting that the theme of cruelty and guilt is implied in the protests of Amnesty International against torture. Perhaps, by referring to it, she wanted to ask me to give her an "amnesty" and not torment her again by mentioning the break. I added that the car might have something to do with her wish to gain some distance from the difficult aspects of our relationship and her wish for safety, as opposed to the acceptance of damage (the old car) and guilt.

She continued by complaining: "I know, you force me to become more independent! Why couldn't you handle me with care and never mention the separation and pain again?"

I replied that, by seeing the problems in this way, she could keep a passive stance and consequently experience the wish for independence and also cope with the difficult aspects of reality as something that I would force upon her.

We were approaching the end of the session when she returned to the problems of her daughter, who plays the violin in the school orchestra. The patient mentioned her own visit to a violin maker, Mr S, where she wanted to buy a string for her daughter's violin. She said she knew that Mr S was an unpleasant man, whom she expected to reject her. But then he had asked her: "Do you have something against me? You looked at me last time in such a strange way!" She replied: "No, not at all!" and then, unexpectedly, he showed her the instrument he was working on. She followed his explanations and noticed its smooth pinewood bottom. It appeared like velvet. She felt that if she hadn't had to leave, she could have listened to his explanations endlessly.

I said, I thought that there was again a change from a cruel, rejecting relationship to a smooth, velvet-like surface that could go on endlessly—perhaps an expression of her wish at the end of this session, for me, like Mr S., to offer her a smooth relationship without end instead of the rough reality.

This was the end of the session. The patient got up from the couch and was breathing deeply. She appeared more thoughtful when she left the session. In the following, final session before the break she was able to allow more contact with feelings of mourning and disappointment when she said in a less self-accusatory way: "Now I see how difficult it is. I know, I am an obstacle to myself."

Discussion

A characteristic feature of this session was the repeated shift between an idealized, timeless atmosphere and a state of mind characterized by passivity and suffering. Both states of mind seemed to bypass any experience of separation by pulling me into a phantasy world where the patient experienced my interpretations either as caresses, like the "simulated" relationship with her daughter, or as punishments, like the stuffing of the geese on her parents' farm. Consequently, whatever I would say, it would mean either tenderness or cruelty, for which I was responsible.

Because the patient would not allow me to exist separately, my comments could not really reach her. This problem seemed to be expressed most clearly in her wish for advice concerning her damaged car, although she said she *did* already know that I wouldn't give a direct opinion. If I had done so, this would have meant a longed-for present. If, however, I refused, as she expected, this meant new proof of my cruelty and confirmation of her expectations of being left alone with her problems.

When I tried to act in neither of these ways, but to interpret her demand symbolically, this was experienced as pressure to become more independent from me. Therefore, she could not really see me as someone who could help her to cope with the impending break. Instead of addressing her feelings of being left alone and empty, she would experience my thoughts as continuously "stuffing" and tormenting her: a misrepresentation that replaced her need by a phantasy of being cruelly invaded by me. If, as seemed likely, she did experience the impending break as a sort of torture, a part of her hated me for it, but another part seemed also to be trying to protect me from her hatred, as she had tried to protect the former German Chancellor. From all these conflicts she hoped to escape by withdrawing into an unreal, "simulated" relationship, in which she could not be herself, nor could I function properly as her analyst.

Nevertheless, the patient did also help me to understand the difficulties in our relationship when she mentioned her visit to the violin maker. Again, there was a rapid change between idealization and a feeling of rejection. However, this man had also asked her: "Do you have something against me?" By mentioning his question, the patient seemed to acknowledge that there was a degree of anger and disappointment inside her, feelings she would otherwise disavow and project into me. She then ended the session in a more thoughtful mood. In the following session she remarked sadly how difficult it was and that she sometimes felt she was an obstacle to herself.

I will illustrate some of these difficulties by quoting material from the first session after the break.

Material from the first session after the break

The patient came to this session saying she was afraid of it. In a somewhat bitter undertone she mentioned that she was having sad days, but hoped that I had nice days with my family. She added that she had imagined being my child: "In my phantasy I have intruded into your family, while being sad and full of hatred towards my father."

After a brief pause Ms R hesitantly mentioned a dream from the previous night, adding that she hoped I would not be disgusted by it. The dream was as follows:

She was a child defecating endlessly, and she became anxious to shit out all that was inside her. Then she saw the enormous piece of shit and while looking at it, she saw it transformed first into a penis, then into a viper, and she was afraid of it. . . .

Once Ms R had related the dream, the atmosphere of the session changed. There seemed to be a feeling of anxiety and excitement, and I felt caught up by the imagery of the dream, my own feelings shifting between interest and disgust. She did not have many associations to this dream, except for her fear of my disgust.

I suggested that the defecation in the dream might represent an attempt to get rid of her feelings of hatred and emptiness during the break when she felt like a child. But then these feelings had been transformed into something first exciting and then threatening, and she expected that I would be either disgusted or excited. In this way the sad feelings had been transformed into disgust, as an excited penis or a dangerous viper attacked her. . . .

When I had ended, she sighed and said that it was her birthday today. . . .

At first I felt angry and interpreted that by wanting me to do something with her excrement-dream, being either disgusted or excited, she could treat the dream as my business, just as she had tried to do with the car problem before the break.

To this she said nothing, and I had a feeling that I had gone too far and had ended by reproaching and attacking her. After a long, oppressive silence, which made me feel guilty, she said she could now feel "a wall of separation between us", whereas she had hoped that in this first session she would be able to talk "endlessly".

When I had recovered a bit, I tried to remind her that in the dream the defecation went on endlessly.

She said she had been dubious whether or not to tell the dream, because she knew that I was to give a lecture in the afternoon. She had imagined that I might be so disgusted that I wouldn't be able to give this lecture afterwards.

I remarked how concretely she seemed to equate the telling with the defecation in the dream and her fear how I might react.

This was nearly the end of the session. In a sadder mood she mentioned the disappointment of her daughter when she had finally met her classmate. The daughter found him speaking about his peers in a very unpleasant way and said: "I am full of these feelings, and I was so disappointed by him!"

Discussion

At the beginning of this session the patient seemed to be in contact with feelings of sadness and disappointment during the break. This allowed her to recall her resentful feelings towards her father and her phantasy of intruding into my family. In a way, I think, this also included an acceptance of a feeling of envy, which was not just aimed at stealing the goodness from the object, but also directed against my relations with my family. With the telling of the dream, however, the atmosphere of the session changed, and, as if it were an announcement of a later enactment, the patient spoke of her fear that I would be disgusted (Feldman, 1998; Segal, 1991, pp. 64ff; Weiß, 2002). In the dream the painful feelings during the break seemed to be transformed into faeces, destined to be evacuated and to produce a reaction of either disgust or excitement.

This was re-enacted in my subsequent interpretation. When the patient responded with a sigh, mentioning that it was her birthday, she conveyed the feeling that my interpretation had been a terrible birthday present. I felt angry, and I went on to confront her, as if I needed to keep separate, pushing the responsibility for the dream's meaning back into her. Perhaps, at a concrete level, she experienced this as the transformation of an excited penis into an attacking viper.

During the following silence I felt I had gone too far. When the patient spoke reproachfully of the "wall of separation between us", she seemed to confirm my guilt feelings, but perhaps she also realized a sense of separateness. Then she mentioned her hope that she might have spoken endlessly in this first session after the break. This helped me to see the underlying enactment and to interpret the equation between the speaking and the defecating in the dream. This became very obvious when she spoke of her fear that I wouldn't be able to give the lecture that afternoon, which seemed to include an idea of enviously attacking and poisoning me. At the very end of the session she seemed to see herself a bit more separate when she mentioned her daughter's disappointment with the boy in her class. The daughter found him guilty of bad behaviour, as he had spoken about his classmates in such an unpleasant way.

Further course of the analysis

Despite the impasse that had been created, in the following sessions the patient seemed better able to acknowledge ambivalent feelings and to tolerate a sense of separateness. This was illustrated by a series of dreams that concerned my connections with other people and the relationship between her parents. The emergence of these images allowed her to acknowledge a relationship between her parents, and this was accompanied by intense feelings of envy, jealousy, and guilt. In such moments there seemed to be more space for interpretations that were not experienced either as caresses or as cruelty. It was these moments of symbolic thinking that made me hope that the patient could, at least temporarily, emerge from her timeless universe in order to face reality and to enable small steps of development to take place.

At other times, however, especially when painful feelings of envy and guilt seemed unbearable, she would retreat, once again, into her timeless romantic universe. My interpretations were then seen as desired sweets that could not be given up or, alternatively, they were experienced as punishments to which she submitted with a passionate suffering. Sweetness and bitterness, however, were no different: with both experiences the patient seemed to avoid separateness.

The pressure to re-enact this situation in different ways proved to be a recurring challenge in this analysis. I felt guilty either because I had been cruel or because I had allowed myself to be seduced by the music of her romantic idealization. The problem was how to extricate myself and resist being pulled too far in either of these two directions. Sometimes I felt as if there was no way out, and whatever I said, we would end in a stuck situation where cruelty was very obvious.

On one occasion she mentioned a book on Prometheus, describing in great detail the cruel punishment he suffered from the divine eagle. At this time she experienced my interpretations as tormenting and tearing her into pieces. She also pointed out that in the end Prometheus—who triumphed over Zeus through his immortality and the endlessness of his suffering—was fused to the rock to which he was chained. This reflected a masochistic version of her timelessness as compared to the previous one, in which romantic imagination provided an illusion of endlessness, uniqueness, and infinity. Both versions were actually very destructive and seemed to contain envious experience that was either split off or projected. While in the romantic illusion separation is denied and envy is dealt with by idealization, in the masochistic scenario the sadistic impulses and guilt, connected with envy, are projected into a vengeful object. Sometimes, as in the Prometheus myth, this may take the form of stirring up envy in others (Klein, 1957, p. 258).

Conclusion

The myth of Prometheus illustrates how the phantasy of a greedy, "destructive introjection" (Klein, 1957, p. 181) may lead to a fear of a retaliating object. Prometheus was punished for tricking Zeus and for stealing from him—first the good food, and then the fire. In the imagery of his lifelong punishment, cruelty and guilt are projected, and perverse gratification is gained from endless suffering. As the further course of this analysis revealed, my patient was able to reconcile this masochistic scenario with her romantic version of timelessness by arguing that if she suffered long enough, she *would* one day be redeemed by the love of her analyst.

This argument seemed to be part of a complex belief system, in which reality was suspended and a perverted hope was clung to in order to obstruct psychic development. Because of its suffusion with envy this form of "love" may be understood as a pathological organization operating on the basis of –L (Bion, 1962a).

As long as the atmosphere of the sessions was dominated by a longing for uniqueness and infinity, my interpretations could not really reach the patient. She could prevent this by isolating the aesthetic and sensual elements of my words from the content of what I had said. Due to this romantic transformation central elements of her subjective experience were being continuously abducted into a timeless sphere, thereby producing *"psychic unreality"*. In this state of mind reality was only half-accepted, and envy was eliminated by creating a *"romantic perversion of the reality of time"*.

Whenever the patient was confronted with the reality of loss, she saw herself as the victim of a cruel situation for which I was held responsible. Romantic infinity would then be turned into endless suffering, which also protected her from an awareness of separateness. Both scenarios were erotized, static, and timeless. They were linked together in different ways and based on misconceptions of the reality of time, which would allow only endless longing or eternal suffering. In the first case the patient experienced my interpretations as *love without words*, in the second as *words without love*, without allowing emotion and meaning to come together.

In the brief moments when she was able to give up her splitting and to acknowledge the reality of the oedipal situation, she felt exposed to painful feelings of hatred, mourning, and guilt. However, when these feelings became unbearable she would retreat once again into one of the two varieties of her defensive organization, into which I was then recruited.

It was only when these movements could gradually be identified that my patient felt more able to emerge from her *psychic retreat.* When she allowed contact with difficult aspects of reality, this encouraged her to resist and to feel less addicted to a pathological organization that was based either on a romantic or a masochistic misrepresentation of the reality of time.

11

Envy and the negative therapeutic reaction

Michael Feldman

In a well-known passage, Freud writes:

> There are certain people who behave in a quite peculiar fashion during the work of analysis. When one speaks hopefully to them or expresses satisfaction with the progress of the treatment, they show signs of discontent and their condition invariably worsens. One begins by regarding this as defiance and as an attempt to prove their superiority to the physician, but later one comes to take a deeper and juster view. . . . They exhibit what is known as a "negative therapeutic reaction". [Freud, 1923b, pp. 49–50]

Freud argued that we were dealing in these cases with an unconscious sense of guilt, "which is finding its satisfaction in the illness and refuses to give up the punishment of suffering" (p. 50).

Freud goes on, in an interesting passage, to refer to the situation when the sense of guilt is the product of an identification with someone who was once the object of an erotic cathexis. "A sense of guilt that has been adopted in this way is often the sole remaining trace of the abandoned love-relation and not at all easy to recognise as such" (Freud, 1923b, p. 50). (The likeness between this process and what happens in melancholia is unmistakable). Here, Freud is clearly referring to what we would now term guilt in relation to a damaged internal object.

While in Freud's terminology it is the *unconscious sense of guilt*, "which is finding its satisfaction in the illness and refuses to give up the punishment of suffering", in the clinical material I give in this chapter one can see the extent to which it is the *patient* who is "finding satisfaction in the illness", and being attached to an object relation that involves the *punishment of suffering*. I am suggesting that in the patient I describe the pain evoked by the (unconscious) experience of envy gives rise to a withholding and tormenting relationship with his object, which manifests itself as a form of negative therapeutic reaction.

Joan Riviere, in her 1936 paper, elaborates what Freud terms the "deeper and juster view" that we need to understand the negative therapeutic reaction in terms of the patient's suffering from an unconscious sense of guilt. She writes, "The common assumption is that even when the analyst has fully understood and interpreted the material, the superego of certain patients is strong enough to defeat the effects of analysis" (Riviere, 1936, p. 305). She suggests that "The superego of the . . . neurotic . . . has always been placated by his sufferings from his sense of guilt, and by his symptoms, which are a real cause of inferiority and humiliation to him. . . ." However, in what she terms "character cases", the superego could never be placated in these ways (ibid., p. 305).

She suggests that in these cases the patient has to defend himself against the psychic reality where all his loved and hated objects—now experienced within himself—are felt to be catastrophically damaged.

> All the injuries he ever did them in thought or deed arose from his 'selfishness', from being too greedy and too envious of them, not generous and willing enough to allow them what they had, . . . from not loving *them* enough, in fact. [Riviere, 1936, p. 315]

She emphasizes that unconsciously the patient's chief aim is to make reparation for the damage he feels he is responsible for.

> Our offer of analysis to make . . . [the patient] well and happy is unconsciously a direct seduction, . . . a betrayal; it means to him an offer to help him to abandon his task of curing the others first, to conspire with him to put himself first again, to treat his loved

> objects as enemies, and neglect them, or even defeat and destroy them instead of helping them. [Riviere, 1936, p. 316]

However, as Riviere points out, the patient's wish to make his objects better, and so become well and good himself, is impossible, both externally and internally, "for his sadism is still unmanageable". In his inner world, the loved ones whom unconsciously he aims to make well and happy "are also . . . the objects of all his hatred, vindictiveness and murderous impulses!" (Riviere, 1936, p. 318).

Faced with the despair regarding this internal situation and the patient's doubts about his reparative capacities (especially in view of the force of his sadism), a characteristic organized system of defence is called into play. In this, the manic reaction that Klein and Deutsch have also described, the essential feature is omnipotence and the *omnipotent denial of psychic* reality.

> The *denial* relates especially to the ego's object relations and its *dependence on its objects*, as a result of which *contempt* and depreciation of the value of its objects is a marked feature, together with attempts at inordinate and tyrannical *control and mastery of its objects.* [Riviere, 1936, p. 308]

The patients' inaccessibility

> is one form of their *denial*; implicitly they deny the value of everything we say. They literally do not allow us to do anything with them, and in the sense of co-operation they do nothing with us. *They* control the analysis, whether or not they do it openly. . . . Such patients often manage to exert quite a large measure of real control over the analyst—and can even do this when we are quite aware of it. [p. 309]

Thus, while Riviere seems to be emphasizing the defensive aspect of this organization, she gives a vivid description of an on-going object relationship characterized by envy, denial of dependence, contempt, and tyrannical control.

Karen Horney's (1936) important paper, published in the same year as Riviere's, focuses more directly on the patients' "defiance and . . . attempts to prove their superiority to the physician"—that is, the hostile, envious, and competitive elements, in her explanation of the negative therapeutic reactions. She gives a clinical example: A lawyer with widespread, subtle inhibitions in almost every life situation "could not even dream of ambitious aims", nor take any steps towards attaining goals that were in proportion to his abilities. When the analyst explored the possibility that he really was intensely ambitious, "he recalled flashes of fantasy in which he was reforming the system of justice in the whole world". Horney writes, "He must have felt relief for a brief time, but immediately he went into reverse gear, saying to himself, 'You don't think you feel better after this!' Then he showed an increase in symptoms along the whole line" (Horney, 1936, p. 28). What is impressive—and unusual—about this material is the way Horney focuses on the negative therapeutic reaction *as it occurs within the session.*

Horney argued that the move towards recovery and success evoked hopelessness and despair because, for the patient, "success is equal to crushing others, and maliciously triumphing over the crushed adversaries, an attitude necessarily leading to a fear of retaliation with two aspects: a fear of success and a fear of failure." The device to ward off this danger might be formulated: "I had better stay inconspicuously in a corner, or remain sick and inhibited" (Horney, 1936, p. 37).

Horney noted that Freud also believed that fear of success was the main source of the negative therapeutic reaction. However, while he emphasized the unconscious feeling of guilt, Horney's focus was on anxiety—specifically anxiety deriving from the patient's rivalrous and envious attacks on the object. She acknowledged that such anxiety and unconscious guilt were closely related, although sometimes one, sometimes the other predominated.

Horney was less pessimistic than Freud about the therapeutic possibilities with patients showing a negative therapeutic reaction, and she makes a number of interesting and important, modern-sounding points regarding technique with such patients. She points out that

> To deal adequately with the negative therapeutic reaction it is necessary in the first place to recognise it as such. This is not difficult in cases in which it comes out in rather dramatic form as described by Freud . . .

but

> an inexperienced analyst may become uncertain and discouraged without recognising in a detached fashion that this is the very effect the patient designs to produce in him. The same forces in the same combinations may, however, operate in an insidious manner, skilfully masked in pseudo co-operation, or

> behind a recognition and admiration of the analyst, including calling attention to some superficial improvement made. [Horney, 1936, p. 43]

The technical principles she recommends involve, first, observing and uncovering carefully the emotional reactions of the patient to the analyst—and, as we might now add, the analyst to the patient. She observes two rules when analysing patients showing a negative therapeutic reaction: first, she chooses to work directly with only those parts of the patient's material that relate to the reaction to the analyst; and, second, she refrains from making any constructions of the past. She argues that the attitudes of the adult patient are not directly based on the events of childhood—past events are modified and mediated by the events that have occurred between past and present.

Thus, as Spillius (2007a), in her valuable discussion of Horney's paper, points out: "her overall view is . . . that the negative therapeutic reaction involves a hostile attack on the analysis and on the analyst" (p. 65), and she agrees with Freud's first view: that the negative therapeutic reaction occurs because of "defiance and . . . an attempt to prove . . . superiority to the physician".

While both Riviere and Horney make reference to the patient's envy as a factor in the negative therapeutic reaction, Klein (1957) undertook a much deeper and more extensive exploration of the central role of envy, and the defences against it, in relation to the negative therapeutic reaction. Envy interferes with the development of a clear sense of what is good and bad.

> From the contention that envy spoils the primal good object, and gives added impetus to sadistic attacks on the breast, further conclusions arise. The breast attacked in this way has lost its value, it has become bad by being bitten up and poisoned. . . . Excessive envy increases the *intensity* of such attacks and their *duration*, and thus makes it more difficult for the infant to regain the lost good object. [Klein, 1957, p. 186]

She illustrates the point thus:

> the analyst has just given an interpretation which brought the patient relief and produced a change of mood from despair to hope and trust. With some patients or with the same patient at other times this helpful interpretation may soon become the object of

> destructive criticism. It is then no longer felt to be something good he has received and has experienced as an enrichment. . . . The envious patient grudges the analyst the success of his work. [Klein, 1957, p. 184]

She goes on to say that if the analyst's help has become spoilt and devalued as a result of the envious criticism, he cannot accept his interpretations with conviction and assimilate them, because

> it is characteristic of envy that it *implies* robbing the object of what it possesses, and spoiling it. [Klein, 1957, p. 188; emphasis added]

> Excessive envy, an expression of destructive impulses, interferes with the primal split between the good and bad breast, and the building up of a good object cannot sufficiently be achieved. [Klein, 1957, p. 192]

Later, Klein writes,

> To enable the patient to face primary envy and hate only becomes possible after long and painstaking work. . . . the deepest and earliest implications (of envy) experienced in the transference situation, are extremely painful, and therefore difficult, for the patient to accept. [Klein, 1957, p. 221]

I suggest that it is not that the envy is an *expression* of destructive impulses, but that the envy *evokes* the destructive impulses. I believe here Klein is conflating two issues: she vividly describes the painful and unwelcome conscious or unconscious experience of envy, and what gives rise to it. However, it is not the *envy per se* that "implies" the robbing and spoiling. It seems to me, rather, that one of the consequences of the arousal of envy is the *mobilization* of the sadistic impulses, the need to rob, to poison, and to spoil and to triumph, with the accompanying gratification and excitement.

I believe it is these responses that are evoked by envy, that are the "manifestation of the death instinct". In trying to formulate the link observed clinically, Klein suggests that "spoiling and devaluing are inherent in envy." (p. 217) I would argue that while the pleasure and gratification in these destructive, spoiling reactions and the devaluation and undermining of the goodness of the object do, of course, partially or wholly, defend against the experience of envy, they are not *in themselves* the expression of envy, or "inherent" in envy.

Klein goes on to describe how she believes the projection of the infant's envy and its re-introjection in the form of what she terms the "envious superego" interferes with attempts at reparation. If the individual's envious and destructive impulses are felt to have spoiled the good object, this leads not only to feelings of persecution, but also to feelings of guilt and the need for punishment, "which finds satisfaction by the increased devaluation of the self" and hence a vicious circle is set up (p. 231). "The more strongly had the envious and destructive impulses been split off, the more dangerous the patient feels them to be when he becomes conscious of them." Klein suggests that the analyst should gradually help the patient towards the painful insight into the internal splits.

> The destructive sides are again and again split off and regained, until greater integration comes about. As a result, the feeling of responsibility becomes stronger, and guilt and depression are more fully experienced. When this happens the ego is strengthened, omnipotence of destructive impulses is diminished, together with envy, and the capacity for love and gratitude, . . . is released. Therefore the split-off aspects gradually become more acceptable and the patient is increasingly able to repress destructive impulses towards loved objects instead of splitting the self. This implies that the projection on the analyst, which turns him into a dangerous and retaliating figure, also diminishes, and that the analyst in turn finds it easier to help the patient towards further integration. That is to say, the negative therapeutic reaction is losing in strength. [Klein, 1957, p. 225]

As Spillius (2007a) pointed out, Rosenfeld believed that the negative therapeutic reaction essentially involved a struggle between the analyst and a mad, narcissistic part of the patient, for the allegiance and loyalty of the dependent, infantile part of the patient. It is after a session in which there has been successful emotional contact between the analyst and the dependent part of the patient that a negative therapeutic reaction is most likely to occur:

> This negative therapeutic reaction is due to a powerful counterattack of the omnipotent narcissistic and often megalomanic part of the patient which was felt to have been dislodged through the progress of the analysis and which reasserts its power by attacking and overpowering the infantile dependent part to re-establish the status quo and to regain control over the ego. [Rosenfeld, 1975, p. 223]

In her own discussion of "Varieties of Envious Experience", Spillius (1993) gives careful consideration to the question of the extent to which envy may be part of the patient's conscious experience. She points out that while Klein was, on the whole, concerned with unconscious envious reactions, other authors—including Spillius herself—describe varieties of more or less conscious experiences of envy.

In the next section of this chapter I propose to track negative therapeutic reactions as they occur within the analytic dialogue. The clinical material I was confronted with led me to the working assumption—which I believe is also consistent with Klein's use of the concept—that I was dealing with the consequences of the *unconscious* experience of envy.

I use material from a session with a young man to illustrate some of the theoretical issues to which I have referred. I believe that this material allows one to infer links between the pain associated with the patient's envy, the excited and triumphant defences that were mobilized, and their destructive consequences for his relationship with his objects, including his relation with his analyst. It was also possible to follow his preoccupation with objects felt to be weak and damaged, the conscious and unconscious guilt evoked by this situation, and his consequent identification with such damaged objects as a defence against such guilt. I suggest that these interactions can be observed within the process of a single session, and that they constitute the central dynamics of the negative therapeutic reaction as I observe it in this patient.

The patient has been in analysis for eighteen months. He has recently graduated from a prestigious institution, where he was regarded as having considerable talent, but he repeatedly disappointed and frustrated his teachers and just managed to avoid failing his course.

Patient's background

Mr O's father, an intelligent and capable man who never fulfilled himself in his career and never felt fulfilled in his marriage, had developed a progressive neurological disease a few years before the analysis and died after a relatively short time. Mr O portrayed his mother as someone who was "good" with very young children, but was otherwise rather inadequate. He has a brother and sister who are much older than he, and until he first went to school, he and his mother had been very close. During his university studies Mr O had to face a series of losses and disappointments, as well as his father's progressive illness, and he became overtly depressed, unable to work, feeling hopeless and seriously suicidal.

He dreads being pulled back to take care of his mother, who is over-weight and without initiative. He is disturbed about any signs—such as his weight or his lack of achievement—that link him with his mother. At other times Mr O finds himself espousing his father's critical and contemptuous attitude (especially towards his mother), which also makes him uncomfortable. He sees himself as immature and dependent on others, although he can be the "life and soul" of a party. Friends and teachers are charmed and impressed by him and offer help, but invariably end up frustrated and perplexed at the failure of their efforts.

Mr O is repeatedly late for his sessions, particularly if the previous session has been helpful. He offers a variety of explanations, often elaborate and "analytical", in a disarming fashion that evokes in me a complex mixture of interest, sympathy, and frustration.

The session reported below took place just after Mr O's final examinations. He insistently told me that in spite of the work he had done at the last minute and the help he had had from his teachers, he was going to fail. Indeed, for some days he repeated in a triumphant voice that he *had* failed. It turned out that he had *just* been allowed to pas provided he completes his project in the next few months.

Clinical material

Mr O arrives for a Friday session 10 minutes late, for the third time in succession.

"Strange, I was thinking as I was coming in the door, in some ways I'm not getting into the rhythm of this, in some ways I'm getting into it all too well. Leaving the flat on Wednesday a bit late, getting here late, leaving on Thursday closer to time, and still getting here late, and leaving today on time and still getting here late. So I will have to adjust my meaning of 'on time'."

(Silence.)

Mr O observes his recurrent lateness with an engaging jokiness, which subtly tries to ensure that his behaviour is not taken seriously by either of us: on the contrary, he rather admires the way he contrives to get into the rhythm of arriving exactly ten minutes late. He speaks in a quasi-insightful way, with implicit references to previous interpretations I have made about the frustrating control he exercises. He assumes that I hope that my interpretations will affect the way he comes to the sessions, but he subtly takes over a superior analytic position and demonstrates to me that there is little I can do about the situation.

The patient goes on to tell me about an interview for a promising job his friend has arranged for him the following week. He says, "I haven't really got my stuff ready for it. Since I was told about it, I have resolutely done other things than prepare for it—until last night, when hopefully I turned a corner and started doing something. But the same old patterns are still there. Back in that room surrounded by so much stuff—with the best intentions—so many things in there I planned to sell on Ebay. Fill about half the room. So much stuff that I am supposed to be using to complete my project—never do—just like my Dad with his shed, and his garage, and *his* stuff he planned to do things with—and never did" (sigh).

One can understand this material in terms of Mr O's unconscious sense of guilt. He identifies with a figure that has been attacked and reduced to weakness and ineffectiveness partially paralyses him, entrapping him into repeating the "same old patterns". One can see this not only in relation to an incapacitated father—I believe it is possible to see the evolution of this process in the course of the session. Having described how he postpones doing his work, as he postpones leaving for the sessions on time, he remarks that "hopefully" he has turned a corner. This is then characteristically followed by "but still—same old patterns", and his description of being surrounded by "stuff" that he has been unable either to use creatively or to dispose of. The analyst—like the father in his phantasies—is repeatedly offered a more hopeful prospect, linked with the patient's "best intentions", and invited to believe that his work might lead somewhere. However, the analyst's capacities and functions become invaded and taken over by the patient and any progress undermined. This process renders the analyst helpless and weak, his work ineffective, piled up in the shed or the garage of the patient's mind. It is the internal object that he continuously reconstructs in this fashion that he becomes identified with, and entrapped by, and this introjective identification impairs his development.

Mr O then mentions that he was going to try to find a place to live that was much nearer to my consulting room, but adds that the job he was applying for was at the other end of town.

After a pause he continues: "The last thing—it isn't really the last thing, shouldn't be the last thing—my Mum had an operation on Friday. She was having her heart jump-started for this heart arrhythmia. They said it would be very hard to correct if she'd had it for a while. They tried the procedure three times, and it didn't work, and she remains as she was. For years we thought she had no energy because she was over-weight and her legs were giving in and couldn't support her. It was a relief for everyone, especially her, to find out there is actually a medical problem behind her lack of energy—she wasn't getting enough blood flow from the heart, it wasn't just *her*. It's like me coming here and starting to realize there is underlying stuff to my not finishing things. It was a relief for her to realize she wasn't just being lazy—she actually had a medical problem, but it wasn't solved."

Mr O is briefly uneasy that I might think the way he makes his mother's condition the "last thing" indicates there is something wrong with his attitude to his mother. I believe he is also referring to an aspect of himself that is active in the session, but at that moment located in his mother. He seems to recognize how difficult it is for me to reverse the condition that has been present in him "for a while", and while I might hope my interventions would serve the function of "jump-starting" something in him, I am faced with an underlying problem that is proving to be intractable. I am invited to become either impatient or critical (as his father did), trying repeatedly and unsuccessfully to nudge him into functioning more effectively. He portrays himself as being gripped by a process that interferes with him being able to move on, get anywhere on time, achieve anything, or allow anyone else to achieve anything with him. He recognizes that there is, as he puts it, "underlying stuff" to his not finishing things: he is not just being lazy, there is something wrong. I believe here we have some indication of his awareness of the manifestations of the negative therapeutic reaction.

Mr O goes on to ask, in a hesitant way, what alternative possibilities there are for the times of his sessions, if he were to start a new job. He tells me that David has said that if he came to work there, they are quite relaxed and flexible about his hours. "The reason David mentioned this is he was thinking about when I would fit in the analysis."

In addition to the realistic issues involved, I believe Mr O indicates his anxiety and uncertainty about my willingness to persist with my efforts, in the face of the frustrations and difficulties. He manages to get his friend David to think about the problem and to take a positive and constructive view of the possibilities, so that I might believe the analysis will survive if *I* make efforts to accommodate his needs. He presents himself in a propitiating, even appealing way, which is intended to get me to hope and to try. However, he then makes a characteristic move to challenge such hopes.

"I think David is slightly over-stating it, because he's a contract worker there, whereas I'd be full-time. So I don't think I could negotiate a break mid-morning to come here, particularly without explaining what I was doing, which I don't want to do. It's amazing how hard it is for me to actually ask you. Now I realize I've gone back to doing what I used to do—laughing or smiling when I've got nothing to laugh about. Interesting to realize I've more or less got out of that in the course of the last however-many months—now it's back.

The aspect of the patient (represented by David) that *is* capable of thought and concern about his analysis, and the prospect that the work here would be properly supported, becomes immediately attacked and undermined. I think it is indeed difficult for the patient to deal with a situation in which he needs something from me, and he becomes anxious about having provoked me and jeopardized my goodwill. Instead of being able to stay with this situation, in which he feels more anxious, vulnerable, and dependent, he moves into a manic, triumphant state, with the mocking laughter and his observations: "It's amazing . . .", "Now I realize . . ." "Interesting to realize . . ." subtly undermining and reducing my role.

I do not take this up directly but make a comment about the difficulties he is facing and his anxious need for me to reassure him about my willingness to accommodate to his needs. I think he also wants me to believe he could make efforts to protect his analysis, which would involve acknowledging the significance of him coming to analysis, not only with colleagues at work, but more importantly, with himself.

(Silence.)

"Yeah."

Mr O goes on to say that he has been looking at the work he has been arranging the previous night. He has always found it hard to talk about his own work, to explain it, get it clear in his head. And yet other people see him as quite decisive. They take notice of his opinions—on abstract thoughts, or other people's situations—as long as no one is relying on *him* to put anything into effect. If he were asked to comment on David's work, he would offer opinions on how to improve it, and, to be honest, he would probably be right. However, he realizes that he doesn't know how to think about his own work, and feels he has no judgement. He was just sitting there last night, feeling completely useless.

In response to my intervention, Mr O seems to be more in contact with his difficulties in getting things clear in his head and in being able to think about his own "situation" in any useful way. He seems able to acknowledge how much he relies on his analyst, like his friend David, to function properly. In response to such feelings of inadequacy, and his envy of others' capacities, he tends to take over the function of providing a critique of the analyst's work, where he feels his judgements are probably right. . . .

I comment on the extent to which, although he feels he is capable of making perceptive, powerful judgements of the work of others, he feels *his* thinking and his work was repeatedly undermined by something inside him.

Mr O responds by speaking in a complex way that has a patronizing tone to it. He refers to what I said about undermining, and says "it is obviously more complex underneath, but that is the net result". He isn't sure he believes that is true—*he* thinks maybe he is being weak and not getting on with things, not sorting them out. He has to force himself to try to look at it, to accept that maybe that is the situation. He doesn't trust himself to take responsibility. It brings to his mind that his father didn't, and his mother still doesn't, trust him to take responsibility.

He goes on to say that it is interesting that on the weekend his brother commented on the fact that his mother treated Mr O like a three-year-old, "with all the friendly and hostile implications of that". He said it seemed perverse that he has ended up in a profession that involves him taking a great deal of responsibility. If he wanted no responsibility, he could have been an artist or something. "But anyway, the strange thing here is I get the idea you don't really know yet—I hope it is a yet, you don't know yet or have a handle on what the block in me might be."

I know *I* certainly don't think I know. Strange thing here, in some ways my mind has to work around this big black monolith in the middle of my head. We do the same here—we've been going around and checking the boundaries of this for ages."

I say that what I suggested—and I thought he had understood—was that there is something active that goes on inside him. I thought it was difficult for him to tolerate my interventions, and to make use of them, especially when he felt himself to be small, and not able to see and understand everything. He then felt driven to become the one who was the adult, the professional in possession of the broader picture, taking responsibility. He became rather pleased and proud of his own constructions, his imagery, like a big black impenetrable monolith. By contrast, he seems to take some pleasure in emphasizing what I do not know or have a handle on, and he isn't sure whether I ever would. Instead, we are condemned to just going round "checking the boundaries". (At this point Mr O yawns.)

I say I think he is indicating how difficult it is for him to listen and to make use of what I offer him—namely something he has not constructed for himself, that is already known to him. This difficulty threatens any prospects of change or development.

"Yeah. What you are saying about the monolith idea—I agree it is not right. I was thinking as you were . . . (yawn) finishing that—about the question am I one or the other, which way should it work or does it work. That's what I wish I could have pinned down, and looked at, know what it is that I'm . . . that's the scary thing. O.k. without the monolith idea, we've still been talking around it for months, and it's still only in the corner of my eye. I know there is something just outside my range of vision that holds me back, or stops me from moving forward or pushes me to one side or stands in front of me, or whatever."

Mr O continues talking in an increasingly elaborate and excited way, debating whether he believes there is a dark force that controls him, that is not his responsibility, or whether he shares his family view that whatever is inside his head is his responsibility to get control of. Or it isn't really an outside force, or an inside force, just another part of him messing him around, and he should just bloody well buck up and sort it out.

Eventually he says he feels these ideas are just spinning around each other, and he is getting confused with what he is saying. "I just wish that someone—I suppose here that means you, could say here's what it is, here's the problem, do this, take two of these pills, it'll be all right. But of course that's not possible, and I'm going to have to have some form of breakthrough, suddenly being able to grab whatever it is in my peripheral vision. I have no idea how that can happen, and that scares the hell out of me. I could be here for the rest of my life skirting around the outside of it and never seeing what the hell it is I'm screwing up with or because of . . . (sigh). As you've said before, a whole side of me feels despair at that. But then the part of me that probably *is* the blackness, the blocking, whatever, I can feel it thinking, well, you know (see here I'm doing the smiley voice again)—I can feel it thinking that means I'm complex, I'm difficult, and that's a victory in itself, in some kind of bloody awful way."

I believe we can see in this material the detailed expression of the negative therapeutic reaction in the patient. Mr O had briefly registered the experience of being in contact with an analyst who was able to recognize his difficulties and take them seriously. However, while I was speaking, he became distracted and unable to make sense of what I was saying. His brief, but "scary" recognition of how much lay only in the corner of his eye, just outside his range of vision (or thinking), was quickly displaced by the escalation of an excited, triumphant manic process, reflected in his manner of speaking and briefly acknowledged by his reference to becoming confused, his "ideas just spinning around each other". His envious response to the perception that, by contrast, I retain the capacity to think, to observe, and to judge is to attack my analytic potency. I, too, become someone who doesn't know, who doesn't have a handle, and the two of us are portrayed just going around the big black monolith that has been erected in his head, hopelessly checking the boundaries.

At best, "someone" could say here's the problem, do this, take two of these pills, it'll be all right. Thus my analytic function is destroyed, and in desperation I can only offer him advice or pills. Indeed, the way the patient takes my interpretations, dismantles them, spins the words and ideas around, taking over any explanatory functions, does indeed create a degree of confusion and helplessness in the analyst. The patient can briefly acknowledge the triumphant satisfaction in being able to undermine and defeat me, and in creating a hopeless atmosphere. However, I suspect the "scariness" of "something" lying just outside his range of vision is also an indication of his paranoid anxiety. He dreads some retaliatory response from the parental figure sitting behind him who is repeatedly subjected to his hostile and devaluing attacks.

> Returning now to the session: I describe the shift that has taken place from the experience he had of having been helped to see some things more clearly, that had made him anxious and uncomfortable. His head became filled with a powerful black monolith that one could only go round and round admiring, but on which one could make no impact, and this seemed to give him a feeling of pleasure and triumph.

Mr O responds by saying that that is *not at all* what he consciously wants, and if he does want it, he doesn't know why. He *doesn't* want to feel victorious about this or find it pleasurable. He goes on to say that it is the same part of him that wanted to commit suicide in the past—the part of him that wants to prove everybody wrong by giving up—prove to everybody how bad it all is—make all the people he knows miss him. If he were suddenly gone, people would realize how much they missed him. He adds, "This is all horrible."

I think the patient has actually heard and understood what I said to him, and he seems briefly able to acknowledge, in a helpful way, that the function of this "committing suicide" is to prove me wrong, to fill me with feelings of inadequacy and guilt, and to make *me* give up. I think as he speaks, he illustrates the struggle between a positive, cooperative impulse and a strong inclination to undo almost all the points I have made with a triumphant smile on his face. He seems to be indirectly confirming that he *is* aware of deriving pleasure from doing things to frustrate and torment, depriving me of any pleasure or satisfaction from my understanding or my work, and making me fail. He is prepared to go to any lengths to defeat his object, even to the point of phantasies of destroying himself.

Discussion

In this chapter I have tried to explore the mechanisms that seem active in the negative therapeutic reaction. I believe one can see the interactions between the patient's envy, the manic triumph used as a defence, and the consequences of his introjective identification with damaged and weakened objects.

I have suggested that it was possible to see how the patient could, at times, recognize and understand an interpretation and feel briefly relieved and helped. However, this positive response was difficult to sustain as it exposed him to a painful awareness of his own limitations, things he felt unable to grasp or understand, that he felt his analyst *could*. At such moments he was driven to grab whatever was in his peripheral vision, as he put it, but which continued to elude him. I believe the material illustrates the way in which the envy and desperation aroused by the awareness of differences between himself and his object repeatedly led to him taking over the qualities and functions of his object. This resulted in manic and triumphant excitement, accompanied by quiet sadistic mockery and contempt. He was gratified by his capacity to provoke feelings of helplessness and despair. This was made explicit when he referred back to the period in which he was filled with suicidal thoughts, as a means of triumphing over his objects, with the accompanying gratification and pleasure.

This triumphant, manic process repeatedly gave rise to phantasies about his objects being robbed and weakened: his mother's physical emotional and intellectual inadequacies, his father's limitations and disappointments and his eventual death from cancer. This was inevitably re-enacted in the analysis, so that I, too, was reduced to inadequacy and helplessness, and he portrayed the two of us just going around the margins, never really getting a handle on anything. It was clear in the material, I think, that he not only felt guilty and persecuted in relation to the objects thus invaded and undermined, but his manic superiority alternated with his introjective identification with such figures—unable to use their legs, their minds, or their potency properly. Thus, in the course of the session, in the course of the analysis thus far, and in his life, Mr O alternated between states in which he showed considerable talent and promise, which evoked expectations and hopes, and a state of paralysis and incompetence that puzzled and tormented him and those around him.

12

Reflections on *Envy and Gratitude*

Irma Brenman-Pick

Klein's *Envy and Gratitude* represented a crucial breakthrough in understanding. While much interest and excitement followed the publication of the work, reactions to it seemed to polarize: among some analysts there was an excessive attribution of envy of the breast in almost all situations, while among others there was an absolute rejection of the very idea. Both extremes provided cosy positions for analysts to occupy: appropriating goodness, the analyst either rejected the very idea of primary envy—including in herself—or massively projected it into the patient and focused upon it there. Either position obviated the need for more difficult reflection and could be used to avoid any consideration of the analyst's own propensities. It is the work of struggling with these issues, and the envy this evokes, that is the focus of my chapter.

Klein herself had described a much more intricate picture than those overheated and partial reactions, and here I revisit and emphasize some of the complexities of her original formulations. Very significantly, Klein writes of "vicious circles" in which envy unites with guilt. I want to show ways, too, in which envy unites with omnipotent excitement and cruelty. I will also suggest that envy and jealousy are not only to be differentiated from each other, but intertwine and fuel each other. Furthermore, as Klein suggests, envy is exacerbated by deprivation and, indeed, also fuels feelings of deprivation because of the way in which it prevents the subject from benefiting from that which is available. In this chapter I illustrate these themes, briefly, with some thoughts about Shakespeare's *Othello* and, at greater length, with two clinical illustrations, one more florid, the other more subtle.

Envy's vicious circles

Klein famously quotes from *Othello*:

> But jealous souls will not be answer'd so:
> They are not ever jealous for the cause,
> But jealous for they are jealous; 'tis a monster
> Begat upon itself, born on itself.
>
> [*Othello*, III.iii]

For Klein, these lines illustrate envy. She suggests that Shakespeare does not always differentiate between jealousy and envy, and that it is the envious person who "can never be satisfied because his envy stems from within and therefore always finds an object to focus on" for ostensible justification. She goes on to cite another passage from the play, which she feels, conveys exactly the meaning of envy as she is describing it.

> Oh beware my Lord of jealousy:
> It is the green-eyed monster which doth mock
> The meat it feeds on
>
> [*Othello*, III.iii]

Shakespeare shows us that Othello was tormented by Iago; yet only at the very end of the play does he

> . . . demand that demi-devil (Iago)
> Why he hath thus ensnar'd my soul
>
> [*Othello*, V.ii]

The tragedy is that this question comes after the murder of Desdemona, not before. Yet even now Othello is not asking himself why he is susceptible to—indeed, powerless against—Iago's provocations. Instead he asks why Iago tried to trap and destroy him. I would like to consider though, what it was that made Othello so susceptible to Iago's provocations.

In a discussion of Othello, Harold Bloom (1999) suggests that Iago's most brilliant insight is that if he was reduced to nothingness by Cassio's preferment, then how much more vulnerable must Othello be, lacking Iago's intellect and game-playing will. Anyone would be pulverized, he says. Indeed, Klein assumes that we are all born with the potential to spoil things in an envious way. What is it that makes some more able than others to hold on to feelings of goodness and gratitude in a way that modifies envious feelings? One factor seems to be linked with the mother's capacity to bear the infant's propensities and projections, as well as her own propensities, and to work through the inevitable difficulties evoked. Such qualities in the mother, in good circumstances, support the infant to cope with these vicissitudes too, but they also evoke considerable envy.

Should Othello be understood as "constitutionally" excessively envious, or might this be compounded by the problem that the noble Lord, in his "nobility", has not made room for dealing with his hatred? Even after he has murdered Desdemona, he insists:

> For naught did I in hate, but all in honour
>
> [*Othello*, V.ii]

Othello, it can be argued, appropriates absolute goodness. Caught up in his elevated ideal, he "ennobles" himself and projects evil into Iago. Of himself, he says that he is not easily jealous! He is all "honour", and the "demi-devil" resides exclusively in Iago. He is then particularly vulnerable to the "ensnarement" of his soul by a vengeful Iago, who, in turn, projects and insinuates into Othello his doubts about his own lovability.

Klein has suggested that what is particularly envied is the relative absence of envy in others. I would suggest, further, that what we may envy in others may be less to do with the absence of envy in them, and rather more to do with their capacity and strength to do psychic work in struggling to take on board and stay with these difficult propensities in a way which allows for them to be worked with internally.

> For example, a young patient ostensibly worships and consciously envies "genius". She appears desperate to be a genius and at times manically sees herself as such. She speaks of me on such occasions as though I, too, were a genius, and as though she en-

> vied me that. In this way, one might say, she "ennobles" me. And we can be in love with each other's "genius". In such a superior position I would, of course, be free of envy. In this state of mind she views me as one who just sits in my chair, and "it all comes to me as from heaven". Following each interpretation I make, I am then experienced as sitting back and congratulating myself on my genius, and she joins me in this self-applause. I suggest that she speaks as though I have succeeded in appropriating "genius", and now I believe myself to be absolutely merged with—we might say in projective identification with—a "genius breast". The envious attack behind this, I am suggesting, is then not on my supposed "genius" but on my struggle to work with and through such issues.
>
> When I interpret along these lines, she says that she knows, though, that I listen and that it must be tough to have to listen to all her crap. It seems that my interpretation has caused her to ricochet from identification with "genius" to the abject purveyor of "crap". So either she is a genius, or she is crap. Presumably the same applies to me. Here the—crapping—attack is on my, and her, capacity to work. When she says I listen, the reality is that I have to work to think about—and perhaps struggle with—not only her "crap" parts, but also my own. For example, what truth, or how much truth, might there be in this picture of me as a narcissistic analyst, and so on? The worship of omnipotence involves an envious devaluation of the working object and of the internal struggle. I am struck by the way work is denigrated by this patient and, frequently, more widely in the culture.

To return to Othello: Shakespeare's play invites scrutiny of the protagonist's special vulnerability. As the play opens, Othello is cast as a black "outsider" in Venice. There are frequent pejorative references to him as "the Moor", and indeed Iago says to Desdemona's father, Brabantio:

> Even now, now, very now, an old black ram
> is tupping your white ewe.
>
> [*Othello*, I.i]

And, later, Brabantio to Othello:

> Oh thou foul thief. . . . She (Desdemona) shunned the wealthy curled darlings of our nation . . . (to) run for her guardage to the sooty bosom of such a thing as thou. . . .
>
> [*Othello*, I.iii]

Do we imagine that Othello deals with the painful feelings that thus may be evoked, or does he, in his "nobility", circumvent them? While he may indeed have noble qualities, he may also, as I suggested, be narcissistically vulnerable. Meanwhile Iago has been passed over for promotion, which was given, instead, to Cassio, who is preferred by Othello: Iago, filled with hate and vengeance, is intelligent enough, as Bloom stressed, to be perceptive about Othello's weaknesses and to know how to work on his (denied) pained feelings as a black outsider, rather than to have to work on his (Iago's) own pained feelings of rejection and exclusion.

We might give thought, then, as to who has projected what into whom? How far has Othello projected into Iago the rejected, deprived, envious parts of himself, projections that return to overwhelm him, and how far is Othello, as the black outsider, the recipient of Iago's projections? And is he, furthermore, a recipient who in his narcissistic vulnerability lacks the inner strength to cope with these projections?

Klein stresses that deprivation of good mothering increases envy. No doubt there are other environmental factors too, including the projection of envious feelings into the child by parents or siblings. The vulnerable child may be ripe for such projections, just as, socially, the denigrated Moor may become a particularly vulnerable target for the projection of envy.

Such complex situations are examples of Klein's "vicious circles", and it is often impossible to be sure where the circles began. She speaks of the vicious circle of envy, destructiveness, and persecution, and further differentiates envy from jealousy. Envy, she maintains, implies the subject's relation to one person only. "Envy is the angry feeling that another person possesses and enjoys something desirable—the envious impulse being to take it away or to spoil it" (1957; p. 181) "Jealousy", on the other hand, "is based on envy, but involves a relation to at least two people; it is mainly concerned with love that the subject feels is his due and has been taken away . . . by his rival" (p. 181).

Klein does not consider the especially painful consequences when the two—envy and jealousy—come together, although, to a greater or lesser extent, they are entwined. Othello may be envious of Desdemona's goodness as well as jealous of her relationship with Cassio, and Cassio's with her. While envy may come before jealousy, as Klein suggests, it seems to me that they are such intimate bedfellows, so closely intertwined, that it would be difficult to know where the one begins and the other ends.

Furthermore, in her view envy features in a two-person relationship. Yet is that ever absolutely the case? While what the neonate knows or feels about the "third" may be a vexed question, from very early on the object may be felt to be in a relationship with the actual father or an "internal penis". In an "idyllic" state of mind this may be negated; yet when the infant is frustrated, as inevitably he will be, there is that which gets in the way of satisfying him. Klein suggests that then he feels that the breast feeds itself; but the breast may also be experienced as feeding someone else or being in a relationship with someone else. The father, or internal father, in whatever form, may then be experienced as an obstacle to absolute total satisfaction.

Because envy is felt to be so reprehensible an emotion, the infant would then experience the other as the "non-envious" preferred one, and this would intensify jealousy as well as envy. The subject feels both unworthy of being loved and guilty for being so envious and jealous of the "other" who is loved—an extraordinarily painful state of affairs, a very "vicious circle" in which jealousy and envy fuel each other.

Self-ennoblement as a defence against envy

In psychoanalytic literature there has been considerable debate about the negative therapeutic reaction. An interesting question is the degree to which this is promoted by envy or by guilt. The following clinical material illustrates, I hope, that it is not an "either/or" but, more probably, a combination of both, further exacerbated, as I have suggested above, by jealousy. This creates "vicious circles", which are then extremely difficult to break. More specifically, I explore some of the myriad ways in which we may defend ourselves against an awareness of our own envious nature. I illustrate how a self-"ennoblement", as I have described in Othello, can function as a defence against such an awareness: powerfully and overtly in Patient A and, in a more hidden, subtler way in Patient B.

Patient A

A few years into analysis, a young, newly married patient, the admirer of genius mentioned earlier, created havoc with a very dramatic breakdown. She had begun the analysis in a similar state. She had at that time just arrived from South America and had become panic-stricken and an insomniac. Her mother had flown over, and a psychiatrist was also looking after the patient. Her self-absorption and omnipotence at that time was such that, for example, in our first meeting that July, with a mixture of desperation and seduction about how especially gifted yet distressed she was, she insisted that I sacrifice my summer holiday to take care of her. She was outraged that I did not agree to this.

She believed that from early infancy she had been left in a day nursery for long periods, to enable her young mother to complete her studies. She portrayed her father as generous but hot-tempered and tyrannical, and her mother as engaging in, even enjoying, "victimhood". From the outset she saw herself as the victim of my tyrannical arrangements, or, alternatively, I was to be victim of her tyranny. Her identification with a tyrannical father gave force to a belief in her power to control.

Some three years later, Patient A had made very considerable progress, and was now committed to working in the analysis and in a job, as well as furthering her studies in international politics. I was therefore somewhat shocked when, during a summer holiday, she again broke down, indulging in renewed florid behaviour. In these situations she created mayhem. Her mother had again been called for, and there was this time a threat to the continuation of the analysis. This breakdown had all the features of a negative therapeutic reaction.

During the term preceding this second breakdown, we had worked, *inter alia,* on a dream she had brought, in which

Army units were gathering to go on ships. One ship was named the Moshe Dayan (he was a General in the Israeli Six-Day War, he was the one with one eye, she explained); *the soldiers are mostly blacks* (like in the British and American armies, she said, where blacks, because they are poor, are used to do the fighting).

She said of Dayan that he was a corrupt man who had stolen archaeological treasures; he was power-mad. His daughter was much nicer; she was liberal and had exposed herself to the risk of visiting the settlers, who had thrown acid or hot water in her face.

Essentially I had interpreted her fears that I would be the one-eyed Dayan, a narrow-sighted/narrow-minded cruel superego (Brenman, 1985), appropriating all goodness, thus impoverishing her and putting "blackness" into her (the poor black soldiers). I had also taken up ways in which she appropriated all consideration and tyrannically took this to be her right. In this she was united with Dayan, the tyrannical father. While I had considered ways in which she (enviously) attacked a more admired (Dayan's liberal daughter) analyst, with hindsight, following this second breakdown, I realized that I had not appreciated the intensity and seriousness with which the forces of envious destructiveness were gathering inside her, nor the full extent of her secret admiration for the violent settlers or for the one-eyed Dayan. One might ask, with Othello, why did those "demi-devils" so ensnare her soul? How does a particular mixture of deprivation unite with attachment to omnipotent vengeful cruelty, becoming a *modus vivendi*? In part, it seems to me that in the face of real deprivation—now my holiday, in the past the day nursery—she feels able omnipotently to exploit the situation (use the poor soldiers) like Dayan, to take/steal more than she is entitled to and not feel any need to consider the needs of others. She is admiring of these skills.

A couple of years later, much work having been achieved, Patient A returned from a holiday break, for the first time conveying that she had really enjoyed the holiday. The second Monday back she spoke, again, of having had a good weekend. She had been with her husband to the theatre where an actress friend of her husband's was performing: it was good, yet she had had the wish during the performance to create pandemonium by pushing her panic button. How much was the urge to excited panic provoked by jealousy (her husband's friendship with the actress, herself not being centre-stage) or envy, not only of the contribution of others, but also of her new capacity to enjoy her life, together with guilt that she now has such a rich life? Her guilt leads her to feel that she does not deserve this. She had spoken of a friend who fouls thing up for herself in a masochistic way. Is the return to sadomasochism a combination of all three? I return to this question below. I note, however, at the same time, the considerable improvement in her. She is able to experience this whole event as a "good weekend" and is able to hold the wish to push the panic button until she can tell me about it on Monday, and for now, at least, not to enact it.

The following day she was anxious, becoming insomniac again. She spoke of a boss who tortures her by making impossible demands and finding fault all the time; what particularly hurt her was that another senior colleague, with whom she had previously had a good relationship, had been ensnared by this boss and joined forces with him. She conveyed this to be a powerful seduction, which in the end succeeds in establishing total power. In the session she was guiltily reminded of the way she used to treat her husband, and also me. She recalled how that had excited her, and now, she said, it makes her feel really bad. I interpreted that what she feels may have been particularly hurtful to me was the way in which she pulled (ensnared) into such attacks parts of herself that had previously been in a good relationship with me and with her husband. She feared that we would now join forces in making impossible demands on her to put things right.

She now remembered that her worst breakdown (two years previously) had occurred just when things were going better. She had then just resumed her studies, and now she feared that if she thinks about successfully completing them, she would become excited by the way she can blow it all up. "That is what I get caught up with: it is the power of being able to do that. It makes me feel so special." She went on to say that she had read in the newspaper about a reckless driver who killed a 26-year-old doctor. She said that she felt envious because this person (the victim) already had her PhD at 26. "There was a lot in the newspaper about the mother's terrible distress; and the awful thing is that the cruelty of this killing excites me."

This was a much more open acknowledgement of the cruel excitement than had previously been expressed. It seems to me that it is the hateful destructiveness that makes her feel so powerful. Without that powerful excitement, she feels vulnerable to very difficult feelings of being left out when the couple get together (her husband and the actress, the two bosses, I with my husband on holiday), together with her envy (of my work and contribution to her improvement and also of her own achievements—for example, she may soon have her PhD and had reported feeling better over the weekend). This combines with her guilt about the distress her destructive and self-destructive behaviour has caused to her mother and to the "mother" in me. Yet she admires this destructiveness and becomes excited by its "genius" in that it defends her against these painful feelings, as in her admiration for the Dayan/settler figures.

She spoke about becoming excited when she reads, for example, about a Cabinet Minister's daughter dying of drug addiction: "It is very terrible to get so excited." I took up not just the *Schadenfreude* about that situation, but her excitement at her own addiction to cruelly killing off her own improvement. This improvement is also evident in her increased capacity to acknowledge these feelings honestly and openly. At the same time there is such excitement about the particular cruelty to me (the mother) in the now even greater opportunity for disappointing and thwarting, and for renewed destruction. In this excitement she believes herself to be engaged in an endless intercourse, identified with a cruel father and a victim mother—a very terrible intercourse at the expense of the child.

There is an addiction to real sadistic cruelty, where someone is attacked not for being bad but for being good. How it excites her to see the parental distress in the face of this addiction of the child. At the same time that excitement feels to her to be, in her words, "very terrible". But now she can create new excitement with just how reprehensible that is. The intensified excitement, then, is to make it all "so terrible" that it cannot be thought about more quietly. If she lets go of this excitement, she is confronted with real pain, not only because she feels guilty in relation to me, but also because her destructiveness is also in conflict with the patient who really values the work we have done together, the patient who also feels deeply loving and grateful both to her husband and to me.

While I have highlighted the somewhat florid nature of this patient's excitement in cruelty, I am also mindful of her generosity—shown, too, in the very hard-working and courageous way she struggles with these difficult issues, her genuine appreciation of her analysis, and her love for her husband too. Yet this more loving side of her is repeatedly "ensnared" by envious destructiveness, linking envy with mania and perversion.

I am reminded here of Oscar Wilde's lines:

Yet each man kills the thing he loves
By each let this be heard
Some do it with a bitter look
Some with a flattering word
The coward does it with a kiss
The brave man with a sword.

[Wilde, *The Ballad of Reading Gaol*, v. 4]

The example that follows is that of a far less destructive and more integrated patient, who attacks not with a sword, but with a kiss: a more subtle enactment of secret envious excitement.

Patient B

A professor in a speciality associated with the caring professions sees me following an earlier analysis: he is concerned that he works/tries too hard. He begins a session by telling me that he had a dream:

An analyst (my colleague) was giving a talk about a patient with an aortic aneurysm. An email my patient had written was up on billboards—he was embarrassed by that and somehow tried to push away a glass of wine.

He associates to hearing a talk by this analyst and then goes on to say how he, the patient, has challenged his Head of Department, who had accused him of not working hard enough on their joint project. He told her to stop being so meddlesome. After all these years, this is the first time he has done this: actually spoken his mind. There was an email correspondence with her after that, which he associated with the email on billboards.

He goes on to say that he thinks this came out of our talk last time—my showing him so clearly how "concerned" he was being about my fit of coughing and offering to get me water, and so on, and not being able to say that he was furious that my cough had "meddled" with his session. He emphasizes again that it is a great relief to be able to speak his mind. He goes on to say that she (the Head of Department) has announced that she is going to retire, and he is worried about what has he done to her.

I interpret that, on the one hand, he is offering me a bouquet: all this stress on it being the first time, and so forth; on the other hand, he is worried that I, like his senior colleague, am hurt and damaged, and that I would retire/give up. I think that he is both bringing me a bouquet and trying hard—too hard?—to restore me, yet also telling me to stop meddling.

"Oh dear", he says—that reminds him of the expression: "a bouquet of barbed wire". Here again he is cooperative, adds a colourful illustration of my interpretation, but does he also aim to go one better than me? In this way he is, perhaps, rather like a child healthily understanding, but also competing with the parents. He associates further to the aortic aneurysm. His father has been very ill; he mentions his parents' ages, clearly—unconsciously—linking them with my husband's and mine. He says that his mother is always on to him about her symptoms; he is so pleased that his younger sister is now a doctor and can deal with mother. When he goes home, he is so self-effacing, he never thinks of himself as a professor; his secretary, with whom he gets on very well, tells him that he is not at all like a professor.

I suggest that he is offering to get on well with me and not to notice that he is a professor and a doctor and I am not; with amazement he says, "are you not a doctor?" He quickly realizes: "that is absurd, but I really did not think of you as not a doctor." This double negative appears to negate the possibility that he could even be thought of for a moment as upstaging me.

I suggest that I had been invited to interpret that he puts himself down—but actually he is telling me how well he gets on with his secretary, and how good he is at not pulling rank with me—even while he puts me down. He believes that I could not cope with my envy of what he has that I do not. Yet in the dream there is this glass of wine being pushed away, which, I think, represents his intoxicated triumph over the objects towards which he is consciously so solicitous.

Patient B insists that this can't be so: "You are so successful", he says, "how could I think that you could possibly be envious of me?" I point out that he treats me as someone who is so fragile that I could not possibly cope with any feelings of envy of what he has that I do not. So he has all the capacities, and I have to be brought mental equivalents of glasses of water or bouquets, albeit of barbed wire.

I further draw attention to his aged (analytic) parents and his worry, or phantasy, that they and we (I and my husband) would be envious of his relative youth and health: we, with all the symptoms (coughing) and fears of old age, as though, like his mother, I bring him these symptoms to be treated, and he treats them, by "kindly not noticing" or, when they can't be ignored, with offers of glasses of water. He says that his father, who is a self-made businessman, has always been so ashamed of his background, of not having the patient's education, yet when his sister qualified, father could say: "I really am so proud, but I do envy you the opportunities you have had, and the education." As Oscar Wilde said, it is the brave man who can admit his envy.

I interpret that he feels that father's love for the sister, and her achievements, seems to be greater than his envy of her, and it gives him the strength and courage to be honest. Perhaps he feels that I, too, might not need him to try/work so hard to have the possibility of my envy of him negated or covered up. I thought that, instead, he, the patient, feels somewhere very bad, even ashamed, of his need to "cover up" his feelings of envy of father/me, as well as jealousy, say, of his sister's relationship with his parents.

Patient B says that in his previous analysis, one part of him was

> always (secretly) dismissing his analyst's interpretations as "you're just envious of me". I think that may have been what he was doing, possibly not only in his previous analysis, but earlier in this session, and even now. I think that what he envies in his father is not only his strength and his capacity to love and support the family, but also his ability to acknowledge his envious feelings; that when he ostensibly protects me, he reduces me, and then fears a murderous envious attack from me. He says: "It is strange that you say that: my wife had thought that it was dangerous for me to come to the session on the tube today" (it was 7/7—the anniversary of the bombings on underground trains and buses in London). I understand this as an association to my speaking of his fear of my murderous envy of his qualifications and his youth; he fears my vengeance. Certainly it seems that what is around is something quite murderous: the bouquet of barbed wire conceals bombs. (Interestingly, Klein stresses the anal quality of the envious attacks—and we see in both these patients, now the bombs, and the earlier references by Patient A to my listening to her "crap".)

In common with many children of depressed mothers, this patient is caught up in a vicious circle. He experiences a mother who, he believes, in part, at least, cannot cope. Yet in the session what we see is that the analyst is not only experienced as not able to cope but also, he believes, like his mother, shows him her symptoms and then he offers to look after her/me (e.g. offers me water for my cough or brings me a "bouquet"). In that process he hates that mother/analyst who is looked after by him, precisely when he feels not looked after: that, instead, his session is "meddled with" by my cough but also by my interpretations, which fail to "look after"/collude with his omnipotent solutions to his problems. So not only is there some evidence of a "not-coping" (coughing) me, but he further undermines me, reducing me to being a person who cannot cope with anything. For this he feels unconsciously responsible and guilty, yet how unfair it is that he should have to feel responsible for his mother's depression or for my cough. So he feels responsible for me and at the same time despises me: he can neither challenge that person, nor can he be challenged, he believes, by this depressed mother or ostensibly envious analyst.

Conclusions

The two cases I have used as illustrations here have certain features in common with the predicaments in *Othello.* Although the circumstances and many aspects of their characters are, of course, quite different, Patient A and Patient B share qualities of self-aggrandisement, secretly congratulating themselves on their "genius" in defending themselves from the pain of experiencing envy and jealousy. In fact, the problem is not the envy so much as the ostensible absence of envy. As is so often said in the public domain, it is not the original transgression but the cover-up that does for you! Together with this goes a more overt or more covert threat of excited, explosive—as Klein suggested, "anal"—outburst, in different ways threatening, and even creating, pandemonium.

Like all other qualities, envy might be thought of as constitutional. Klein stressed this, while also speaking of the nurture, which might modify this. I lay stress not so much on an excess of inborn envy, but on the escalating cycles where there is an absence of support to deal with this difficult propensity. There appears in these cases to be scant space for thought, or for doing the internal psychic work necessary to deal with envy and the concomitant jealousy. Instead, there is an immediate murderous reaction. Yet what I believe such people most envy is precisely their objects' capacity to work through the problems of the combinations of loss, envy, jealousy, and the associated guilt.

13

Being envious of envy and gratitude

Peter Fonagy

Melanie Klein's 91-page monograph, *Envy and Gratitude*, published half a century ago, sold for about 63 pence. But its price is just about the only anachronistic aspect of this remarkable treatise, which took psychoanalysis into a domain where it had not, until that point, established itself with any degree of comfort. This impressive work explores vicissitudes of character formation in terms of the relative dominance of two opposing infantile affect states: envy and gratitude. The suggestion that the predominance of envy over gratitude at moments of gratification could have pernicious consequences was to have a profound impact on clinical practice and theoretical developments, but it also aroused much controversy, which is perhaps interpretable as an example of envy. The concept of envy is remarkable for providing a bridge between the clinical concerns of psychoanalysis and the science of mind evolving in other disciplines in parallel with progress in psychoanalytic thought. In this brief chapter I shall consider a few examples of the application of Mrs Klein's concept in this broader psychological domain.

Defences against envy

The richness of the concept of envy is rooted in the dynamics of envy. Envy is less remarkable in its direct manifestations than the myriad of instances where we note the sometimes extreme steps taken by the individual to protect themselves against its experience. Narcissistic defences of idealization and devaluation can both be seen as protecting against an annihilating envious attack on the object, either by placing it out of reach or by making it unworthy of the wish to possess and control. The idea that underneath an apparent denigration of the object may be a hidden and far more deadly wish to annihilate born of admiration is clinically very helpful. To interpret denigration as defending against desire often has little if any impact, but turning the patient's conscious mind towards a destructive desire achieves a sense of "feeling felt" (Damasio, 1999, p. 280). Sometimes envious attacks are forestalled by the creation of total confusion or by generating a fantasy of total control that can profoundly interfere with reality testing (Rosenfeld, 1965). Envy can also be projected, generating social situations where others are manipulated to feel envious while the subject experiences righteous indignation, coupled with enormous relief. Mrs Klein showed how frequently these defensive manoeuvres turn to action, and in many cases it is the defence against envy rather than primary envy itself that undermines the possibility of good relationships developing.

Professional groups are not immune from such defensive actions, often treating significant progress made by others as threatening precisely because inspiring ideas by definition belong to others. They are felt to be under the control of other minds and thus cannot but stir up envy. Consequently, as Mrs Klein described, love is stifled and aggression is intensified in order to circumvent the guilt that envy can arouse. I have little doubt that the concept of envy—cogent, clear, and immensely powerful as an explanatory construct—succeeded in stirring up envy, which may account for both the derogatory reaction of some critics and the idealization of the concept by others. Spillius (1993) draws attention to the "storm of protests" that followed the introduction of the concept (see, for example, Joffe, 1969; Zetzel, 1958). By contrast, the extensive use of the concept of envy could be an indication of its defensive over-valuation. In 1970, 48 articles had used the concept; in 1980 it was 82; by 1990, there were 107; and by 2000, 147 papers included in the PEP archive had used the concept with increasing approval and sophistication (e.g. Etchegoyen, Lopez, & Rabih, 1987; Gabbard, 2000). Is the number of patients manifesting envy increasing? Or is it our own attitude to our work that is changing, and this shift reflects the increased recourse to this idea? Apparently, Klein herself felt that the concept of primary breast envy had been "worked to death by some of her adherents" (Grosskurth, 1987). Yet there are many facets of this concept that justify its position at centre stage of modern psychoanalysis.

Envy and the genetics of pathology

For Klein, the degree of envy experienced by an infant is the key index of the child's constitutional risk for psychological disturbance. She postulated envy as existing from the beginning of life and more or less equated it with sadism. She suggested that her early writings on the child's sadistic attacks upon, and projective identification with, the mother should be recast in terms of envy. Klein regards primary envy as a constitutional factor that can explain the pathological paranoid–schizoid position: the envious attacks on the good object bring with them a premature experience of depressive anxiety about damage to the good object, and this interferes with the primal differentiation between good and bad in the object and in the self. The breakdown of normal splitting opens the way to the confusional states of psychosis and creates a barrier to working through the paranoid–schizoid position and proceeding to a normal experience of the depressive position. Klein's monograph attempted to map a biological aspect, a constitutional predisposition to destructiveness, that characterizes certain individuals, the subjective experience of whom has remained a mystery to most of us, but whose constitutional predisposition to interpersonal violence continues to shock and bewilder (Feinberg, Button, Neiderhiser, Reiss, & Hetherington, 2007; Wamboldt & Reiss, 2006).

Naturally, Klein's approach to biology was in terms of libidinal fixation, but it is the sadistic character of the expression of oral and anal concerns that retain the poignancy of her contributions. The leap forward is offered by the understanding of the dynamics of envy and how the working through of this heretofore little-understood sentiment is an essential precondition for the experience of a genuinely mutual relationship. The biological aspect turns out to be crucial. Study after study of twins, some reared apart, confirms the overriding importance of biological predisposition (e.g. Bolton, Rijsdijk, O'Connor, Perrin, & Eley, 2007; Kim-Cohen, Moffitt, Taylor, Pawlby, & Caspi, 2005; Silberg, Rutter, Tracy, Maes, & Eaves, 2007). Often these studies are advanced in opposition to psychoanalytic claims in relation to the uniquely formative character of the parent–infant relationship (e.g. Fairbairn, 1954; Winnicott, 1965). Yet psychoanalysis is as much about understanding how biological predisposition expresses itself via subjective experience as it is to do with understanding the influence of the childhood parental environment. As Freud (1905d) observed: "The constitutional factor must await experiences before it can make itself felt; the accidental factor must have a constitutional basis in order to come into operation" (p. 239). The claim that genes cause human behaviour is absurdly reductionistic. Behaviour is invariably the product of mental experience (Sandler & Joffe, 1969). An understanding of the psychic reality of genetic causation is a major contribution of Kleinian psychoanalysis. For Freud the instincts were unrepresented and thus intrinsically unknowable (Freud, 1915e). Their functioning could only be inferred through the conscious or unconscious ideational contents or affects. By contrast, Kleinian theory has always considered instinctual drives as being knowable. Freud's suppositions concerning the representation of the drive in Kleinian theory become equated with the drive as inborn phantasy involving objects or part objects (Isaacs, 1943). Along these lines, envy, a concept present in psychoanalytic theory from the 1920s (Joffe, 1969), is suggested by Mrs Klein to be not a drive-derivative, but an innate drive with experiential phenomenological properties in and of itself.

The inborn nature of envy and gratitude has far-reaching implications beyond the usual criticism that complex emotions generally held to belong to a somewhat advanced stage of development are antedated and allocated to the most immature phase of life—in fact, birth itself (Joffe, 1969; Yorke, 1971; Zetzel, 1958). These criticisms were, interestingly, made by psychoanalysts who themselves, for theoretical reasons, largely precluded the direct study of infancy and were not in a good position to argue about the cognitive capacities of infants. As it happens, the unfolding of a rich stream of psychological research with infants has provided quite a textured picture of the rapidly unfolding capacities of pre-verbal infants, with many surprisingly early "acquisitions" such as counterfactual reasoning and rational imitation (Gergely, Bekkering, & Kiraly, 2002; Gergely & Csibra, 2006), inferring and attributing false beliefs to others that represent counterfactual states of reality (Onishi & Baillargeon, 2005; Surian, Caldi, & Sperber, 2007) or understanding pretence actions of others that represent fictional states of reality (Onishi, Baillargeon, & Leslie, 2007). Such findings suggest that pre-verbal infants do possess all the basic cognitive prerequisites for mentalization. If this complex of affects is constitutional and operative with effective energy from the beginning of life, then Melanie Klein may have been correct to suggest replacing Freud's concept of instinctual drives, libido, and the destructive instinct with a mentalized set of motives in the infant.

Envy and gratitude are inborn and call into being the ego mechanisms of splitting and projection, which, in turn, lead to complex and sophisticated psychic processes. Among psychoanalytic constructs, envy stands out as one of the most useful in understanding the psychic mediation of the influence of genetic predisposition. For example, the widely accepted constitutional predisposition to depression (e.g. Bergen, Gardner, & Kendler, 2007; Kendler, Gatz, Gardner, & Pedersen, 2006; Orstavik, Kendler, Czajkowski, Tambs, & Reichborn-Kjennerud, 2007) can be reconciled with psychoanalytic accounts via the assumption that the phenomenology of depression originates in a superego figure on whom envy has been projected, which therefore comes to be experienced as persecutory and interferes with thought processes and with every productive activity and, ultimately, with creativeness (Rosenfeld, 1959).

The narcissism of envy (envy and the self)

So, what is the source of envy? Envy for Melanie Klein is rooted in the phantasy of spoiling the good object by, in phantasy, placing bad parts of oneself into it, with the express intent of spoiling and destruction. There is an essentially narcissistic aspect to envious destruction, which accounts for the disorganizing effect it has on the self (Rosenfeld, 1971). As Segal (1993) pointed out: "Envy is necessarily an ambivalent feeling, since it is rooted . . . in need and admiration" (p. 59). It is part of "my self", however despicable, disgusting, and disfiguring, that I use to destroy the thing that I seek but do not possess. Thus envious destruction always entails a "colonization" of the object of the attack by an alien, unmetabolized part of the self. This makes the envied object felt to be of the self. It continues to be felt to belong to the self even when it has played its part as a vehicle for bad aspects in destroying what has been attacked. Envious attacks are therefore qualitatively different from other types of aggressive interaction in that they reflect both an "*unheimlich*" [uncanny] familiarity and a very deep antipathy with the envied object. This peculiar combination sets envious attacks apart from other acts of destruction, at least phenomenologically, and provides a challenging account of the addictive character of certain types of violence. It explains the strange pride that violent individuals experience in relation even to horrific acts of destruction. Otherwise, why would a criminal revisit the scene of the crime? Or indeed, why do those engaged in horrific mass murder, such as ethnic cleansing, report a striking feeling of moral uplift associated with their actions?

The key to understanding the clinical importance of recognizing the envious character of an attack lies in this insight about the strange duality of comfort and hate. Bion (1962a) vividly describes the emotional situation in which the infant feels fear that it is dying. The infant splits off and projects its feelings of fear into the breast, together with envy and hate of the undisturbed breast. Bion points out that it is precisely because of the state of envy (which precludes a reciprocal relationship) that the fear component in the fear of dying becomes so destructive. The fear projected into the breast spoils the breast, and it is no longer present to reassure, soothe, or protect. The breast is felt enviously to remove the good or valuable element in the fear of dying (the urge for safety) and force the worthless residue back into the infant. The infant who started with a fear that he was dying ends up by containing a nameless dread. To my way of thinking, Bion, using Klein's constructs, clearly describes the phenomenology for the infant of the state of affairs that attachment theorists describe as the disorganization of the attachment system (e.g. Green & Goldwyn, 2002; Hesse & Main, 2000; Solomon & George, 1999). Attachment theorists are primarily concerned with the infant's relation to an object who is the source simultaneously of terror and reassurance. Klein's concept (with Bion's elaboration) moves this beyond the mechanistic description provided by the computer metaphor of the internal working model to evoke the embodied subjective experience of this dynamic (Fonagy & Target, 2007).

Control and life

Envy, according to Mrs Klein, is a deceptively simple emotional experience. It does not have the complications of jealousy, where the child has to conceive of the mental state of at least one other person in addition to the object. Envy does not entail triangulation (Cavell, 1998; Von Klitzing, Simoni, & Bürgin, 1999) or even much of an intersubjective state of mind (Trevarthen & Aitken, 2001; Tronick, 2007). It is "an angry grudging feeling" that is about not wanting another person to possess or enjoy something that one oneself finds desirable, to prefer spoiling it to giving it away, to allow it to exist exclusively under one's control or not at all. Klein had noticed that envy and the death instinct have a key common feature: they attack life and sources of life. This implies the possibility of envious attacks on one's own being if the crucial criteria of possession and control are not met. Mrs Klein implies that as humans, we might prefer death to existence if the all-important criterion of control is not satisfied. One of the pains that the individual seeks to avoid by self-annihilation and object-annihilation is the pain caused by the awareness of the existence of an object that is hated and envied (Segal, 1993). The annihilation is both an expression of the death instinct in envy and a defence against experiencing envy by annihilating the envied object, which is felt out of control of the self and/or the self that could desire the object. The more intense the experience of being out of control, the stronger the urge to bring an end to the need by destroying the self.

The importance of envy for social science in general and issues pertaining to the unequal distribution of health across social groups in particular has become apparent only relatively recently. It surprised many in the closing decade of the twentieth century to learn that the biggest risk factor for coronary heart disease (CHD) is neither cholesterol nor smoking but, rather, the nature of an individual's work, the control they have over their job, and the social support they have available to them (Marmot, 2006; Wilkinson, 1996, 2000). Even more interesting is the increasing body of research suggesting that the risks for many chronic diseases in adult life are set very early: during the first decade of life, or even in infancy (Barker, 1990; Power & Hertzman, 1997). A relatively recent study reported questionnaire responses of 17,421 adult health plan members with Kaiser Permanente who were routinely asked for information on adverse childhood experiences (ACEs) while being assessed for medical and physical problems Most types of problems were found to be extremely accurately predicted by ACEs (Felitti, 2002; Felitti et al., 1998). In studies such as Michael Marmot's investigations of cardiovascular disease among Civil Servants in Whitehall, personal control repeatedly emerged as a key factor in predicting the relative freedom from almost all disease experienced by those at higher grades of the service compared to individuals sharing their workspace but with a great deal less control over available resources. A sense of control ensures longevity; its absence creates risks to health across most organ systems. This phenomenon challenges understanding unless we appreciate Melanie Klein's insights into primitive frustrating emotional experiences that are recreated by observing someone else having control over something good that remains beyond one's own sphere of agentive action. We can only assume that in such instances unmentalized envious attacks turn against the body as well as the mind.

Attachment and gratitude

Bowlby's key objection to classical psychoanalysis was the unqualified assumption of early object relationship based on the mere gratification of oral needs. It would be too much to ask of a single work that it should revolutionize the nature of love as well as of hate. Yet I think that Mrs Klein's classical concept of "gratitude" has implications for a modern conceptualization of attachment. Klein was at one with Freud, Abraham, Anna Freud, and others in seeing the development of love as rooted in oral gratification: "The more often gratification at the breast is experienced and fully accepted, the more often enjoyment and gratitude and accordingly the wish to return pleasure are felt" (p. 189). However, she makes a stunning addition to this assumption when she qualifies the development of trust and gratitude by attributing to the infant "the ability to accept and assimilate the loved primal object without greed and envy interfering too much" (p. 188). She assumes constitutional differences to exist between infants in terms of the extent to which they are able to psychologically process (metabolize) experiences of being given to. In other words, love cannot conquer all. Against the background of destructive envy, love cannot be heard at all. Of course clinical work with adoption, and the distress of adoptive parents hoping but failing to undo envious destructiveness created by a combination of genetic predisposition, earlier deprivation, and maltreatment, reminds us of exactly such an absence of complementarity between love and aggression (Bimmel, Juffer, Van IJzendoorn, & Bakermans-Kranenburg, 2003; Howe, 2006; Lieberman, 2003; O'Connor, Marvin, Rutter, Olrick, & Britner, 2003). Sensitivity may be necessary, but it is certainly not sufficient under such extreme conditions.

This was also a difficult lesson for attachment theorists to learn. Attachment theory began by understanding aggression as a defensive response to the frustration of attachment needs: "I have described repression of yearning for the lost object, displacement of reproaches against it, denial of the reality of loss, splits in the ego, the role of projective identification, and the use as defences both of aggression and of the care of a vicarious figure" (Bowlby, 1963, p. 540). Mrs Klein places the boot of violence on the other foot. Aggression is not seen as purely a reaction. In her theory, gratitude (love) is made possible by the assimilation of inborn aggression. Excessive aggression will disorganize attachment to a point where evolutionarily established signals of caregiving no longer have their anticipated effect. Klein's theory can be read as a description of the disorganization of attachment, which is marked by the failure normally to process positive signals of having been emotionally understood or affectively contained. Klein could be wrong about her emphasis on oral gratification as the basis of the attachment system (we know that the attachment system has biological triggers, the neuropeptides of vasopressin and oxytocin, which are specific to activating parent–child, child–parent, and romantic bonds (see Insel, 2003; Lim & Young, 2004; Lim, Wang, Olazabal, Ren, Terwilliger, & Young, 2004), but she is charting a new passage in highlighting the complementary quality of attachment and destructiveness, with the latter not being reducible to the frustration of the former (Fonagy, 2003). On the basis of large-scale longitudinal observational studies, developmentalists now generally accept that aggression peaks in infancy, and that it is the failure to desist from aggression that leads to problems of conduct in childhood, rather than aggression emerging *de novo* in response to environmental adversity (NICHD Early Child Care Research Network, 2004; Tremblay et al., 2004). Social processes that were previously thought to generate or promote aggression work by interfering with the socialization of aggression, much as Klein suggested. This has, of course, important implications for prevention as well as therapy.

Sensitivity, caregiving, and attunement will not deliver an antidote to destructiveness in some people precisely because this stimulates the wish to attack and destroy, rather than meeting the assumed frustrated need against which aggression and violence were assumed to be defensive reactions. In fact, the more care-giving such individuals receive, the more is a reaction of envious destruction bound to follow. Those whose attachment system is not disorganized (most of us) find this reaction inexplicable, yet we also know that it is as ubiquitous as any of the phenomena Freud (1901b) included in the "Psychopathology of Everyday Life". This helps us to understand why it is that some patients react to a helpful interpretation that clearly brings relief with destructive criticism and mostly the analyst is not allowed that moment of self-satisfaction which led Freud to light up his cigar and apocryphally exclaim that it was only a cigar (Elms, 2001) Mrs Klein pointed out that the better the contact we make with the envious patient, the more sensitive and attuned our intervention, the more we are going to be criticized. We have to wait for the deep truth of this to sink in before responding. But ultimately we have to rise to the sheer impertinence and provocativeness of the statement. An Alice-in-Wonderland world is conjured up where each act of goodness receives its just punishment. In another apocryphal story, an exasperated Chair of Department is said to have exclaimed: "I don't know why X is attacking me! I have never done anything for him!"

Conclusion

In this chapter I intended to celebrate Melanie Klein's contribution by showing its relevance to current thinking in developmental psychopathology. Kleinian analysts are often accused of not having a developmental model, which some (more self-critical members of the group, e.g., Spillius, 2001) own up to. While Kleinian theory was courageously adultomorphic and was never intended to be experimentally explored in the observational laboratory, it peculiarly might just turn out that Mrs Klein's fictitious developmental ideas were more relevant to the scientific basis of the discipline and closer to reality, as established in infant laboratories, than most of us were willing to acknowledge.

14

Vicious circles of envy and punishment

Henry F. Smith

The analyst's attention

In the last several decades, on both sides of the Atlantic, there has been a shift in the analyst's attention towards the moment-by-moment movement of the clinical session, especially within the transference. In the United States we have seen the change in the advent of self psychology, with its focus on the detailed conscious experience of the patient; in the relational school, with its emphasis on the ongoing enacted interaction with the analyst; and in contemporary conflict theory, where Gray (1994) introduced an "inside the hour" focus on moments of conflictual interference, especially in the transference, and Brenner (2002) argued from another perspective that every mental event—every thought, affect, or action—is, when it is observed analytically, a compromise formation, made up of the conflict among wishes (or drive derivatives), defences, self-punitive trends, and painful affect. In his view it is these immediate clinical phenomena that command the analyst's attention, rather than the larger abstract agencies of the mind—the id, ego, and superego—which should be discarded as misleading in their simplifications.

The shift is also evident among the contemporary British Kleinians, who are less inclined than their predecessors to offer the patient early developmental reconstructions or to point out evidence of large abstractions such as the death instinct, as if they could not only be inferred but were concretely represented in clinical material. Instead of these, they offer a much more immediate scrutiny of the patient's use of the analyst and the analyst's interventions than has been associated with traditional Kleinian technique. Contrast the close attention to nuances in the here-and-now transference that we have come to recognize in the work of Joseph (1989) or Feldman (2007) with the following description by Klein (1957) of her own work in *Envy and Gratitude*:

> The gist of my interpretations was that her grievance about the missed analytic sessions related to the unsatisfactory feeds and unhappiness in babyhood. The two cakes out of the "two or three" stood for the breast which she felt she had been twice deprived of by missing analytic sessions. [Klein, 1957, p. 205]

In some sense *Envy and Gratitude* straddles both the older and the newer ways in its rhetorical focus. Reading it now, one cannot escape the feeling of listening to a moral drama played out between good and evil, between persecutory internal objects and good ones, or, for that matter, between envy and gratitude. For the most part the entities at war seem to represent pure cultures, as if the mind were divided into a series of split entities and affects: purely good and purely bad objects, pure envy and pure gratitude. I think this rhetorical splitting stems both from Klein's interest in early states of mentation, where, in principle, the splitting of such states is part of development, and from her longstanding interest in drives in conflict with each other. This stands, incidentally, in contrast to Brenner (1982), for whom drives or, more accurately, drive derivatives (wishes)—he makes a point that drives are only an abstraction and never observable—are never in conflict with each other unless one drive derivative is defending against the other. Both libidinal and aggressive drive derivatives are expressed in every psychic moment, finding expression in every compromise formation.

On the other hand, running as a leitmotif throughout *Envy and Gratitude*, is her repeated acknowledgement that there are no pure states: "This does not mean that some element of guilt does not enter into the most genuine feelings of gratitude" (p. 189) or "Since the need for a good object is universal, the distinction between an idealized and a good object cannot be considered as absolute" (p.

193). With Brenner, Klein does not appear to feel that there is any state without conflict, even in infancy: "The absence of conflict in the infant, if such a hypothetical state could be imagined, would deprive him of enrichment of his personality and of an important factor in the strengthening of his ego. For conflict, and the need to overcome it, is a fundamental element in creativeness" (p. 186).

Klein is led to these increasingly complex observations by her own clinical experience, which causes her to modify her pure categories for the sake of clinical truth. But the siren song of the pure or idealized state is almost irresistible, as, shortly before telling us that there is no gratitude without guilt, she speaks of the "*full gratification*" that envy prevents, noting that "the infant can only experience *complete enjoyment* if the capacity for love is sufficiently developed . . . such *unity* means being *fully understood*" (p. 188, italics added). She gives no notice here that fullness and completeness are themselves idealizations or that "complete enjoyment" is an impossibility if conflict is always in the works. In these early pages, phrases such as "full . . . unity . . . fully understood . . . fully accepted . . . fully into play . . . complete enjoyment . . . fully enjoying his feeds" (pp. 188–192) echo insistently throughout the text. At the end of *Envy and Gratitude,* Klein writes movingly, "when love can be sufficiently brought together with the split-off rage and envy, these emotions become bearable and diminish, because they are mitigated by love" (p. 232). Here the end result is a mixed state, but the drama has already been played out internally between the healing of power of love and the destructive power of hate and envy as pure or ideal states in themselves. This is a general psychology expressed in the language of Judeo–Christian morality.

Sprinkled within the qualifiers in this work—and more densely at the beginning than at the end—there remains the sense of goodness as a pure state. Thus Klein says: "A full gratification at the breast means that the infant feels he has received from his loved object a unique gift which he wants to keep. This is the basis for gratitude" (p. 188). She continues: "Hope and trust in the existence of goodness, as can be observed in everyday life, helps people through great adversity, and effectively counteracts persecution" (p. 194). We know what she means, but the idealized moral categories—"full gratification" in the first passage, "the existence of goodness" in the second—are offered here again as if there were no inherent conflict within them or inevitable ambivalence to temper them.

Note, in Klein's concession that guilt will enter even "the most genuine feelings of gratitude", her use of the word *genuine*, yet another expression of an ideal or pure state. While we all adopt words such as *genuine, authentic, full, real,* and *whole* (as in whole-object relation) to qualify the patient's or the analyst's state of mind, the "genuineness" of the patient's presentation—or the lack of it—is something that contemporary Kleinians have taught us to observe. The word is almost a proprietary one in their discourse, and it has proven a unique and durable aspect of the analyst's listening. My point, however, is that there is a seductive moral tone to this language that compels us to look for moments that feel genuine and to be alert to others that feel not so, and there are some countertransferential risks in doing just that, which I discuss in conjunction with the clinical material I present below. However useful the terminology is, it is important to bear in mind Klein's warning that just as there is no pure gratitude without guilt, so there is surely no purely genuine state.

It is probably impossible to analyse or even to think without utilizing idealizations like *genuine* and *real*. As soon as we observe and name anything, it quickly becomes reified and idealized; our psychoanalytic culture, as much as any other, is built on such moral high ground. Thus the morally seductive concept of forgiveness is currently enjoying its moment in the sun, even in psychoanalysis, though not without criticism (Smith, 2007a), and every analytic approach can be shown to have its own idealizations, from the currently much debated idealization of neutrality to the sacrosanct notion of empathy. (I once argued that there is no pure state of empathy and that every such state must have its defensive function, both for the patient and for the analyst, and was told by a self psychologist that I was being hypochondriacal.) My point here is that while pure states and idealized categories are in the nature of concept formation in general and pose a problem for our field in particular, there is something about the moral character of Klein's categories (e.g. *goodness, hatred, envy, greed,* and qualifiers such as *full, complete,* and *whole*) that cannot help but enter the clinical stage as moral forces.

I do not mean to emphasize these concerns at the expense of the real power and meaning of Klein's approach—to miss, that is, the forest for the trees. For it is in the unfolding structure of *Envy and Gratitude* itself that her idealized states are shown to be part of a much more complex pattern, as Klein spins a theoretical and clinical tale that is so precise and intricate in its turnings back upon itself that we recognize a lifelike complexity, until she finally concludes, "complete and permanent integration is in my view never possible" (p. 233).

One of the great contributions of Klein's work is the detail in which she spells out what she calls the "vicious circles" that unfold both in development and in the clinical session as a result of envy: the devalued, envious person attacks the one he/she envies, including the analyst and the analyst's interpretations, but this attack only leads to guilt and further self-attack in response, which compounds the person's devalued state, stirring up more envy, and thus leading to more attack. Also implicit in this work is the "virtuous circle" that results when an individual has internalized the good object and can feel and express love and gratitude as a result, which then "makes it possible to introject a more friendly outer world" (p. 189), thus adding to the goodness within.

Notice how the strategy and structure of the work itself draws the reader into the very circles Klein is describing. Here I have in mind the way in which she keeps circling back on subjects already covered, continually reasserting the quest for completeness and fullness and then qualifying it with disclaimers as to its improbability, thereby immersing the reader in a pattern similar to the clinical circles of which she speaks. The very recursiveness of Klein's writing seems to draw us into the cyclical process of analysis itself. Thus the reader experiences at first-hand—even viscerally—the debate between Klein's own wish for pure states of goodness and love and her realization that they are impossible: the self-same conflict she is spelling out.

We hear this conflict playing itself out in Klein's clinical illustrations as well, the work still straddling two eras: an older, simpler, more certain one and a later one of greater complexity and detail. Klein begins by spelling out her constitutional and developmental view in which literal fixed states abound and where the feeding situation determines important aspects of the adult character. In the interpretation I quoted above, we can note a potential hazard of this theoretical commitment in so far as it encourages analysts to imagine that patients can make direct use of the interpretation of universal and concretized symbols ("the two cakes stood for the breast") and early developmental reconstructions ("unsatisfactory feeds in babyhood"). In contrast, other interventions indicate a distinctly different and more contemporary view, focused on the transferential moment—see, for example: "I interpreted that this was only a minor feature of the dream: the main meaning was that he had torn up my work and was destroying it" (p. 214), or Klein's observation of the appearance in a dream of the phrase "this kept me going" (p. 215) as evidence of how essential the analysis had become to the patient.

Brenner and Klein

We can see the nature of Klein's reasoning and rhetoric more clearly if we contrast it, somewhat arbitrarily, with Brenner's. Where Klein's thinking in *Envy and Gratitude* is cyclical, deepening the territory each time she repeats her ideas with added nuances and drawing the reader into an experience of clinical complexity, Brenner's approach is misleadingly concise and precise. He simply repeats and demonstrates that everything the analyst observes is a compromise formation and must be analysed as such; he repeats this again and again in his writing, until the reader finally gets it. If Brenner is the hedgehog in this duo, Klein is the fox ("The fox knows many things, but the hedgehog knows one big thing"—Archilochus, 700 BCE).

Brenner's theory does not allow for the idea of anything pure about any state—neither love nor hate. Even genuineness must be a compromise formation defending against painful affect, and every good object, every moment of gratitude, must be made up of aggressive as well as loving wishes, defences, and self-punishments; the state of mind in question is simply the outcome of these underlying components vying for expression. In such a system there can be no pure culture of good and bad objects, no gratitude that is not laced with envy, nor envy unmitigated by gratitude, and no pure punishment: every aspect of psychic life, punishment and hatred no less than love, is a mixture of erotic and aggressive drive derivatives, and every moment has its measure of punishment to mete out to both self and object.

To be sure, on this point a comparison between Klein and Brenner is not fair to either one: Brenner's theoretically spare approach yields, when put to the clinical test, a field of observation of vastly increased complexity, a cascade of compromises to be analysed, and Klein could be positively and usefully hedgehog-like in the persistence of her theoretical point of view and clinical practice. Moreover, Klein often uses the terms "*good*" and "*bad*"—like "*love*" and "*hate*"—in a metapsychological sense, as forces or entities operating within the deep structures of the mind, whereas Brenner's focus is on those conscious and unconscious entities that are the end result of these forces, and therefore always mixtures, always ambivalent. Hence, I am comparing them, quite incorrectly, at two different levels of abstraction. (At times it is unclear just what level of psychic life Klein is addressing in *Envy and Gratitude*: sometimes she seems to be speaking of conscious envy and conscious gratitude; at other times she seems to be positing a descriptively unconscious envy that is deeply defended against; and at yet other times she seems to see envy as a kind of metapsychological force and a derivative of the death instinct that, like hate, is at war with other forces that are good and life-affirming.)

Nonetheless, I think we can see the different paths that Brenner and Klein have taken to solve the problem of pure states, Brenner by positing within the details of his theory that they are impossible, and Klein by demonstrating that one state is continually modified by another, while both states remain locked within the vicious circles that underlie the work's argument. My point is that without some check of the sort these analysts develop, the clinician will be led, as we all are, into assuming that things are only as they seem.

Views of punishment

Perhaps we can appreciate more clearly the distinction I am drawing between Brenner and Klein—and hence between certain aspects of North American and British approaches—if we compare their views on punishment. I have already indicated that Brenner sees self-punishment and fear of punishment as a component of every compromise formation and hence every psychic event. Although the issue of punishment runs implicitly through the entire text of *Envy and Gratitude*, Klein only mentions it late in the work, where she speaks first of the "envious superego" that is "felt to disturb or annihilate all attempts at reparation and creativeness . . . [and] to make constant and exorbitant demands on the individual's gratitude." Note that in this instance envy is in conflict with gratitude itself. Next, she says that "to persecution are added the guilt feelings that [stem from the sense that] the persecutory internal objects are the result of the individual's own envious and destructive impulses, which have primarily spoilt the good object." Finally, she adds that "the need for punishment, which finds satisfaction by the increased devaluation of the self, leads to a vicious circle" (p. 231). In this scenario, we watch the forces of good and evil do battle, much as in a medieval passion play (or exercise in moral philosophy), with punishment as a player who appears on stage to play his requisite part in the drama.

In contrast to Brenner's approach, which is to say that punishment is everywhere and in everything, Klein plays out the drama that unfolds in theory—and, as it turns out, in practice—by describing (a) an envious superego powerfully interfering with attempts at creativeness; (b) guilt feelings about spoiling one's good internal objects and creating persecutory ones, leading to (c) the need for punishment, which can find satisfaction in an increased devaluation of the self, which then sets in motion (d) a vicious circle, as the defence against envy leads to more self-punishment, which leads to further devaluation of the self, which, in turn, leads, inevitably, to more envy. I would suggest that the simultaneous or rapidly changing occurrence of these conflicting feelings, impulses, and anxieties, observable in the moment-to-moment movements in the relationship between patient and analyst—the subtle shifts in the session arousing envy or persecutory anxiety—is the cornerstone of contemporary Kleinian technique. And I think we can identify an even tighter vicious circle, implied though not spelled out in the text, as punishment of self leads to punishment of other, which leads to punishment of self, and so on. It is to this latter circle, which serves many purposes simultaneously, that I would now like to turn. I start with an illustration from *Hamlet* (Shakespeare, 1603)

Hamlet and punishment

In the final scene of Act III Hamlet, seeking to avenge his father's death, mistakenly kills Polonius and then immediately attacks his mother verbally, punishing her for her incestuous relationship with his uncle:

> Nay, but to live
> In the rank sweat of an enseamed bed,
> Stew'd in corruption, honeying and making love
> Over the nasty sty!
>
> [*Hamlet*, III.iv.91–94]

Next he is visited by the ghost of his father, following which, with all the loving passion of an oedipal child, he pleads with his mother this night and forevermore to repent and "go not to my uncle's bed". And then he says (and this is my point):

> For this same lord [Polonius]
> I do repent; but heaven hath pleas'd it so,
> To punish me with this, and this with me,
> That I must be their scourge and minister.
>
> [*Hamlet*, III.iv.174–177]

"To punish me with this, and this with me": Hamlet is punished by his deed, even as his deed punishes others. Thus, in this brief sequence Shakespeare captures several truths about punishment: first, that each single act of punishment is at once both punishment of other and punishment of self; second, that as Hamlet is trying to bind his relationship to a father lost and to a mother morally lost, whom he still loves passionately, punishment is a desperate if misguided plea for love; and, third, that punishment, like sadomasochism more generally, is itself a defence against object loss. Note, however, that if punishment is *simultaneously* punishment of self and of others, it creates its own vicious circle, with punishment of others requiring punishment of self (because of guilt) and punishment of self requiring punishment of others (because of envy). Thus the vicious circle is set in motion by a single act of punishment.

We can see these truths in their purest form in the analysis of masochism, where misery is at once both self-punishing and object-punishing, and moral masochism is always also moral sadism—an attempt simultaneously to preserve the object and to destroy it—as what is projected and what is introjected continually and instantaneously trade places. Such complexities come clearest in the countertransference.

An analytic session

I am thinking of a psychiatrist in her late thirties, now in her second analysis. Ms H (as I will call her) complains bitterly that she needs me to love her, but she does so in so self-attacking a tone that I feel attacked both by her request and by her self-attack, at the same time as I become the attacker and feel guilty as a result. To paraphrase

Hamlet, she punishes herself with me and me with her self-punishment. And I find that I, too, wish to punish and to be punished in my work with her.

My patient's attack on herself is also an appeal for me to stop her. Many years ago she had tried to take her own life with the hope that her first analyst would come to her rescue. Now she imagines herself ripping the skin off her face, but she is less overtly self-destructive in action—until you listen to the action in the session and the use she makes of me and my comments.

The session I present takes place six years into the analysis and two days before I am to leave for two weeks. My leaving intensifies the feeling of object loss for both of us.

> Ms H comes in and says: "I'm going too fast. I don't think I have felt this way since I was in analysis before." I feel put on notice: she means when she tried to kill herself. "I feel I'm going to die. I don't really understand why I'm feeling so altogether bereft in relation to your vacation." She says this in a voice that sounds more exhausted and resigned than angry at me, nonetheless posing an analytic question that I am supposed to answer. Her question, with its academic intonation, rings false, given that the stake is survival itself. She needs something from me in exchange for my going away, something to keep her alive. But any feelings of anger or panic have to be mine: she is too tired to have them.
>
> She continues: "I say to myself, look, it will be good, because in the time I have free, I have an upstairs office filled with things to be filed"—thus reducing our relationship to a filing operation. "I have to call five people. This is the kind of thing I do well. I have to call them in person. I feel I'm racing and have nothing underneath me, which of course is not true, but there's the feeling of going so fast there's nothing holding me up."
>
> What Ms H says is, in a sense, true: she has nothing underneath her—but she denies it as soon as she has observed it, an implicit attack on her own insight and any contribution to it that I might make. At this point she starts to weep, but it doesn't sound genuine to me (an aspect of my countertransference that I discuss below). "I don't understand what I'm doing and why I'm feeling so awful. I got into this thing with my printer. It ran out of toner,

and I said to my husband, 'It's out of toner. I don't understand. It was perfectly fine.' He said, 'Just shake it.' I hate asking him for anything." She hates asking him or me for anything, and I feel momentarily pleased that she sees this and that her hatred is so accessible. "He always says, 'I will show you, and you stand there and watch, so next time you can do it yourself.' So he did, and, of course, it didn't work." In addition to her abject dependency on her husband, he, like me, is ineffectual. "He said this morning, 'If you tell me what kind of printer you have, I will go to the store and get it.' But I don't know what kind it is, and if I go to look at it, I'll be late to see you, so I say (I can't bear saying it), 'Could you look at my printer while I'm gone, or it can wait until I get back from Smith's.' And he said, 'I'd like you to go upstairs and tell me, and then I'll go.' I said, 'Fuck it. I can't do it now.'" Again I feel encouraged that her rage sounds genuine, but it is gone in a flash, as she backs away to a kind of self-punitive compliance. "I said to him, 'I can do it Saturday. I know you want me to be responsible.' He said, 'Yes. I do,'" at which point she turns again and in a pleading voice says to me: "Why do I feel so unbearable about you leaving? I don't know why I feel I'm going to die, like I'm giving up the source of life."

In this mix there is a repeated shifting back and forth between a more genuine rage at me and at her husband, as I experience it, and a self-punitive attack that is simultaneously an attack on me and a desperate holding on to me. In fact, the very way she speaks about all this in her familiar defensive misery feels like a continuous punishing assault on our capacity to work together. Ms H feels she is unbearable to me in her misery at the same time as her misery feels unbearable to her—"To punish me with this, and this with me."

Ms H then tells me about an encounter with a supervisor, to whom she was presenting her treatment of a very anxious young woman. Her supervisor said that instead of interpreting the transference directly, she should deal with it in displacement. My patient often complains that I interpret her transference too directly. Of her supervisor, she says: "I hate her. She has this moralism, and that drives me up the wall. I can't stand her. Something about her is very severe, but I felt awful afterward. I tell myself, 'You're being paranoid. She makes you worry that you are pressing the patient too much, but there is this absolutely solid relationship with the patient. It's just that she falls into this place of fear.'"

Hearing about many pressing and punishing figures here—her supervisor, herself, and me, the same people who are simultaneously being punished—I say (and this is my first comment in the session): "I think you are telling me you fall into this place of fear as I am about to leave, but it isn't the only place you inhabit."

Ms H starts to weep again, but again it doesn't sound genuine. She knows I have in mind her rage, but with her forced tears I am the one who ends up feeling angry, not she. Rather than joining her in her place of fear, I have become the punisher, and I feel guilty wondering whether I have simply missed her point of view. She continues, "I know I'll be fine, but I'm so panicked." Now the tears have completely vanished, gone as quickly as they appeared, as she reasserts her fearfulness.

She continues, "I'm scared about the weekend, scared of going into the old place of wanting to rip my skin off. It feels unbearable. I'm trying to figure out how to deal with the panic about you going away. It's the sense of dying that is weird. I'm not one who is afraid of dying. It's like dying inside, which isn't as bad as the self-attack. That's the worst."

I say, "I think you want me to feel I'm leaving you to die, leaving you all alone in this frightening world to rip your skin off."

Ms H dismisses my comment distractedly, "I don't know. I want to say—but I won't, because I know I'm not supposed to"—which feels like an attack both on her impulse to say something and on our relationship—"I want to say, 'Where will you be?' Give me something to hold on to. I feel so borderline. Give me something to hold on to. You would say you'd tell me if I needed you to. I thought, I don't need it. It's coming from a place of boldness. I would really like to know." In other words, she doesn't really need it, she is simply being bold to ask, and I should tell her because, of course, I want to support her boldness. I pause and in that pause—she knows this dance—she takes it back again, each of these takings-back more self-punishing and punishing of me than the last: "But now it's become so shameful, I don't want to ask." And then she asks again, "But I don't want to do without. I want you to give me something to contain the attack on my face, something I can use to comfort myself."

And then suddenly she says in her sweetest voice, "You can't imagine how I just want to paint pictures of where you are. If I could imagine where you were going, maybe to England, maybe you are taking someone who graduated on a tour of Europe or going to Tuscany or something like that. That would be so nice. I get all these vicarious pleasures."

Feeling confined by her sweetness, with her rage and her deprivation left for me to bear, I say, "But you pay a price for these vicarious pleasures. You resent terribly the other person. I give this to the other and not to you."

Again she responds dismissively, "I don't know. It's hard to feel that, it gives me so much pleasure. I'm not in touch with the angry part of me that wants you to feel guilty"—so she did hear my earlier message—"because I so much want to wrap myself around you. It's kind of pathetic, isn't it?"

Further along, Ms H speaks about something she might want to call me about while I'm away, but she won't. "That's the only way I could feel my anger at you. I'll take care of it by myself. I'd rather do everything myself than ask for anything. I'll learn how to be responsible with a vengeance. I won't ask for anything. I won't ask again. I'll pretend everything is good. It's very unfair and cruel. I'll deprive you of me. I won't let you be a source of comfort to me. See, I'd much rather have my vicarious pretty fantasy than feel myself in this position. I hate it. I hate this angry person. This is the anger I hate to feel. I feel it towards my husband. I hate it. I just hate it, because then there's nothing good left. You see, I get rid of all the comfort. I don't know how to stop doing that."

Note that in making these convincing "analytic" observations, she continues to punish me by "doing everything herself" at the very moment of observing how she does just that. She does hate the punishing anger she feels at herself and at me, and I say, "I think you are telling me that I cause you this desperate pain by reminding you of your resentment and hatred."

Ms H says, "Maybe", again withholding any real thinking about my comment. "I don't want to feel it, because it's just too alone in a bad place I can see myself creating. I don't know how to get out of it."

For the moment I take her "creation" of this inner state at face value, and I say, "No, because, as you said, you not only banish anything good about me, you banish anything good about yourself and create this exaggerated 'I live only in hatred'."

I think I may have been too confrontative—that is, too punishing—but she now says with conviction, "Yes. That's exactly what it is. It becomes intolerable", and she is able to hold it briefly before letting it go, "Oh, God, this is scaring me so much. I think it is important, but it is scaring me so much. I'm so scared of what you just said. It's exactly true, but right now I can't find a way to reduce the exaggeration or a way out or a way to let you in or let the good part of me in." And then she begins to sound as if she is parroting my words, turning them back into questions: "Why does it get so exaggerated? I want you to patch up this place real fast. Patch it up. I don't want to be stuck here", the request now clear and bold, if no less punishing, and ultimately doomed. "You make it better. You made it bad." The session is over.

Discussion

"To punish me with this, and this with me." Throughout this session we can hear the vicious circle within which both my patient and I are caught, as her self-punishing misery is also intended as punishment of me, which compounds her need to punish herself, resulting in further punishment of me, and further compensatory self-punishment. At times I feel as if I am a bystander watching a kind of perpetual-motion phenomenon generated by my patient alone. But I am, as it turns out, a necessary participant, for her punishment of me with her self-punishing attacks has the effect of holding me in place as the object she is about to lose. It is a punishment that begs to be loved and comforted at the same time as it makes it impossible to do so, and in all of this I *feel* punished by her self-punishment at the same time as I feel myself to be the punisher of both her and me.

One of the ways in which I participate in her punishment is in my use of the word *genuine*, which you will have noted several times in my description of the session. However accurate a characterization of my experience of the patient's affect at certain moments, it is a judgement—like *real* or *authentic*—that carries a moral tone, one that my patient is adept at picking up, even if I am not articulating it, and this reinforces her sense of me as accusatory. And she is right: there is a degree of criticism expressed in the mere thought that she does not sound genuine. Moreover, I have learned that while she experiences many varieties of rage and sadness, they all feel genuine to her and need to be explored for their individual meaning. Hence there is a danger in our otherwise useful alertness to whether the patient is in genuine contact with herself or with the analyst—namely, that it can blind the analyst to questioning in what way any particular affect, however ungenuine it may sound, is *genuinely* expressive of some inner condition on the part of the patient. This dilemma is reminiscent of the time when we used to say that a patient was "avoiding the transference" until we discovered that that very avoidance *was* the transference. Our awareness of what sounds genuine and what does not inevitably has countertransferential meaning.

In this session my focus is primarily on what is being enacted between us and on my patient's use of me and my comments. While they may be at the back of my mind, I am not aware of assuming or consciously seeking any of the larger and more abstract theoretical ideas that may lie behind either the "North American" or the "British" view of the material. I *am* aware that my sense that every moment is a mix of conflicting elements silently informs my listening. And while I am continually assessing the genuineness of my patient's responses to me, my visceral awareness of the vicious circle that is being played out between us reminds me that I am never dealing with pure states of genuineness, gratitude, or envy.

In all of this my patient's envy of others—anyone, that is, who has goodness and health about them—and her envy, in turn, of me and my comments, is palpable and at various times clear to both of us. Sometimes she expresses what feels to me like heart-felt gratitude for the work I have done with her. But soon afterward her self-punishing attack will reappear. Is it to forestall the envy she feels? Or to deprive herself of what she feels she does not deserve, spoiling the sense of my goodness and her own? I think it is both, for she does not in fact feel the envy at that moment, so quickly is it overridden with shame and self-punishment. She feels no pure gratitude that is not laced with guilt, or interfered with by envy, and no pure envy, for that matter, that is not also a plea to be loved and to be able to feel love and gratitude, as she imagines others do.

Amidst all the turmoil of the session, the patient comes back time and again to her fear of object loss and separateness, repeatedly turning herself around in the vicious circle and turning me around in it too, so that we are both permanently glued to each other in this sado-masochistic, self- and object-punishing unit. I feel it in her transference, which suggests that I am either very sweet or very sadistic. There is no way out, my role is fixed, either as a hated or as a loved object. Both her punishment and her sweetness are designed to prevent any sense of separateness at all—we are either a punishing unit or a sweet one—so that while all the discussion is *about* a separation, she makes certain not to allow awareness of a single moment of separateness within the actual session.

Thus the sado-masochism is played out by me on her, and her on me, and, simultaneously, by each of us on ourselves. But it is designed in part to prevent me from moving away from her *in the session*. Her position of powerlessness, then, is enormously powerful, punishing and appealing for love at the same time as it is a successful defence against object loss. Trapped together in this place in which there is no separateness, there is no possibility for the actual experience of envy—or, for that matter, of real object love.

I want to say something about my patient's confusion. For the most part I think of it as both defensive and gratifying, her need to avoid knowing anything, her need to destroy her own thinking, satisfy her masochism, and keep hope alive that I will fill her with knowledge, with all its sado-masochistic and erotic implications. It is also a defence against envy. If she is so confused, then she cannot feel envy, and her confusion serves as self-punishment as well as punishment of the analyst she envies. We cannot help but wonder, however, whether her confusion also results, as Klein describes, from "uncertainty as to whether the analyst is still a good figure, or whether he and the help he is giving have become bad because of the patient's hostile criticism" (p. 184).

In time my patient would say to me, "I get into a muddle because at a certain point I don't know what is you and what is me." Klein notes that when the predominance of envy prevents identification with a good and whole object, "excessive projective identification, by which split-off parts of the self are projected into the object, leads to a strong confusion between the self and the object, which also comes to stand for the self" (p. 192). This would seem to be important in relation to my patient's fears about the actual separation of the break. The confusion of herself and me, a result of the constant projective identification of parts of herself into me—to control me, to keep me—leaves her bereft not only of me, but of the parts of her own mind, which she needs for thinking and for dealing with her loss.

All of this would qualify as a demonstration of Klein's view of a negative therapeutic reaction, wherein the defences illustrated become "a powerful obstacle to the capacity to take in what the analyst has to give" (p. 220), including any potentially helpful comments I might make. I would only add that, judging by the material I have described, the negative therapeutic reaction is participated in by both analyst and patient as part of an endless circle in which the two are engaged, and there can be no working through of any sort that does not pass through this place of mutual torment. In that sense the negative therapeutic reaction *is* the work itself, analogous to what used to be called the transference neurosis, now enacted in all its precision between the two participants.

In addition to the vicious punishment of this process, it is also a highly gratifying one: the gratification of sadistic and masochistic wishes—what Joseph (personal communication) calls a "happy masochism"—lived out in the interchange, which cannot be avoided. In this sense any interpretation I make, no matter how dispassionately, gratifies the very wishes being interpreted, and all interpretation must be understood as interpretation within an enactment (Smith, 2006, 2007b). There is no working through without some greater understanding of what my patient is doing with me and with my comments—and I with her—as we examine the repeated enactments that are taking place between us moment by moment in the real time of the session.

Notes

This paper was published in a slightly altered version in *The Psychoanalytic Quarterly, 77*, No. 1 (2008), pp. 119–218.

REFERENCES

Abraham, K. (1919). A particular form of neurotic resistance against the psycho-analytic method. In: *Selected Papers of Karl Abraham,* trans. D. Bryan & A. Strachey. London: Hogarth Press, 1927.

Abraham, K. (1924). The influence of oral erotism on character formation. In: *Selected Papers of Karl Abraham,* trans. D. Bryan & A. Strachey. London: Hogarth Press, 1927.

Abraham, K. (1927). A short history of the development of the libido viewed in the light of mental disorders. In: *Selected Papers of Karl Abraham,* trans. D. Bryan & A. Strachey. London: Hogarth Press, 1927.

Alexander, F. (1950). Analysis of the therapeutic factors in psychoanalytic treatment. *Psychoanalytic Quarterly, 19*: 482–500.

Allen, N. (1968). *Shakespeare Survey 21.* London: Cambridge University Press.

Baker, R. (1993). The patient's discovery of the psychoanalyst as a new object. *International Journal of Psychoanalysis, 74*: 1223–1233.

Balint, M. (1959). *Thrills and Regressions.* London: Hogarth Press.

Barker, D. J. (1990). The fetal and infant origins of adult disease. *British Medical Journal, 301*: 111.

Bergen, S. E., Gardner, C. O., & Kendler, K. S. (2007). Age-related changes in heritability of behavioral phenotypes over adolescence and young adulthood: A meta-analysis. *Twin Research and Human Genetics, 10* (3): 423–433.

Bimmel, N., Juffer, F., Van IJzendoorn, I. M. H., & Bakermans-Kranenburg, M. J. (2003). Problem behavior of internationally adopted adolescents: A review and meta-analysis. *Harvard Review of Psychiatry, 11* (2): 64–77.

Bion, W. R. (1948). *Experiences in Groups and Other Papers.* London: Tavistock, 1961.

Bion, W. R. (1959). Attacks on linking. *International Journal of Psychoanalysis, 40*: 308–315. Also in: *Second Thoughts. Selected Papers on Psycho-Analysis* (pp. 93–109). London: Heinemann, 1967; reprinted London: Karnac, 1984.

Bion, W. R. (1962a). *Learning from Experience.* London: Heinemann; reprinted London: Karnac, 1984.

Bion, W. R. (1962b). A theory of thinking. *International Journal of Psychoanalysis, 53.* Also in: *Second Thoughts. Selected Papers on Psycho-Analysis.* London: Heinemann; reprinted London: Karnac, 1984.

Birksted-Breen, D. (1996). Phallus, penis and mental space. *International Journal of Psychoanalysis, 61*: 39–52.

Birksted-Breen, D. (2002). Time and the après coup. *Bulletin of the British Psychoanalytic Society, 38* (8): 12–21.

Bléandonu, G. (1994). *Wilfred Bion: His Life and Works, 1897–1979.* New York: Other Press.

Bloom, H. (1999). *Shakespeare: The Invention of the Human.* London: Fourth Estate.

Bolton, D., Rijsdijk, F., O'Connor, T. G., Perrin, S., & Eley, T. C. (2007). Obsessive-compulsive disorder, tics and anxiety in 6-year-old twins. *Psychological Medicine, 37* (1): 39–48.

Bowlby, J. (1963). Pathological mourning and childhood mourning. *Journal of the American Psychoanalytic Association, 11*: 500–541.

Bradley, A. C. (1904). *Shakespearean Tragedy.* London: Penguin, 1991.

Brenman, E. (1985). Cruelty and narrow mindedness. *International Journal of Psychoanalysis, 66*: 273–281.

Brenman-Pick, I. (1985). Working through in the counter-transference. *International Journal of Psychoanalysis, 66*: 157–166. Also in: E. Bott Spillius (Ed.), *Melanie Klein Today, Vol. 2* (pp. 34–47). London: Routledge, 1988.

Brenner, C. (1982). *The Mind in Conflict.* New York: International Universities Press.

Brenner, C. (2002). Conflict, compromise formation, and structural theory. *Psychoanalytic Quarterly, 70*: 397–417.

Britton, R. (1998). *Belief and Imagination: Explorations in Psychoanalysis.* London: Routledge.

Britton, R. (2003). *Sex, Death, and the Superego.* London: Karnac.

Cavell, M. (1998). Triangulation, one's own mind and objectivity. *International Journal of Psychoanalysis, 79*: 449–467.

Cavell, S. (2003). *Disowning Knowledge in Seven Plays of Shakespeare.* Cambridge: Cambridge University Press.

Cohen, W. (1997). Othello. In: *The Norton Shakespeare: Based on the Oxford Edition.* New York: W. W. Norton.

Coleridge, S. T. (1813). Marginalia on Othello. In: J. Wain (Ed.), *Shakespeare: Othello (Casebook).* London: Macmillan, 1971.

Damasio, A. (1999). *The Feeling of What Happens: Body and Emotion in the Making of Consciousness.* New York: Harcourt Brace.

Davis, M., & Wallbridge, D. (1981). *Boundary and Space.* New York: Brunner/Mazel.

Doolittle, H. (1977). *Visage de Freud.* Paris: Denoël.

Elms, A. C. (2001). Apocryphal Freud. *Annual of Psychoanalysis, 29*: 83–104.

Empson, W. (1951). Honest in Othello. In: J. Wain (Ed.), *Shakespeare: Othello (Casebook).* London: Macmillan, 1971.

Erlich, H. S. (2003). Experience—What is it? *International Journal of Psychoanalysis, 84*: 1125–1147.

Erlich, H. S., & Felsen, I. (1990). Identification patterns of offspring of Holocaust survivors with their parents. *American Journal of Orthopsychiatry, 60*: 506–520.

Etchegoyen, R. H., Lopez, B. M., & Rabih, M. (1987). On envy and how to interpret it. *International Journal of Psychoanalysis, 68*: 49–60.

Fairbairn, W. R. D. (1954). Observations on the nature of hysterical states. *British Journal of Medical Psychology, 29*: 112–127.

Feinberg, M. E., Button, T. M., Neiderhiser, J. M., Reiss, D., & Hetherington, E. M. (2007). Parenting and adolescent antisocial behavior and depression: Evidence of genotype x parenting environment interaction. *Archives of General Psychiatry, 64* (4): 457–465.

Feldman, M. (1998). "Why Patients Tell Us Their Dreams." Unpublished lecture, Westlodge Conference, London.

Feldman, M. (2000). Some views on the manifestation of the death instinct in clinical work. *International Journal of Psychoanalysis, 81*: 53–65.

Feldman, M. (2007). Addressing parts of the self. *International Journal of Psychoanalysis, 88*: 371–386.

Felitti, V. J. (2002). The relation between adverse childhood experiences and adult health: Turning gold into lead. *The Permanente Journal, 6*: 44–47.

Felitti, V. J., Anda, R. F., Nordenberg, D., Williamson, D. F., Spitz, A. M., Edwards, V., et al. (1998). Relationship of childhood abuse and household dysfunction to many of the leading causes of death in adults: The Adverse Childhood Experiences (ACE) study. *American Journal of Preventive Medicine, 14*: 245–258.

Fonagy, P. (2003). Towards a developmental understanding of violence. *British Journal of Psychiatry, 183*: 190–192.

Fonagy, P., & Target, M. (2007). The rooting of the mind in the body: New links between attachment theory and psychoanalytic thought. *Journal of the American Psychoanalytic Association, 55*.

Freud, S. (1901b). *The Psychopathology of Everyday Life. S.E., 6* (pp. 1–190).

Freud, S. (1905d). *Three Essays on the Theory of Sexuality. S.E., 7* (pp. 123–230).

Freud, S. (1911b). Formulations on the two principles of mental functioning. *S.E., 12* (pp. 218–226).

Freud, S. (1912b). The dynamics of transference. *S.E., 12* (pp. 97–108).

Freud, S. (1914g). Remembering, repeating and working-through (Further recommendations on the technique of psycho-analysis, II). *S.E., 12* (pp. 147–156).

Freud, S. (1915c). Instincts and their vicissitudes. *S.E., 14* (pp. 117–140).

Freud, S. (1915e). The unconscious. *S.E., 14*.

Freud, S. (1916a). On transience. *S.E., 14* .

Freud, S. (1920g). *Beyond the Pleasure Principle. S.E., 18* (pp. 3–64).

Freud, S. (1923b). *The Ego and the Id. S.E., 19*.

Freud, S. (1926e). *The Question of Lay Analysis. S.E., 20* (pp. 177–250).

Freud, S. (1930a). *Civilization and Its Discontents. S.E., 21* (pp. 59–145).

Freud, S. (1933a [1932]). *New Introductory Lectures on Psycho-Analysis. S.E., 22* (pp. 3–182).

Freud, S. (1937c). Analysis terminable and interminable. *S.E., 23* (pp. 211–253).

Freud, S. (1941f [1938]). Findings, ideas, problems. *S.E., 23* (p. 299).

Gabbard, G. O. (2000). On gratitude and gratification. *Journal of the American Psychoanalytic Association, 48* (3): 697–716.

Gammill, J. (1989). Some personal reflections on Melanie Klein [trans. M. Meloche]. *Melanie Klein and Object Relations, 7*: 1–15 [available online at www. Melanie-Klein-trust.org.uk].

Gergely, G., Bekkering, H., & Kiraly, I. (2002). Rational imitation in preverbal infants. *Nature, 415*: 755.

Gergely, G., & Csibra, G. (2006). Sylvia's recipe: Human culture, imitation, and pedagogy. In: N. J. Enfield & S. C. Levinson (Eds.), *Roots of Human Sociality: Culture, Cognition, and Human Interaction* (pp. 229–255). London: Berg Press.

Gray, P. (1994). *The Ego and the Mechanisms of Defense.* New York: Jason Aronson.

Green, J., & Goldwyn, R. (2002). Annotation. Attachment disorganisation and psychopathology: New findings in attachment research and their potential implications for developmental psychopathology in childhood. *Journal of Child Psychology and Psychiatry, and Allied Disciplines, 43* (7): 835–846.

Grosskurth, P. (1987). *Melanie Klein: Her World and Her Work.* Cambridge, MA: Harvard University Press.

Guignard, F. (1994). Sigmund Freud et Wilfred Bion: Filiation et commensalité. *Revue Française de la Psychanalyse, 58* (Spécial Congrès): 1619–1637.

Guignard, F. (1995). Le maternel et le féminin: Deux espaces de la vie psychique. *Psychologie Clinique et Projective, 95* (1).

Guignard, F. (1996). *Au vif de l'infantile. Champs psychanalytiques.* Lausanne: Delachaux & Niestlé.

Guignard, F. (1997). Position dépressive et position schizo-paranoïde aujourd'hui. In: *Le mal-être (angoisse et violence).* Coll. Débats de psychanalyse. Paris: Presses Universitaires de France.

Guignard, F. (2001). "Communication à l'atelier sur 'Le genre dans la situation analytique'." Paper presented at Pré-Congrès International des Analystes Formateurs de l'API, Nice, 21 July.

Guignard, F. (2002a). Apories de la transformation dans l'activité psychique du psychanalyste en exercice: Taches aveugles et interprétations-bouchons. *Revue Française de la Psychanalyse* (Spécial Congrès).

Guignard, F. (2002b). Intrication pulsionnelle et fonctions du sadisme primaire. *Revue Française de la Psychanalyse, 4*: 1103–1116.

Guignard, F. (2002c). *La relation mère–fille. Entre partage et clivage,* ed. T. Bokanowski & F. Guignard. Coll. de la SEPEA. Paris: Editions In Press.

Guignard, F. (2006a). "Le psychanalyste et l'enfant dans la société occidentale actuelle." Paper presented at First International Conference of CO-CAP, Buenos Aires, August.

Guignard, F. (2006b). Mais où sont les neiges d'antan? *Revue Française de la Psychanalyse, 5* (Spécial Congrès): 267–273.

Hanly, C. (1984). Ego ideal and ideal ego. *International Journal of Psychoanalysis, 65*: 253.

Hart, C. (1916). *The Student's Catholic Doctrine.* London: Burns Oates & Washbourne.

Hegel, G. W. F. (1812). *Wissenschaft der Logik, 1.* Frankfurt a.M.: Suhrkamp 1990.

Hesse, E., & Main, M. (2000). Disorganization in infant and adult attachment: Description, correlates and implications for developmental psychopathology. *Journal of the American Psychoanalytic Association, 48*: 1097–1127.

Horney, K. (1936). The problem of the negative therapeutic reaction. *Psychoanalytic Quarterly, 5*: 29–44.

Howe, D. (2006). Developmental attachment psychotherapy with fostered and adopted children. *Child and Adolescent Mental Health, 11* (3): 128–134.

Insel, T. R. (2003). Is social attachment an addictive disorder? *Physiology & Behavior, 79* (3): 351–357.

Isaacs, S. (1943). The nature and function of phantasy. In: M. Klein, P.

Heimann, S. Isaacs, & J. Riviere (Eds.), *Developments in Psycho-Analysis* (pp. 67–121). London: Hogarth Press, 1952.

Joffe, W. G. (1969). A critical review of the status of the envy concept. *International Journal of Psychoanalysis, 50*: 533–545.

Joseph, B. (1959). An aspect of the repetition compulsion. *International Journal of Psychoanalysis, 40*: 213–222. Also in: *Psychic Equilibrium and Psychic Change: Selected Papers of Betty Joseph*, ed. M. Feldman & E. Bott Spillius. London: Routledge, 1989.

Joseph, B. (1982). Addiction to near death. In: *Psychic Equilibrium and Psychic Change: Selected Papers of Betty Joseph*, ed. M. Feldman & E. Bott Spillius. London: Routledge, 1989.

Joseph, B. (1989). *Psychic Equilibrium and Psychic Change: Selected Papers of Betty Joseph*, ed. M. Feldman & E. Bott Spillius. London: Routledge.

Kendler, K. S., Gatz, M., Gardner, C. O., & Pedersen, N. L. (2006). A Swedish national twin study of lifetime major depression. *American Journal of Psychiatry, 163* (1): 109–114.

Kim-Cohen, J., Moffitt, T. E., Taylor, A., Pawlby, S. J., & Caspi, A. (2005). Maternal depression and children's antisocial behavior: Nature and nurture effects. *Archives of General Psychiatry, 62* (2): 173–181.

Klein, M. (1924). An obsessional neurosis in a six-year old girl. In: *The Writings of Melanie Klein, Vol. 2: The Psycho-Analysis of Children*. London: Hogarth Press, 1975; reprinted London: Karnac, 1998.

Klein, M. (1932). *The Psycho-Analysis of Children*. London: Hogarth Press, 1975; reprinted London: Karnac, 1998.

Klein, M. (1935). A contribution to the psychogenesis of manic-depressive states. In: *The Writings of Melanie Klein, Vol. 1: Love, Guilt and Reparation and Other Works, 1921–1945* (pp. 262–289). London: Hogarth Press, 1975; reprinted London: Karnac, 1992.

Klein, M. (1940). Mourning and its relation to manic-depressive states. In: *The Writings of Melanie Klein, Vol. 1: Love, Guilt and Reparation and Other Works, 1921–1945* (pp. 344–369). London: Hogarth Press, 1975; reprinted London: Karnac, 1992.

Klein, M. (1946). Notes on some schizoid mechanisms. In: *The Writings of Melanie Klein, Vol. 3: Envy and Gratitude and Other Works* (pp. 1–24). London: Hogarth Press, 1975; reprinted London: Karnac, 1993.

Klein, M. (1952). The origins of transference. In: *The Writings of Melanie Klein, Vol. 3: Envy and Gratitude and Other Works* (pp. 48–56), ed. R. Money-Kyrle, B. Joseph, E. O'Shaughnessy, & H. Segal. London: Hogarth Press, 1975; reprinted London: Karnac, 1993.

Klein, M. (1955). On identification. In: *The Writings of Melanie Klein, Vol. 3: Envy and Gratitude and Other Works* (pp. 141–175). London: Hogarth Press, 1975; reprinted London: Karnac, 1993.

Klein, M. (1957). *Envy and Gratitude.* In: *The Writings of Melanie Klein, Vol. 3: Envy and Gratitude and Other Works* (pp. 176–235). London: Hogarth Press, 1975; reprinted London: Karnac, 1993. [First published as: *Envy and Gratitude: A Study of Unconscious Sources.* London: Tavistock Press, 1957.]

Kubie, L. S. (1939). A critical analysis of the concept of a repetition compulsion. *International Journal of Psychoanalysis, 20*: 390–402.

Lacan, J. (1977). *The Four Fundamental Concepts of Psycho-Analysis,* trans. A. Sheridan. London: Penguin.

Laufer, M., & Laufer, E. (1984). *Adolescence and Developmental Breakdown.* London: Yale University Press.

Leavis, F. R. (1952). Diabolic intellect and the noble hero. In: J. Wain (Ed.), *Shakespeare: Othello (Casebook).* London: Macmillan, 1971.

Leowald, H. (1971). Some considerations on repetition and repetition compulsion. *International Journal of Psychoanalysis, 52*: 59–64.

Lieberman, A. F. (2003). The treatment of attachment disorder in infancy and early childhood: Reflections from clinical intervention with later-adopted foster care children. *Attachment and Human Development, 5* (3): 279–282.

Lim, M. M., & Young, L. J. (2004). Vasopressin-dependent neural circuits underlying pair bond formation in the monogamous prairie vole. *Neuroscience, 125* (1): 35–45.

Lim, M. M., Wang, Z., Olazabal, D. E., Ren, X., Terwilliger, E. F., & Young, L. J. (2004). Enhanced partner preference in a promiscuous species by manipulating the expression of a single gene. *Nature, 429* (6993): 754–757.

Lorca, F. G. (1987). *Poem of the Deep Song.* San Francisco, CA: City Lights Books.

Madigan, S., Moran, G., & Pederson, D. (2006). Unresolved states of mind, disorganised attachment relationships and disrupted interactions of adolescent mothers and their infants. *Developmental Psychology, 42* (2): 293–304.

Marmot, M. G. (2006). Status syndrome: A challenge to medicine. *Journal of the American Medical Association, 295* (11): 1304–1307.

Milton, J. (1975). *John Milton: Paradise Lost* (2nd edition), ed. S. Elledge. New York: W. W. Norton.

Money-Kyrle, R. (1956). Normal counter-transference and some of its deviations. *International Journal of Psychoanalysis, 37*: 360–366. Reprinted in: *The Collected Papers of Roger Money-Kyrle* (pp. 330–342); and in: E. Spillius (Ed.), *Melanie Klein Today, Vol. 2* (pp. 22–33). London: Routledge, 1988.

Money-Kyrle, R. (1968). Cognitive development. *International Journal of*

Psychoanalysis, 49: 691–698. Reprinted in: *The Collected Papers of Roger Money-Kyrle* (pp. 416–433). Perthshire: Clunie Press, 1978.

Money-Kyrle, R. (1971). The aim of psycho-analysis. *International Journal of Psychoanalysis, 49*: 691–698. Reprinted in: *The Collected Papers of Roger Money-Kyrle* (pp. 416–433), ed. D. Meltzer & E. O'Shaughnessy. Perthshire: Clunie Press, 1978.

NICHD Early Child Care Research Network (2004). Trajectories of physical aggression from toddlerhood to middle childhood: Predictors, correlates, and outcomes. *Monographs of the Society for Research in Child Development, 69* (4): vii, 1–129.

Nuttall, A. D. (2007). *Shakespeare the Thinker.* New Haven, CT: Yale University Press.

O'Connor, T. G., Marvin, R. S., Rutter, M., Olrick, J. T., & Britner, P. A. (2003). Child–parent attachment following early institutional deprivation. *Development and Psychopathology, 15* (1): 19–38.

O'Shaughnessy, E. (1992). Enclaves and excursions. *International Journal of Psychoanalysis, 73*: 603–611.

O'Shaughnessy, E. (1999). Relating to the superego. *International Journal of Psychoanalysis, 80*: 861–870.

Onishi, K. H., & Baillargeon, R. (2005). Do 15-month-old infants understand false beliefs? *Science, 308* (5719): 255–258.

Onishi, K. H., Baillargeon, R., & Leslie, A. M. (2007). 15-month-old infants detect violations of pretend scenarios. *Acta Pychologica, 124* (special issue): 106–128.

Orstavik, R. E., Kendler, K. S., Czajkowski, N., Tambs, K., & Reichborn-Kjennerud, T. (2007). Genetic and environmental contributions to depressive personality disorder in a population-based sample of Norwegian twins. *Journal of Affective Disorders, 99* (1–3): 181–189.

Petot, J. N. (1993). *Melanie Klein, Vol. 2: The Ego and the Good Object, 1932–1960.* Madison, CT: International Universities Press.

Pines, D. (1988). Adolescent pregnancy and motherhood: A psychoanalytic perspective. *Psychoanalytic Inquiry, 8*: 234–251.

Power, C., & Hertzman, C. (1997). Social and biological pathways linking early life and adult disease. *British Medical Bulletin, 53*: 210–221.

Riviere, J. (1932). Jealousy as a mechanism of defence. In: *The Inner World and Joan Riviere,* ed. A. Hughes. London: Karnac, 1991.

Riviere, J. (1936). A contribution to the analysis of the negative therapeutic reaction. *International Journal of Psychoanalysis, 17*: 304–320. Reprinted in: *The Inner World and Joan Riviere,* ed. A. Hughes. London: Karnac, 1991.

Riviere, J. (1937). Public lectures: Hate, greed, and aggression. In: *The Inner World and Joan Riviere,* ed. A. Hughes. London: Karnac, 1991.

Rosenfeld, H. (1959). An investigation into the psycho-analytic theory of depression. *International Journal of Psychoanalysis, 40*: 105–129.

Rosenfeld, H. (1964). On the psychopathology of narcissism: A clinical approach. *International Journal of Psychoanalysis, 45*: 332–337. Reprinted in: *Psychotic States.* London: Hogarth Press, 1965.

Rosenfeld, H. (1965). *Psychotic States: A Psychoanalytic Approach.* New York: International Universities Press.

Rosenfeld, H. (1971). A clinical approach to the psychoanalytic theory of the life and death instincts: An investigation into the aggressive aspects of narcissism. *International Journal of Psychoanalysis, 52*: 169–178. Reprinted in: E. Bott Spillius (Ed.), *Melanie Klein Today, Vol. 1: Mainly Theory.* London: Routledge, 1988.

Rosenfeld, H. (1975). Negative therapeutic reaction. In: P. L. Giovacchini, A. Flarsheim, & L. B. Boyer (Eds.), *Tactics and Techniques in Psychoanalytic Therapy, Vol. 2: Transference* (pp. 217–228). New York: Jason Aronson.

Rosenfeld, H. (1987). *Impasse and Interpretation.* New Library of Psychoanalysis. London: Tavistock Publications.

Roughton, R. (1993). Useful aspects of acting out: Repetition, enactment, and actualization. *Journal of the American Psychoanalytic Association, 41*: 443–472.

Sandler, J. (1983). Reflections on some relations between psychoanalytic concepts and psychoanalytic practice. *International Journal of Psychoanalysis, 64*: 33–45.

Sandler, J., & Joffe, W. G. (1969). Towards a basic psychoanalytic model. *International Journal of Psycho-Analysis, 50*: 79–90.

Segal, H. (1957). Notes on symbol formation. *International Journal of Psychoanalysis, 38*: 391–397.

Segal, H. (1964). *Introduction to the Work of Melanie Klein.* London: Hogarth Press.

Segal, H. (1979). *Klein.* Brighton: Harvester Press; reprinted London: Karnac, 1989.

Segal, H. (1983). Some clinical implications of Melanie Klein's work: Emergence from narcissism. *International Journal of Psychoanalysis, 64*: 269–276.

Segal, H. (1991). *Dream, Phantasy and Art.* London: Routledge.

Segal, H. (1993). On the clinical usefulness of the concept of the death instinct. *International Journal of Psychoanalysis, 74*: 55–61. Reprinted in: J. Steiner (Ed.), *Psychoanalysis, Literature and War.* London: Routledge, 1997.

Shakespeare, W. (1603). *The Tragedy of Hamlet, Prince of Denmark.* The Arden Shakespeare. London: Routledge.

Shakespeare, W. (2006). *Othello.* New York: Oxford University Press.

Silberg, J. L., Rutter, M., Tracy, K., Maes, H. H., & Eaves, L. (2007). Etiological heterogeneity in the development of antisocial behavior: The Virginia Twin Study of Adolescent Behavioral Development and the Young Adult Follow-Up. *Psychological Medicine, 37* (8): 1193–1202.

Slade, A., Sadler, L., Dios-Kenn, C., Webb, D., Currier-Ezepchick, J., & Mayes, L. (2005). Minding the baby: A reflective parenting program. *Psychoanalytic Study of the Child, 60*: 74–100.

Smith, H. F. (2006). Analyzing disavowed action: The fundamental resistance of analysis. *Journal of the American Psychoanalytic Association, 54*: 713–737.

Smith, H. F. (2007a). "Is the Concept of Forgiveness Useful?" Paper presented at the 45th IPA Congress, Berlin.

Smith, H. F. (2007b). Voices that changed psychoanalysis in unpredictable ways. *Psychoanalytic Quarterly, 76*: 1049–1063.

Solomon, J., & George, C. (1999). *Attachment Disorganization.* New York: Guilford Press.

Spillius, E. B. (1993). Varieties of envious experience. *International Journal of Psychoanalysis, 74*: 1199–1212.

Spillius, E. B. (2001). Freud and Klein on the concept of phantasy. *International Journal of Psychoanalysis, 82* (2): 361–373.

Spillius, E. B. (2007a). On the influence of Horney's "The Problem of the Negative Therapeutic Reaction". *Psychoanalytic Quarterly, 76*: 59–74.

Spillius, E. B. (2007b). Varieties of envious experience. In: *Encounters with Melanie Klein: Selected Papers of Elizabeth Spillius* (pp. 140–161), ed. P. Roth & R. Rusbridger. London: Routledge.

Steiner, J. (1993). *Psychic Retreats: Pathological Organisations in Psychotic, Neurotic, and Borderline Patients.* London: Routledge.

Steiner, J. (2006). Seeing and being seen: Narcissistic pride and narcissistic humiliation. *International Journal of Psychoanalysis, 87*: 939–951.

Stern, D. (1985). *The Interpersonal World of the Infant.* New York: Basic Books.

Strachey, J. (1934). The nature of the therapeutic action of psychoanalysis. *International Journal of Psychoanalysis, 15*: 127–159.

Surian, L., Caldi, S., & Sperber, D. (2007). Attribution of beliefs by 13-month-old infants. *Psychological Science, 18*: 580–587.

Tremblay, R. E., Nagin, D. S., Seguin, J. R., Zoccolillo, M., Zelazo, P. D., Boivin, M., et al. (2004). Physical aggression during early childhood: Trajectories and predictors. *Pediatrics, 114* (1): e43–50.

Trevarthen, C., & Aitken, K. J. (2001). Infant intersubjectivity: Research, theory, and clinical applications. *Journal of Child Psychology and Psychiatry, and Allied Disciplines, 42* (1): 3–48.

Trollope, A. (1861). *Framley Parsonage.* London: Everyman's Library, J. M. Dent, 1906.

Trollope, A. (1866). *The Last Chronicle of Barset.* London: Penguin Classics, 1967.

Trollope, A. (1883). *An Autobiography.* Oxford: Oxford University Press, 1950.

Tronick, E. (2007). *The Neurobehavioral and Social–Emotional Development of Infants and Children.* New York: W. W. Norton.

Vanier, A. (2000). *Lacan,* trans. S. Fairfield. New York: Other Press.

Von Klitzing, K., Simoni, H., & Bürgin, D. (1999). Child development and early triadic relationships. *International Journal of Psychoanalysis, 80* (1): 71–89.

Wain, J. (1971). *Shakespeare: Othello (Casebook).* London: Macmillan.

Wamboldt, M. Z., & Reiss, D. (2006). Explorations of parenting environments in the evolution of psychiatric problems in children. *American Journal of Psychiatry, 163* (6): 951–953.

Weiß, H. (2002). Reporting a dream accompanying an enactment in the transference situation. *International Journal of Psychoanalysis, 83*: 633–645.

Wilde, O. (1898). "The Ballad of Reading Gaol." In: C. Ricks (Ed.), *The New Oxford Book of Victorian Verse.* Oxford: Oxford University Press.

Wilkinson, R. G. (1996). *Unhealthy Societies: From Inequality to Wellbeing.* London: Routledge.

Wilkinson, R. G. (2000). Social relations, hierarchy and health. In: A. R. Tarlov & R. F. S. Peter (Eds.), *The Society and Population Health Reader: A State and Community Perspective, Vol. 2* (pp. 211–235). New York: New Press.

Wilson Knight, G. (1930). The *Othello* music. In: J. Wain (Ed.), *Shakespeare: Othello (Casebook).* London: Macmillan, 1971.

Winnicott, D. W. (1947). Hate in the countertransference. In: *Collected Papers: Through Paediatrics to Psycho-Analysis.* London: Tavistock Publications, 1958. Reprinted as: *Through Paediatrics to Psycho-Analysis.* London: Hogarth Press; reprinted London: Karnac, 1992.

Winnicott, D. W. (1948). Primary introduction to external reality in society and the growing child. In: *The Maturational Processes and the Facilitating Environment: Studies in the Theory of Emotional Development.* London: Hogarth Press & Institute of Psychoanalysis, 1965; reprinted London: Karnac, 1990.

Winnicott, D. W. (1950). Aggression in relation to emotional development. In: *Collected Papers: Through Paediatrics to Psycho-Analysis.* London: Tavistock Publications, 1958. Reprinted as: *Through Paediatrics to Psycho-Analysis.* London: Hogarth Press; reprinted London: Karnac, 1992.

Winnicott, D. W. (1954). The depressive position in normal emotional development. In: *Collected Papers: Through Paediatrics to Psycho-Analysis.* London: Tavistock Publications, 1958. Reprinted as: *Through Paediatrics to Psycho-Analysis.* London: Hogarth Press; reprinted London: Karnac, 1992.

Winnicott, D. W. (1960a). The theory of the parent–infant relationship. In: *The Maturational Processes and the Facilitating Environment: Studies in the Theory of Emotional Development.* London: Hogarth Press & The Institute of Psychoanalysis, 1965; reprinted London: Karnac, 1990.

Winnicott, D. W. (1960b). The true and the false self. In: *The Maturational Processes and the Facilitating Environment: Studies in the Theory of Emotional Development.* London: Hogarth Press & The Institute of Psychoanalysis, 1965; reprinted London: Karnac, 1990.

Winnicott, D. W. (1962). Ego integration in child development. In: *The Maturational Processes and the Facilitating Environment: Studies in the Theory of Emotional Development.* London: Hogarth Press & The Institute of Psychoanalysis, 1965; reprinted London: Karnac, 1990.

Winnicott, D. W. (1963a). The development of the capacity for concern. In: *The Maturational Processes and the Facilitating Environment: Studies in the Theory of Emotional Development.* London: Hogarth Press & The Institute of Psychoanalysis, 1965; reprinted London: Karnac, 1990.

Winnicott, D. W. (1963b). The mentally ill in your caseload. In: *The Maturational Processes and the Facilitating Environment: Studies in the Theory of Emotional Development.* London: Hogarth Press & The Institute of Psychoanalysis, 1965; reprinted London: Karnac, 1990.

Winnicott, D. W. (1965). *The Maturational Processes and the Facilitating Environment: Studies in the Theory of Emotional Development.* London: Hogarth Press & The Institute of Psychoanalysis; reprinted London: Karnac, 1990.

Winnicott, D. W. (1969). Physiotherapy and human relations. In: *Psycho-Analytic Explorations,* ed. C. Winnicott, R. Shepherd, & M. Davis. London: Karnac, 1989.

Winnicott, D. W. (1970). The basis for self in body. In: *Psycho-Analytic Explorations,* ed. C. Winnicott, R. Shepherd, & M. Davis. London: Karnac, 1989.

Yorke, C. (1971). Some suggestions for a critique of Kleinian psychology. *Psychoanalytic Study of the Child, 26,* 129–155.

Zetzel, E. R. (1958). Review of *Envy and Gratitude*: A study of unconscious sources, by Melanie Klein. *Psychoanalytic Quarterly, 27*: 409–412.

Zimmer, C. (2006). Silent struggle: A new theory of pregnancy. *The New York Times,* 14 March.

INDEX

www.ingramcontent.com/pod-product-compliance
Ingram Content Group UK Ltd.
Pitfield, Milton Keynes, MK11 3LW, UK
UKHW022002180926
475701UK00003B/147
* 9 7 8 1 8 5 5 7 5 7 3 5 6 *